W9-BXZ-405

Cycling the San Francisco Bay Area

30 Rides to Historic Sites and Scenic Places

Carol O'Hare

Bicycle Books – San Francisco

First printing 1993

Printed in the U.S.A.

Cover design: Kent Lytle, Lytle Design, Alameda, CA
Cover photograph: Neil van der Plas
Frontispiece photo by Surrey Blackburn, Angel Island Association

All photographs by the author except where credited

Maps by Susan Cronin-Paris (route maps) and Rob van der Plas
(locator maps)

Earlier versions of some of the rides described in this book first
appeared in *A Bicyclist's Guide to Bay Area History*, published by
Fair Oaks Publishing Company.

Published by:
Bicycle Books, Inc.
PO Box 2038
Mill Valley, CA 94492
U.S.A.

Distributed to the book trade by:
USA: National Book Network, Lanham, MD
Canada: Raincoast Book Distribution, Vancouver, BC
UK: Chris Lloyd Sales and Marketing, Poole, Dorset

Publisher's Cataloging in Publication Data:
O'Hare, Carol
Cycling the San Francisco Bay Area: 30 Rides to Historic Sites and
Scenic Places.
Series title: The Active Travel Series
Bibliography: p. Includes Index.
1. Bicycles and bicycling—touring guides.
2. San Francisco, guides.
I. Title
II. Authorship

Library of Congress Catalog Card No. 93-83823

ISBN 0-933201-57-5, Paperback original

Acknowledgements

Many people have contributed to this book. My thanks go to Bud O'Hare, Karen Hunt, Beverley Fritsch, and Pete Blasberg, who have accompanied me on these rides over the years. I am grateful to Elaine de Man for editing the manuscript, to Susan Cronin-Paris for drawing the maps, and to photographers Betty Johnston, Surrey Blackburn, and Wayne Gravelle.

I also wish to acknowledge all those who generously offered historical information about their towns, including: Russ Kingman, Jack London Bookstore, Glen Ellen; Dorothy Soderholm, Napa County Historical Society; Mrs. William Aguilar, Napa; John Wichels, Yountville; Emeline Martin and Virginia Mossi, Petaluma; Gail Woolley, Palo Alto/Stanford Heritage Association; Bea Lichtenstein, Historic Preservation Society of Santa Clara; Kitty Monahan, New Almaden Quicksilver County Park Association; and Barbara Bunshah, Livermore History Guild.

About the Author

Carol O'Hare began cycling in 1982, after she moved to the San Francisco Bay Area from the East Coast. She also developed an avid interest in local history and has often combined these two activities. In 1985 she wrote and published *A Bicyclist's Guide to Bay Area History*, which she revised a few years later. She has led many rides to historic sites for her bike club, Western Wheelers, and for community college groups.

Wayne Gravelle

A native of Minneapolis, Carol has a B.A. degree from the University of Minnesota and an M.S.W. degree from Boston University. She has worked as a laboratory technician, health counselor, and health educator.

She now spends her time writing, traveling, hiking, doing historical research, and, of course, cycling. She resides in Sunnyvale, California, with her husband (whom she met on her first bike club ride).

Foreword
by
Elaine Mariolle

When I first began cycling seriously ten years ago I was drawn to fast, long-distance rides. Although I enjoyed the scenery and the challenge of the terrain, I mostly focused on getting to my destination. But over the years I've learned that there's more to a bike ride (and to life) than just reaching a goal.

All those places (and people) along the way are important and worth exploring. Cycling, like life, should be a process to be enjoyed and savored. That is why I really like what Carol O'Hare has done in her book, *Cycling the San Francisco Bay Area*. She gives cyclists reasons to slow down, look around, and appreciate their surroundings.

My favorite parts of the book are the historical and architectural notes that are served up with the flair of a professional tour guide. Carol also does a great job of outlining a range of interesting routes from leisurely to challenging, with maps and directions that are clear and easy to follow. Even though I am a Bay Area native and long-time cyclist, I discovered new things with Carol's book and you will too. Everyone who cycles in the Bay Area should have a copy of this book.

[Elaine Mariolle, women's winner of the 1986 Race Across America, is co-author of *The Woman Cyclist*. Her columns and articles on bicycling have appeared in the *San Francisco Chronicle*, *California Bicyclist*, and other publications.]

Table of Contents

Introduction

The San Francisco Bay Area offers some of the best cycling you can find anywhere. A temperate climate permits year-round riding. The terrain, from flat valleys to rolling foothills and challenging mountains, has something for everyone. The natural beauty is exceptional, with a magnificent coastline, lovely landscapes, extensive parklands, and the extraordinary bay. Cities and towns of all sizes invite exploration, and interesting historic sites abound.

The scenic beauty of the Golden State is undeniable, but when I first moved to California from the East Coast, I was unconvinced that it had much to offer in the way of history. As I began to explore my adopted state, however, I quickly learned how wrong I was. The Bay Area, especially, has a unique charm that includes a fascinating variety of historic places, and I discovered that one of the best ways to experience it is by bicycle. This book was written to help you discover that as well.

The book describes rides in each of the nine counties that make up the Bay Area: Sonoma, Napa, Marin, Solano, Alameda, Contra Costa, San Francisco, San Mateo, and Santa Clara. Although different from each other in many ways, each has historic sites and scenic places that will appeal to all.

Bay Area Weather

The Bay Area is known for its microclimates, and weather may change dramatically from one area to another, as well as from season to season. But you will find that any time of year can be good for riding.

It seldom rains during the summer months, but fog tends to form along the coast and move inland through the Golden Gate and other gaps in coastal mountain ranges, providing a sort of natural air-conditioning. So, while the inland valleys remain hot, San Francisco and coastal areas may be cool and foggy, particularly in the morning, as the fog usually burns off by midday. Westerly winds, which increase in the afternoon, are also strongest during the summer.

By September, the fog and wind patterns change, bringing sunny, warm weather to all of the Bay Area. With winter comes rain, although there are many clear days between storms and temperatures remain comfortable. In the spring the hills are green and wildflowers are in bloom, a lovely time for cycling.

How to Use This Book

The 30 rides described here vary greatly in length and difficulty. Some are short and easy, suitable for a relaxed family outing, while others offer the distance and challenge sought by more experienced cyclists. You can follow a route exactly as described or incorporate it into a ride of your own design. In some areas, you can combine two rides.

The ratings I have given these rides are, of course, subjective. They take into account mileage, terrain, road conditions, and traffic. Generally, an *easy* ride is short, flat, follows bike lanes or roads with adequate shoulder, and avoids heavy traffic. A *strenuous* ride, on the other hand, is longer, usually includes demanding climbs, may be on narrow roads with no shoulder, and sometimes involves traffic. *Moderate* and *moderately strenuous* rides fall in between. I have tried to provide enough descriptive detail about each tour to allow you to choose those rides that will best suit you.

The distances given are not exact but tell you approximately how many miles each ride is, how far it is to the next turn or stopping point, and how long the hill ahead of you is going to be.

My aim has been to furnish all the information you will need to plan a pleasurable outing. In addition to route descriptions and historical lore, I have included the location of campgrounds and hostels in case you want to plan an overnight stay. Museums of interest and their hours are also noted, as well as restrooms and places to buy food.

You may find that these excursions take longer than expected, so be sure to give yourself plenty of time for checking directions, enjoying the scenery, visiting museums and historic sites, and eating a meal or snack.

The facts presented here were checked for accuracy just before the book went to press. However, museum hours change, and budget cuts may force facilities to be open less frequently, so you may want to call ahead to obtain up-to-date information. Road surfaces may also improve or deteriorate, and occasionally, buildings are torn down or moved. If you find any errors or changes, please let me know (see page 4 for the publisher's address).

Beginning Your Ride

Before setting out, make sure your bicycle is in good working order and that you are prepared to fix a flat tire. Wear a helmet to protect your head from injury in case of an accident or a fall. A map of the area will be useful if you miss a turn or want to explore areas off the described route. You may also want to bring along a lock so you can visit places of interest without worrying about your bike. Since many of the buildings described here are not public property, please respect the privacy of the occupants. And don't forget to obey the traffic laws. This is even more important in light of the increasing numbers of automobiles and bicycles sharing the road.

Although written for cyclists, this book can also be used by those who wish to make the tours by car, and parts of the routes may be comfortably covered on foot.

Have a pleasant and safe journey as you explore the San Francisco Bay Area by bicycle.

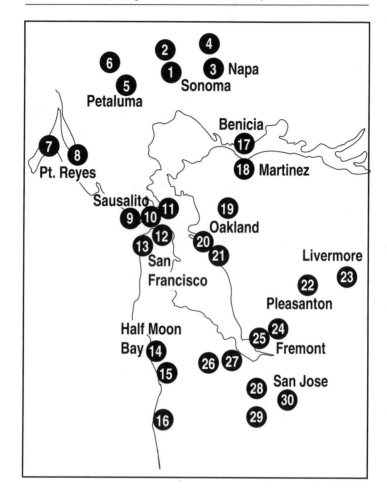

1. Sonoma

Distance: 10 miles plus 3.5-mile side trip

Rating: *Easy*, following flat city streets and country roads. Traffic may be heavy near the Plaza, especially on weekend afternoons.

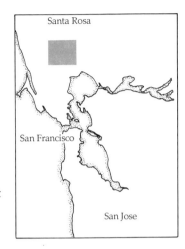

Highlights: Sonoma is one of the most historic towns in the state. It is the location of the last established mission, site of the founding of the "Republic of California" by the Bear Flag Party, and home of General Mariano Vallejo, one of the most important men of his time. The tour also includes visits to two wineries.

Location: On Highway 12, between Vallejo and Santa Rosa in Sonoma County, less than an hour's drive northeast from San Francisco.

Mission San Francisco Solano on 114 East Spain Street in Sonoma. The oldest part dates to 1825, the chapel to 1840.

courtesy Redwood Empire Association

Sonoma Plaza

Ride south on First Street East to circle the Plaza. (If traffic is heavy, or if you wish to spend more time examining the buildings surrounding the Plaza, you may decide to lock your bicycle and do this part of the tour on foot.)

The Sonoma Plaza, the largest of its kind in California, was laid out in 1835 by General Vallejo and over the years has seen many uses. Mexican and Indian soldiers drilled on it in the late 1830s, horse races and duels were held here, and soil from the Plaza was used to make adobe bricks for the buildings surrounding it. By the 1870s the Plaza was bare of trees, and livestock of all kinds had grazed and trampled the ground. In the 1880s, the Sonoma Valley Railroad covered half of the open space with tracks, coal yard, depot, car barn, and other railroad buildings.

The first step in beautifying the Plaza came in 1890, when a city lawsuit forced the railroad to remove its equipment.

Bear Flag Revolt

The Bear Flag rebellion was probably one of the most colorful events in California history. In the 1840s, large numbers of Americans, lured by rumors of free land, began arriving in California. Met by restrictions prohibiting them from owning property and fearful of being driven out of California by the Mexican government, a group of settlers decided to take matters into their own hands. On June 14, 1846, with the unofficial backing of Captain John C. Fremont of the U.S. Army, they captured the unresisting Pueblo of Sonoma and arrested Vallejo. Even though Vallejo supported annexation of California by the United States, he was imprisoned for two months at Sutter's Fort in Sacramento.

The Americans announced the establishment of a free and independent Republic of California and raised a homemade flag—the Bear Flag—over Sonoma. Less than a month later, after the Mexican capital at Monterey was captured, the flag was replaced by that of the United States. Unfortunately, the revolt prevented the peaceful annexation of California by the United States and made war with Mexico inevitable. Although the California Republic was short-lived, the Bear Flag is now the official flag of the state of California.

Several years later, landscaping by the Ladies Improvement Club resulted in the present parklike setting. Today the Plaza contains hundreds of trees and shrubs, a rose garden, a duck pond, a playground, picnic tables, restrooms, a monument to the Bear Flag rebellion, and the city hall.

Also located in the Plaza, at 453 First Street East, is the 1913 Carnegie library, which now houses the Sonoma Valley Visitors Bureau. Here you can obtain additional information and maps of Sonoma and the surrounding area.

As you circle the Plaza, it is hard to miss the Sebastiani Theater on the left, an impressive two-story pink structure with a 72-foot tower. Samuele Sebastiani is best known as the founder of the winery that bears his name, but he was also responsible for the construction of several significant buildings in Sonoma. The theater, one of his major projects, is a typical movie palace of the 1930s.

Turn right on East Napa Street. As you reach Broadway (Highway 12), you will see the Mission Revival style City Hall, built between 1906 and 1908 of stone from local quarries. All four sides are identical, so merchants on each side of the Plaza would be satisfied that the building "faced" their direction.

Pause here for a look down Broadway, once the grand boulevard entrance into Sonoma. This spot also marks the end of El Camino Real, the road that connected all the missions.

Continuing on Napa, go right at the next intersection to view the buildings along First Street West. The two-story Leese-Fitch Adobe on the corner, at No. 485-495, was built about 1836 and was successively owned by two of General Vallejo's brothers-in-law. Near the other end of the block is the Salvador Vallejo Adobe, at No. 415-427, constructed in the early 1840s for the General's brother.

The Sonoma Hotel is at the intersection with Spain Street. When it was built in the 1870s, stores and saloons occupied the lower floor, and there was a social hall on the second. Converted to a hotel in the 1920s, it still offers travelers a place to stay the night.

Turn right on Spain Street. The building at No. 18 is the Swiss Hotel, a Monterey Colonial style adobe home constructed in 1840 by Salvador Vallejo, who was married to the sister of General Vallejo's wife. It became a hotel in the 1880s and is now a restaurant.

The open space next to the Sonoma Cheese Factory was the site of La Casa Grande, the home completed in 1840 for completion. The house, constructed of locally quarried basalt rock, may have cost as much as $250,000, money Swift had made in the gold fields. Swift's good fortune did not last, however. His wife divorced him, financial reverses beset him, and he was killed when his mule threw him over an embankment. The house is now a private country club.

Vallejo's Home, Lachryma Montis

Return along Temelec and Almeria to Arnold Drive, watching for traffic as you turn left. From Arnold, go right on Leveroni. At the stop sign after the bridge over Sonoma Creek, turn left onto Fifth Street West, as you head toward General Vallejo's home, Lachryma Montis, to compare it with Swift's. Continue on Fifth all the way into town, crossing Highway 12 (which now follows Napa Street). After a few more blocks, turn right, just past Claudia, onto a paved bike path.

You will soon see the buildings of the Vallejo Home State Historic Park to your left across the open field. Turn left when you come to the narrow road lined with cottonwood trees.

In 1851 General Vallejo built this fine, two-story Victorian Gothic Revival residence, with its twin porches, dormer windows, and elaborately carved wooden trim. The house was prefabricated in the East and shipped around Cape Horn to California. Vallejo named his estate Lachryma Montis ("mountain tear") for the free-flowing spring on the property. Grapevines, fruit trees, decorative trees and shrubs covered the land.

General Vallejo and his wife lived at Lachryma Montis for over 35 years. But as the General suffered one economic setback after another, it became necessary to sell nearly all their vast land holdings. During his last years, Vallejo lived quietly, spending his time reading and writing letters to his many children and friends. He also authored a five-volume history of California and was an active supporter of the California Horticultural Society. He died in 1890 at the age of 82 and was buried in nearby Sonoma Mountain Cemetery.

In addition to the house, the park contains several other interesting buildings to investigate. A brick warehouse, originally used to store wine, fruit, and other produce, is known today as the Swiss Chalet and serves as a museum. There are also picnic tables under the trees by the pool and restrooms near the entrance. When you are ready to leave, ride back out to the bike path and continue on your way.

As you cross First Street West, notice the Depot Hotel on the left. Built in 1870 of stone from General Vallejo's quarries, it was originally a home with walls 16 inches thick. It was acquired by the railroad in 1888 and used as a saloon for travelers. Today it is a restaurant.

Continue along the bike path to the park where the Sonoma Valley Railroad Depot is located. This replica of the original 1880 building houses the Sonoma Valley Historical Society museum. The bike path on which you are riding is actually the old railroad right-of-way.

General Mariano Vallejo

Mariano Guadalupe Vallejo was born in 1807 in Monterey, the Spanish capital of Alta California. He joined the military at the age of 16 and rose rapidly through the ranks, becoming the Commander of the Presidio of San Francisco in 1831. Arriving in Sonoma in 1835, he was responsible for reducing the mission to the status of a parish church, freeing the Indian workers, and distributing the mission lands and other assets to the general population.

As a reward for his efforts, Vallejo was granted 44,000 acres of prime agricultural land which he called Rancho Petaluma. With additional acquisitions, Vallejo eventually owned 175,000 acres. This vast empire, together with his extensive military and civil powers, made Vallejo one of the wealthiest and most influential men in California while it was a Mexican province. He surveyed and established the town of Sonoma, gave land grants to private citizens, and directed military affairs.

His circumstances suddenly changed when he was imprisoned by Americans during the Bear Flag Revolt in 1846. After he was freed and allowed to return home, Vallejo found that his rancho had been stripped of its horses, cattle, and other commodities. His vast political and economic power had evaporated. He continued to play a part in government, however, as a delegate to California's 1848 constitutional convention and then as a state senator. After his unsuccessful attempt to establish a state capital at what is now the town of Vallejo, he limited his political activities to the local level and served two terms as mayor of Sonoma.

After a block and a half, at 315 Second Street East, you'll see the Vella Cheese Company to the right, housed in a 1905 brewery. Vella, along with the Sonoma Cheese Factory on the Plaza, makes Monterey Jack, the only type of cheese native to the West.

Historic Wineries

As you approach the end of the bike path on Fourth Street East, you will ride through vineyards belonging to the Sebastiani Winery. The winery buildings are located to the right on Fourth Street East.

Samuele Sebastiani came to California from Italy and worked in the stone quarries on Schocken Hill. By 1904 he had saved enough money to buy both an old winery and these vineyards, which had been planted by the mission padres in 1825 and were later owned by Vallejo. Sebastiani's son and grandson have followed in his footsteps, producing both bulk and premium wines. Sebastiani's 1923 Craftsman style home can be found just past the tasting room.

From here you may either return to the Plaza or continue to another historic winery. The 3.5-mile roundtrip to Buena Vista Winery is scenic and nearly flat, although the last narrow section can be difficult to navigate if there is much traffic. To return to your starting point from Sebastiani's, proceed south down Fourth Street, turning right at the first corner after the tasting room onto East Spain Street. (The remainder of the route description continues below.)

To reach Buena Vista Winery, ride north on Fourth Street and turn right onto Lovall Valley Road, opposite the bike path. When the road seems to end, go left on Seventh Street, then right, staying to the right back onto Lovall Valley, following the signs to Buena Vista. When you reach Old Winery Road, turn left and ride along the narrow, eucalyptus-lined driveway to its end at the winery.

The Buena Vista Winery, one of California's oldest, was founded in 1857 by Agoston Haraszthy, a Hungarian count who constructed the massive stone buildings and dug cellars deep into limestone hillsides. He imported hundreds of European grape varieties and made Buena Vista one of the state's leading wine producers. Unfortunately, the count came to an untimely end on a trip to Nicaragua in 1869 when he disappeared in the jungle, some say eaten by alligators.

The winery remained in operation, run by two sons who had each married one of Vallejo's daughters, until the earthquake of 1906. In the 1940s the buildings were restored and the winery reopened. Today the actual wine-making is done elsewhere, but you can take a self-guided tour of the cellars and enjoy the tasting room. There also are shady picnic facilities and restrooms on the grounds.

Leaving Buena Vista, retrace your route back to the Sebastiani Winery on Fourth Street, and turn right at the corner onto East Spain Street.

Route Continues

After a short distance along East Spain, you will come upon two more old houses of note. On the left, at No. 245, is an early wood frame home, dating from the 1850s. On the corner, at No. 205, is an adobe with a two-story veranda. The back section was built of wood in 1846. The adobe part in front has walls 22 inches thick and was added in 1851 after the owner struck it rich in the gold fields.

To your right is Schocken Hill, the location of one of the largest granite and basalt quarries in the Sonoma area. In the

Buena Vista Winery at the end of Old Winery Road in Sonoma. Founded in 1857, it is one of California's oldest wineries.

courtesy Buena Vista Winery

23

1880s and 1890s, quarries were Sonoma's third most important industry, after wineries and dairies. The quarries furnished paving blocks for the streets of San Francisco, Petaluma, and San Jose until the use of asphalt destroyed the business.

The two-story Blue Wing Inn, on the left at No. 139, dates from about 1840. This Monterey Colonial style adobe was probably built to house soldiers and travelers and later served as a saloon and stage depot.

At the end of the block is the Plaza and the end of your ride through the historic town of Sonoma.

Additional Information

Sonoma State Historic Park: Across from the Plaza along East Spain Street. Open daily 10:00 AM to 5:00 PM. Includes the mission, barracks, and Vallejo's home. Admission fee. (707) 938-1519.

Sonoma Valley Visitors Bureau: 453 First Street East. Open daily 9:00 AM to 5:00 PM. (707) 996-1090.

Sonoma Cheese Factory and Deli: 2 West Spain Street. Serves sandwiches and sells picnic supplies. You can also watch Sonoma Jack cheese being made. Store open daily 8:30 AM to 5:30 PM. (707) 996-1931, (800) 535-2855.

Toscano Hotel and Kitchen: 20 East Spain Street. Open for free tours weekends 1:00 to 4:00 PM, Mondays 11:00 AM to 1:00 PM. Lobby open for viewing daily 10:00 AM to 5:00 PM.

Sonoma Valley Historical Society Museum: In Depot Park, 270 First Street West. Open Wednesday through Sunday 1:00 to 4:30 PM. Small admission fee. (707) 938-9765.

Vella Cheese Company: 315 Second Street East. Offers cheese samples. (707) 938-3232, (800) 848-0505.

Sebastiani Vineyards: 389 Fourth Street East. Open daily 10:00 AM to 4:00 PM for tastings and tours. (707) 938-5532.

Buena Vista Winery: End of Old Winery Road. Open daily 10:00 AM to 5:00 PM. (707) 938-1266.

Bike Rental: Goodtime Bicycle Company, 18503 Sonoma Highway, Boyes Hot Springs. (707) 938-0453.

2. Sonoma Valley

Distance: 25 miles plus 3-mile side trip

Rating: *Moderate* except for the challenging mile-long climb on the side trip to Jack London State Historic Park. The ride to Kenwood also involves a narrow road with little shoulder. Part of the route is unshaded and may be hot during the summer.

Highlights: Although the Sonoma Valley is a premier wine-growing region, the highlight of this ride is Glen Ellen and the early 20th-century home of author Jack London. You will also explore the charming town of Kenwood and the last home of General Mariano Vallejo, the outstanding native Californian of his day.

Location: Less than an hour's drive northeast of San Francisco on Highway 12.

House of Happy Walls, Jack London State Park, Glen Ellen. Built 1919 by the widow of Jack London as a memorial to her husband, it is now a museum.

courtesy Redwood Empire Association

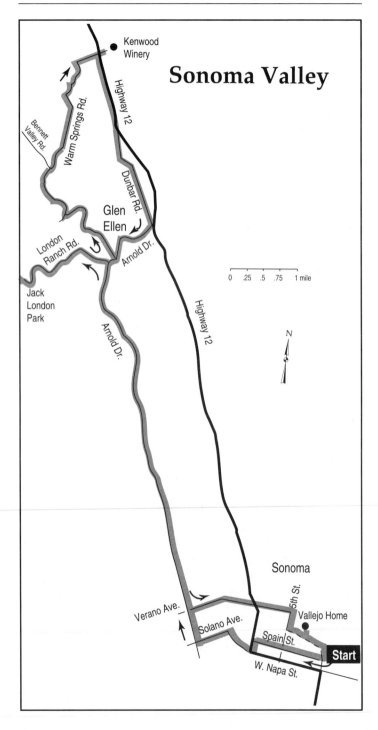

Begin your ride at the Plaza, located along Highway 12 in the center of Sonoma, one of the state's most historic towns. There is free parking behind the buildings of the State Historic Park on the north side of the Plaza, off First Street East. Allow plenty of time at the end of your tour to explore this fascinating area. (See Sonoma Ride, page 13.)

From the Plaza, ride west on Spain Street, past the Sonoma Hotel and the entrance to the Vallejo Home (you'll visit this on your return). In the next block, at 400 West Spain, you will see the large Italianate house built in 1870 for one of General Vallejo's daughters.

At the end of West Spain Street, about a mile down the road, make a left turn onto the Sonoma Highway (Highway 12), and then go right at the next intersection onto Riverside Drive. Cross over the narrow bridge, continuing past the stop sign to the next left turn, which is Solano Avenue. Hidden behind the trees, at 400 Solano, is the house that once belonged to Spanish Kitty Lombard, a madam from San Francisco's wild Barbary Coast.

You are now riding through the small community of El Verano, one of several resort towns built around local hot springs just after the turn of the century. Continue along Solano for half a mile, and go right when you reach Arnold Drive. Traffic may be heavy here, but the road is mostly flat with a good shoulder much of the way.

The 6-mile route to Glen Ellen takes you past vineyards, old farms, new homes, and through the pleasant, shady grounds of the Sonoma Developmental Center. Established in 1891, it was the first hospital west of the Mississippi for the care of the mentally retarded. From here it is just over a mile to Glen Ellen, best known as the home of Jack London.

Glen Ellen

Glen Ellen is a quaint little town that had its start when General Vallejo built a sawmill along Sonoma Creek in the 1840s. Frenchman Joshua Chavet settled here in 1856 and established vineyards and a winery. The town was named in 1869 after the wife of another vintner, and the post office was established two years later.

The town's boom period began when the railroad reached Glen Ellen in 1879, bringing large groups of tourists to camp or stay in cottages and hotels. By the turn of the century, the tiny town had become a boisterous place with numerous hotels, saloons, and brothels. Several brick buildings constructed by Chavet after a 1905 fire destroyed much of the town still exist today.

Jack London State Historic Park

Jack London came to Glen Ellen on vacation in 1903, shortly after publication of his first major novel, *Call of the Wild*. Here he met Charmian Kitteridge whom he married in 1905 after divorcing his first wife. He and Charmian made Glen Ellen their home for the rest of their lives.

London was born in San Francisco in 1876 and grew up in Oakland. In his early years he earned his living as a newspaper boy, fisherman, hobo, seaman, and gold miner in Alaska's Klondike. He was a handsome, hard-working, hard-drinking man with socialist ideals, a love of books, and a passion for writing. He sold his first story at the age of 22 and was America's highest-paid author by the time he was 30. In his short lifetime (he died of uremic poisoning at the age of 40) he wrote 51 books, nearly 200 short stories, and numerous articles.

Jack London State Historic Park is located on a wooded hillside outside of Glen Ellen and includes London's ranch, the House of Happy Walls museum, and the ruins of Wolf House. To reach the park, take London Ranch Road, across from the country store (a good place to buy picnic supplies). The 1.3-mile climb to the park is moderately strenuous, the first part being the steepest. On the way, you will pass the Glen Ellen Winery, located on one of Sonoma Valley's historic wine estates.

The entrance to the park is at the end of the road. Allow one to two hours to see everything and perhaps enjoy a picnic lunch.

Just inside the entrance, turn right toward the overflow parking lot and the trail that leads to the Londons' beloved Beauty Ranch where Jack practiced scientific agriculture and entertained his many friends. There are stone barns, concrete silos, and the "Pig Palace," a luxurious circular building he designed for his hogs, all located on a half-mile walk. You will also see the small 1862 cottage where Jack London lived, wrote, and died.

To the left of the park entrance, through the parking lot, is the path to the House of Happy Walls, the stone house built by Charmian London in 1919 as a memorial to her husband. She lived alone here until her death in 1955 at the age of 84. Today the building houses a museum and includes the South Sea collection gathered on the couple's two-year sailing voyage, as well as other London memorabilia. (Restrooms can be found near the parking lot.)

From the museum, be sure to take the half-mile trail down through the trees to the ruins of Wolf House. The Londons began building it in 1911, using native volcanic lava boulders and redwood timbers. It contained 26 rooms, 9 fireplaces, and a courtyard reflection pool. Late one night in 1913, just a few weeks before the Londons planned to move in, this magnificent house was mysteriously destroyed by fire. It was never rebuilt. All that is left are the stone walls and chimneys, an eerie monument to the author's dream.

Three years later, Jack London suddenly died. As he wished, his ashes were buried on a wooded knoll off the trail to Wolf House near the graves of two pioneer children. The site is marked by a huge lava boulder, too large for use in Wolf House. Charmian's ashes are here also. When you have finished exploring this beautiful park, return to Glen Ellen, enjoying the exhilarating downhill run. At the bottom of the hill, turn left on Arnold Drive. (If you do not want to do the

Novelist Jack London's "Wolf House" in Glen Ellen. Built of native volcanic lava and redwood timbers, it was gutted by fire in 1913, just before the Londons were to move in.

courtesy Redwood Empire Association

10-mile round-trip to Kenwood, turn right to return to Sonoma.)

From Arnold, go left at Warm Springs Road (at the sign for Morton's Warm Springs), heading toward the town of Kenwood. This shady, narrow road winds along a pretty little creek, though you may encounter some traffic. After about a mile you'll pass the ruins of an old pool, a remnant of a turn-of-the-century resort.

About 2.5 miles from Glen Ellen, turn right at the intersection to stay on Warm Springs Road (Bennett Valley Road goes left). The road is even narrower here, but traffic is very light. Just before you come to Kenwood, you'll pass Morton's Warm Springs, which has three public swimming pools that are all heated by natural hot springs.

Kenwood

Once part of Rancho Los Guilicos, the little community of Kenwood sprang up in the 1880s after the railroad arrived. As you enter town, you'll see the 1888 stone depot on the right, across from Jake's Deli (a good place to buy lunch).

Kenwood soon became the center of a major ranching and agricultural region, while tourists flocked into town to enjoy the hot mineral springs. Then the train quit running in 1936, leaving the town small and unspoiled. Be sure to visit the Gothic style community church that faces the plaza. Kenwood Vineyards, one of several wineries in the area, is located across Sonoma Highway (Highway 12), opposite Warm Springs Road. It was founded in 1906 as the Pagani Brothers Winery, and the tasting room dates from that time.

After exploring Kenwood (more restaurants can be found along the highway a few blocks north), you'll return to Glen Ellen by riding south on Highway 12, the former stage and railroad route between Sonoma and Santa Rosa. You'll have wonderful views of mountains and vineyards along this scenic road, but traffic moves fast and may be heavy at times. The shoulder is also rather narrow, so exercise caution.

After less than 2 miles, however, you'll leave the busy highway and turn right onto Dunbar Road, a quiet country lane where you can relax and admire the old farms and newer homes along the way.

Dunbar ends back at Arnold Drive. From here you can see Glen Oaks, a grand stone mansion across the highway, built in

1860 by Colonel Charles Stuart. The town of Glen Ellen was named for his wife.

Turn right on Arnold, and in another mile you'll be back in the center of Glen Ellen.

To return to Sonoma, ride on Arnold for approximately 5 miles until you reach Verano Street, opposite a small, white-steepled church. Turn left at the traffic light and continue on Verano across Highway 12 to its end at Fifth Street West. Follow the road to the right, and after about 3 blocks, just past Linda Drive, make a left onto the paved bike path.

Vallejo's Home

In a short distance, you will see the buildings of General Vallejo's home to your left, across the open field. Turn left when you come to the narrow, tree-lined road that leads to his estate, Lachryma Montis, now part of Sonoma State Historic Park.

General Mariano Vallejo, one of the wealthiest and most influential men in California, built this fine two-story Victorian Gothic Revival residence in 1851. Besides the house, the park has a museum and several other smaller buildings, including restrooms near the entrance. (For more information on General Vallejo and Lachryma Montis, see Sonoma Ride, page 13.)

Bud O'Hare

Kenwood Community Church. This Gothic style church is on the Plaza in Kenwood.

After exploring Vallejo's estate, ride back out to the bike path and continue on your way. At Depot Park, follow the bike path that goes to the right. This will bring you to the parking lot behind the state park buildings on the Plaza and the end of your tour of the beautiful and historic Sonoma Valley.

Additional Information

Shone's Country Store: Center of Glen Ellen. Open daily 6:30 AM to 9:00 PM. (707) 996-6728.

Jack London Historic State Park: End of London Ranch Road in Glen Ellen. Open daily 10:00 AM to 5:00 PM. Entrance fee for automobiles, bicycles free. (707) 938-5216.

Glen Ellen Winery: 1883 London Ranch Road. Open daily for tasting and self-guided tours 10:00 AM to 4:30 PM. (707) 935-3000.

Morton Warm Springs: 1651 Warm Springs Road in Kenwood. Open May to September. Fee to use the pools and picnic grounds. (707) 833-5511.

Jake's Delicatessen: 405 Warm Springs Road, Kenwood. Open daily 8:00 AM to 7:00 PM. (707) 833-1350.

Kenwood Winery: 9592 Sonoma Highway, opposite Warm Springs Road. Open daily 10:00 AM to 4:30 PM. (707) 833-5891.

Sugarloaf Ridge State Park: 2605 Adobe Canyon Road, north of Kenwood off Highway 12. Campsites and hiking trails. Three miles up a steep and narrow road in the Mayacamas Mountains. (707) 833-5712.

Bike Rental: Goodtime Bicycle Company, 18503 Sonoma Highway, Boyes Hot Springs. (707) 938-0453.

See Sonoma Ride, page 24, for more resources.

3. Napa

Distance: 8 miles

Rating: *Easy* ride on flat city streets. There is likely to be some traffic to contend with, however, especially near the downtown area.

Highlights: Napa was once a major river port and the center of the Napa Valley wine country. This ride offers a glimpse of the city's glorious past, with many outstanding examples of 19th-century commercial and residential architecture.

Location: Off Highway 29 in southern Napa County, north of Vallejo and an hour's drive northeast of San Francisco.

Manasse Mansion at 443 Brown Street in Napa. Built in 1889, it is now a bed-and-breakfast inn.

Betty Johnston

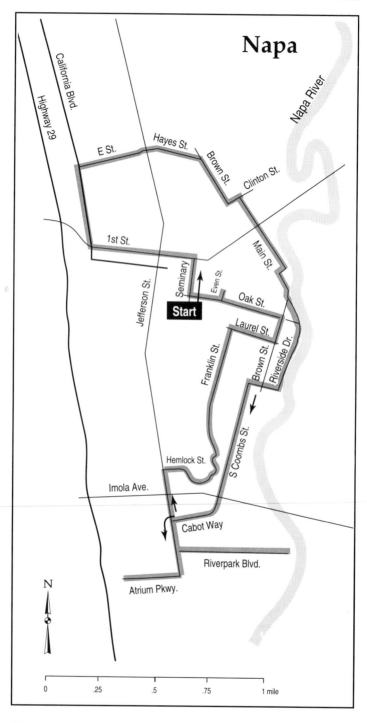

Napa

Napa River

California Blvd.

Highway 29

E St.

Hayes St.

Brown St.

Clinton St.

1st St.

Main St.

Jefferson St.

Seminary

Even St.

Oak St.

Start

Laurel St.

Franklin St.

Brown St.

Riverside Dr.

S Coombs St.

Hemlock St.

Imola Ave.

Cabot Way

Riverpark Blvd.

N

Atrium Pkwy.

| 0 | .25 | .5 | .75 | 1 mile |

Ride through the City of Napa

Begin your ride through Napa at Fuller Park, located at the intersection of Jefferson and Oak streets. To reach the park from Highway 29, take the First Street exit to Central Napa, turn left on Second Street and right on Jefferson. (Restrooms are available in the park.) The surrounding neighborhood is well known for its many fine examples of 19th-century architecture, ranging from small cottages to splendid mansions.

From the park, ride north on Seminary Street, noting the beautifully restored Eastlake style house on the corner, at No. 705. At the other end of the block, at No. 741, you'll see one of the most elaborate homes on this tour with its profusion of spindles, turned columns, and brackets. This 1892 Queen Anne was designed by popular local architect Luther Turton for the family of William Andrews, a grocer.

Continuing on Seminary, cross Third and Second streets, then turn left onto First Street, a busy one-way street that often has considerable automobile traffic but still has room for bicycles. At the corner of Jefferson Street is the stately 1905 Noyes Mansion, at 1750 First Street, designed in the Colonial

History of Napa

The original town site of Napa was surveyed in 1848 by Nathan Coombs, and its first building, a saloon, was erected a year later. Napa grew quickly, and with its drinking establishments, theater, reading room, band, and other amenities, became a favorite retreat for miners seeking to escape the winter weather in the gold fields. In 1852, European grape cuttings were planted south of town, and Charles Krug produced the first European-style wine in the Napa region a few years later.

The wine industry flourished, partly because of the city's location on the navigational head of the Napa River. First schooners plied her waters, and then a steamship line to San Francisco was established in 1850, providing inexpensive and reliable transportation to the metropolitan marketplace. The city of Napa controlled the region's trade for almost a century, until the advent of the motor trucking system brought an end to the river's usefulness, and the city's importance faded. Today the river is used mainly for recreation.

Revival style by Luther Turton for Frank Noyes, owner of a lumberyard. Turton was also the architect for the 1892 house across the street at 1005 Jefferson.

As you continue riding along First Street, you'll find a delightful assortment of mansions and cottages that date from the 1870s to the early 1900s. On the corner of the next block, at No. 1910, there is an 1902 Turton-designed, brown shingle house that is now one of several bed-and-breakfast establishments in Napa. The house next door with the steep pitched roof, at No. 1926, is also by Turton. Across the street at No. 1929, the elegant home with a Mansard style roof dates from 1875.

At the traffic signal, make a right turn onto California Boulevard where you'll have a bike lane and will pass the posh hotel, Inn at Napa Valley. Continue on California for a few blocks, turning right when you reach E Street, which will take you through a neighborhood of less imposing homes and cottages.

Once you recross Jefferson, E Street becomes Hayes Street. When it ends, turn left onto Yount Street and note the remains of the historic Lisbon Winery, built in 1882 by Joseph Mathews, a native of Portugal who pioneered the exportation of fine Napa wines to Europe and developed a prize-winning sherry. Before Prohibition, there were several other wineries along the riverfront, but they no longer exist.

From Yount Street, ride south on Brown Street until the road ends at Clinton, where you'll go left to Main Street. On the corner is the old sandstone Pfeiffer Building, now the Andrews Meat Co. & Delicatessen, the oldest surviving commercial structure in Napa. Built in 1875 as a brewery, it later became a saloon (and possibly a brothel), and for 50 years was a Chinese laundry.

Main Street

Turn right on Main Street, which parallels the river, to see more of downtown Napa's historic buildings. If traffic seems too heavy for sightseeing, you may want to walk your bike along the sidewalk. The Napa Opera House, at 1018 Main, served as the social center of the community from 1879 until it closed in 1914 as a result of the decline in traveling shows and the increased popularity of movies. After sitting empty for more than 50 years, the Opera House is now being restored and will once again offer performing arts and cultural events.

The Winship Building, at 948 Main, is an example of Luther Turton's commercial architecture. It was commissioned in 1888 by a doctor for his second-floor practice and street-level stores and now houses offices and specialty shops. Next to it, at 975 First Street, is the elegant Semorile Building, also designed by Turton for an Italian grocer. It is distinguished by the unusual combination of brick, stone, and wrought iron on its façade.

Additional historic buildings are located off Main Street. The stone Goodman Library, at 1219 First, is another Turton design. Built in 1901 with funds donated by George Goodman, it was used as a library until 1963 when it became the home of the Napa County Historical Society.

Part of the Napa County Court House, located one block to the right on Third Street, dates from 1878. Farther down Third you can see the tall, slim spire of the First Presbyterian Church, constructed in 1874. A California Historical Landmark, this wooden Victorian Gothic structure is well preserved inside and out.

Continue along Main Street until it ends at Fifth, and turn right. Here is the brick Hatt Building, originally a grain mill dating from 1884. Take the first left at Brown Street, then go left again onto Riverside Drive for a peaceful ride along the Napa River. After half a mile, when Riverside ends, go right

Queen Anne Victorian at 741 Seminary Drive in Napa. It was built in 1892 for William Andrews, a grocer.

Betty Johnston

on Elm, then left at South Coombs Street. In half a mile, after crossing Imola Avenue, the road becomes Cabot Way and takes you through a modern suburban neighborhood.

Spreckles-Sheveland Ranch

At South Jefferson, make a left turn and go a quarter mile to Atrium Parkway, where you turn right. You're now riding through what was once a large 1890s ranch owned by sugar tycoon Adolph Spreckles of San Francisco. Here Spreckles bred and trained race horses, including several Kentucky Derby winners. The ranch at one time extended all the way from the river to the hillside across Highway 29 and from Imola Avenue south past the Meadows senior residence. There were barns, two race tracks, a marble pool, and a 35-room mansion, as well as other, smaller ranch houses. The mansion was destroyed by fire in 1928, and in 1940 most of the property was sold to the Shevelands who converted some of the buildings into apartments. From the road, you can see the stud barn with the cupola on top and the house where the jockeys lived. Although the Sheveland Ranch is now greatly diminished in size, it is still home to members of the family.

Return to South Jefferson and turn left, passing the Napa Yacht Club, an exclusive housing development with its own marina. Homeowners here can pilot their yachts right up to their own backyard docks. For a closer look, go right at River-park Boulevard, the first street past the yacht club, and ride a half mile to the river, along the tree-lined road that once connected the Spreckles ranch to their boat landing.

Return to South Jefferson and continue north, once again crossing Imola. The first right turn takes you away from the traffic and onto Hemlock Street which loops around a quiet neighborhood. At Cesta, go right, then left at South Franklin Street. You'll soon pass the Napa Women's Club at No. 218, housed in a former primary school dating from 1901.

Napa Mansions

The block past Pine is lined with redwood trees and is one of the prettiest in town. The 1886 mansion at No. 313 belonged to Samuel Holden, who was president of the Sawyer Tanning and Woolen Mill, a bank director, city council member, and college president. At the other end of the block, at No. 397, is the Italianate Sawyer house, built in the late 1870s for the founder of the mill. From Franklin, go right onto Laurel, then left when you reach Brown Street, where you'll see two of Napa's most impressive old residences. The house at No. 443 was built in 1889 for Edward Manasse, who developed a new process for tanning glove leather and was a partner in the tanning mill. The fine home at No. 485 was constructed about the same time for Edward S. Churchill, a banker and vintner. The porch and columns were added later. This building is on the National Register of Historic Places, and both residences are now bed-and-breakfast inns. Turn left on Oak Street where, on the right at No. 1120, you will pass a three-story home with a mansard roof. When it was built in 1872 for George Goodman, Sr., it faced Brown Street, but now apartments fill its front yard and block its view. Goodman had a general store and started the first bank in Napa.

At the next corner, on the left, there is a large brown shingle home at 486 Coombs. Located directly behind the Churchill mansion, it was built in 1893 by Edward S. Churchill for his son, Edward W. In another block, at 492 Randolph Street, is the house built in the 1880s by George Goodman, Sr., for his son George, Jr. It is a typical Queen Anne style with corner tower and elaborate entrance porch.

Migliavacca Mansion at Fourth and Even Streets in Napa. Designed by Luther Turton, it was built in 1895 for $4,000.

After another 2 blocks, make a right turn onto tiny Even
Street to see the fanciful Migliavacca Mansion, on the corner
of Fourth Street. Also designed by Luther Turton, this
residence with its three-story tower was built in 1895 for
Giuseppe Migliavacca and his family of ten children at a cost
of $4,000. Migliavacca was in the wine business and associated
with the Bank of Italy, forerunner of the Bank of America.
Originally located several blocks away, the house was moved
to this site to make room for a new library.

Return to Oak Street, going right as you head back to Fuller
Park and the conclusion of your ride through this historic port
city.

Additional Information

Napa County Historical Society Museum: 1219 First
Street, Napa. Open Tuesday and Thursday noon to 4:00
PM. (707) 224-1739.

Andrews Meat Co. & Delicatessen: 1245 Main Street.
Open Monday through Saturday 8:30 AM to 5:30 PM.
Sandwiches. (707) 253-8311.

Napa Visitors and Conference Bureau: 1310 Napa Town
Center, Napa, CA 94559. Open weekdays 9:00 AM to 5:00
PM, Saturday 10:00 AM to 3:00 PM. (707) 226-7459.

Napa Chamber of Commerce: 1556 First Street, Napa, CA
94559. Open weekdays 9:00 AM to 5:00 PM. (707) 226-7455.

Bike Rental: Bryan's Napa Valley Cyclery, 4080 Byway
East, Napa. (707) 255-3377.

4. Napa Countryside

Distance: 31 miles

Rating: *Moderate*, because of some rolling hills, although much of the route is flat. You may encounter headwinds on your return (especially in the afternoon). Summer weather in Napa Valley is hot and dry, perfect for grape-growing but potentially hard on cyclists. This ride is especially pleasant in the fall, when vineyards turn red and gold and grapes are being harvested.

Highlights: This ride takes you from the city of Napa with its many old homes into the countryside, past acres of vineyards and numerous wineries to the historic town of Yountville.

Location: Napa Valley is located in Napa County, along Highway 29, about an hour's drive northeast from San Francisco.

Cycling the Napa countryside along the Silverado Trail.

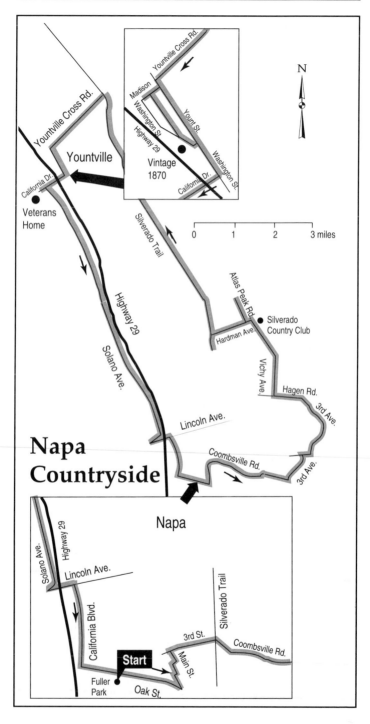

Ride through the City of Napa

Begin your ride at Fuller Park in Napa, located at the intersection of Jefferson and Oak streets. To reach the park from Highway 29, take the First Street exit to Central Napa, going left on Second Street and right on Jefferson. (Restrooms are available in the park.) Ride west on Oak Street, away from Jefferson, and on your way out of town you'll see a number of the Victorian-era homes Napa is noted for. At the corner of Oak and Randolph Street, 492 Randolph, is the 1880s Queen Anne style house built for George Goodman, Jr., by his father, who owned a general store and started the town's first bank. The large brown shingle home at the next corner, 486 Coombs, was constructed in 1893 for Edward W. Churchill by his father, a banker and vintner. It is located directly behind the elder Churchill's mansion at 485 Brown, a fine home built around 1889. This elegant structure, now a bed-and-breakfast inn, is on the National Register of Historic Places. On the other side of the street at 1120 Oak, there is a three-story home with a mansard roof built in 1872 for George Goodman, Sr. Continue along Oak until it ends at Riverside Drive, where you go left and ride along the Napa River. A century ago, the river served as a main transportation route into the Napa Valley and was

History of Napa Valley

The Napa countryside, known around the world for its extensive vineyards, excellent wines, and natural beauty, is one of the Bay Area's most popular tourist destinations. Nearly one hundred wineries can be found around Napa Valley today, but little remains of its original inhabitants, the Napa Indians who lived in this area for centuries. When pioneer George Yount arrived in 1831, he estimated that the Indian population in Napa Valley numbered between 10,000 and 12,000. But, as happened in other areas, the Indians did not survive the invasion by white settlers. Thousands died during a cholera epidemic in 1833, and within a decade the native population was decimated.

The city of Napa was laid out in 1848 by Nathan Coombs. Early settlers quickly recognized the area's potential, and the first European-style wine was produced in 1858 by pioneer vintner Charles Krug. Napa Valley has been an important wine-producing region ever since.

instrumental in the development of the area's wine industry. But as water transportation became less important, commercial development occurred away from the river, and now it is mostly used for recreation.

When Riverside ends, turn right onto Brown and right again at Fifth Street. From here you can see the brick Hatt Building, originally a grain mill dating from 1884. Follow the road left onto Main Street.

Turn right at Third Street, just before Veterans Memorial Park. This takes you over the Napa River on a narrow bridge and then across busy Soscol Avenue. As you cross Silverado Trail (Highway 121), angle to the right on Coombsville Road, named for Nathan Coombs, the town founder. You will have a bike lane here and a gradual uphill.

Napa Countryside

The Tulocay Cemetery, on the left, is the final resting place of many of Napa's citizens, including Mammy Pleasant, infamous madam and voodoo queen, and Cayetano Juarez, the owner of Rancho Tulocay who donated part of his land grant for this cemetery in 1859. Bicycles are not allowed in the cemetery, so if you wish to explore it, you will have to do so on foot.

As you continue along Coombsville Road, you will soon be out of the city and into the countryside with views of open fields and the hills beyond. Turn left when you reach Third Avenue in about 1.5 miles. After less than a mile, Third goes to the right and the road narrows, though traffic is light. You will ride by acres of vineyards, along a tree-lined ravine, and past the Napa Valley Country Club. After a couple of miles, the road angles left and becomes Hagen Road. In a half mile you'll see the Welcome Grange, officially known as the Mt. George Farm Center, where meetings have been held since 1916.

Make the next right turn onto Vichy Avenue, and ride along rolling hills until Vichy ends at Monticello Road (Highway 121). Turn left, then take the first right onto Atlas Peak Road.

After a block, you will come to the Quail Ridge Wine Cellars. Originally the Hedgeside Winery, it was constructed of native stone in 1885 for Morris Estee, a national leader of the GOP. The architect was Hamden McIntrye, who also designed Inglenook Winery and Christian Brothers Greystone Cellars in Napa Valley. There are 450 feet of tunnels, hand dug into the hillside by Chinese laborers, still used for aging wine. The house next door was part of the winery but has since been converted to a private residence.

The entrance to the Silverado Country Club is just over half a mile farther along. The country club is located on what was once the 1,200-acre estate of John Miller, the youngest Union general during the Civil War. The club house and restaurant are in the original mansion, built in 1889 around an earlier adobe.

After viewing General Miller's home, continue on Atlas Peak and take the first left at Hardman Avenue. When you reach the Silverado Trail, turn right for a ride along the eastern side of Napa Valley. There may be some fast-moving traffic, but the road has wide, smooth shoulders and is mostly level with only an occasional rolling hill.

This is the most scenic part of the ride, taking you past numerous wineries and miles of orderly rows of vineyards. To the east is the Howell mountain range, and across the valley is the Mayacamas range. It's hard to argue with the words of George Yount who, when he first set eyes on Napa Valley, said, "In such a place I should love to live and die."

After 6.7 miles of pleasant riding, turn left at the Yountville Cross Road, which will take you 2 miles across the valley to the town of Yountville.

Silverado Country Club on Atlas Peak Road in Napa. It was originally a mansion for a Civil War general.

Along the way, you'll pass the entrance to the Napa River Ecological Reserve on the right, just after crossing the river. You may want to stop and take a short walk to the river, where you can rest in the shade of the oak and laurel trees. Church groups held summer gatherings here beginning in 1851, and as many as 4,000 people stayed in the campgrounds during the 1870s.

Yountville

As you enter historic Yountville, the road ends at Yount Street, named for the first white settler in the Napa Valley, George Calvert Yount.

Yount, a native of North Carolina, spent several years in Sonoma with General Vallejo and became a Mexican citizen. In 1835, as a reward for his loyalty and service, Vallejo granted him over 11,000 acres of land in the heart of Napa Valley, which Yount called Rancho Caymus. With the help of local Indians, Yount built a log blockhouse, then an adobe along the river, about a mile north of the present town. He planted the first vineyards in the valley, raised cattle and sheep, maintained fruit orchards, and built both a sawmill and grist mill. In 1855 he commissioned a surveyor to lay out a town called Sebastopol on the southern edge of Rancho Caymus. Two years after Yount's death in 1867, the town was renamed in his honor. Yount is buried in the cemetery at the north end of town.

Ride to the left onto Yount Street. You will soon pass the Yountville Community Church, which has a traditional white steeple and dates from 1876. The Town Hall, a little farther along, is located in the 1930 grammar school building. Next you'll come to the old Magnolia Hotel on your right, at No. 6529. This brick and stone structure was built in 1873 as a hotel, but it has since served as a bordello, a center for bootlegging during Prohibition, and as a 4-H Club meeting place. After years of being boarded up, it has been restored as a bed-and-breakfast inn.

Vintage 1870

Yount soon merges with Washington Street, the major thoroughfare in town. Here, you'll go to the right to see Yountville's prime tourist attraction, Vintage 1870, a massive, ivy-covered brick complex of restaurants and specialty shops housed in historic winery buildings.

Gottlieb Groezinger, a German immigrant, established this winery in 1870 as the center of an immense agricultural complex. The main building, a two-story livery stable, and a distillery still remain. The small structure in front was built in 1868 by Sam Brannan as a depot for his privately owned Napa Valley Railroad.

By the time Groezinger built his winery, Yountville was a thriving farming community and a rest stop for the valley's freight and stage lines. Then nearly everyone began planting grapes, but within two decades an infestation of *phylloxera*, a tiny, aphid-like insect that feeds on grape roots, destroyed the vines and brought financial ruin to many. Groezinger's enterprise survived, however, until Prohibition closed its doors. The buildings were scheduled for demolition in the 1960s but were converted instead to the shops you see today, changing Yountville from a small, rural residential community to a popular tourist destination. The winery is now on the National Register of Historic Places.

Hungry cyclists can choose from two restaurants here, although weekend crowds can be daunting. (There are several other restaurants on Washington.) Public restrooms are located in both the front and rear buildings.

Vintage 1870 on Washington Street in Yountville. Shopping complex is housed in winery buildings dating from 1870.

courtesy Redwood Empire Association

Continuing along Washington, you'll pass a charming little brick restaurant at No. 6534, which was the Wells Fargo station in Groezinger's time. At the next corner, angle right, and go straight ahead onto Jefferson Street, which takes you away from the tourist congestion and through a neighborhood of homes from Yountville's pioneer days. The red house on the right, 6610 Webber Street, is an 1850 farmhouse that belonged to Captain John Grigsby, a participant in the Bear Flag rebellion in Sonoma. Originally situated on the outskirts of town, it was moved to this location in the 1870s, and now, with various additions, is a bed-and-breakfast inn.

Another old house can be found at the corner of Madison Street, on the right. The mother of John Wichels, the town historian, was born here in 1876. Mr. Wichels was born in 1898 in the house across the street with the picket fence. Ride left on Madison for one block, back to Washington Street. To the right is the city park where restrooms are located. You can purchase picnic supplies at the Yountville Market, a deli and cafe, located to the left at 6770 Washington.

When you are ready to leave Yountville, you can either ride down Washington past Vintage 1870 or return to Yount Street, following it to the intersection with Washington, where you'll turn left.

California Veterans Home

After a few blocks, at the stop sign, turn right on California Drive. This takes you under Highway 29, across the railroad tracks, and to the entrance of the Veterans Home of California. Continue up the tree-lined drive to reach the buildings of this spacious and peaceful facility.

Established in 1884 by veterans of the Mexican and Civil wars, the Veterans Home was been operated by the state of California since 1897 as a residence for retired and disabled veterans. To see the 1918 Armistice Chapel Museum, go left at the top of the hill a very short distance, making a right turn at the parking lot between Kennedy Hall and the Administration Building. Ride through the lot and across the street. Standing in the middle of the grassy plaza is the old chapel, now a museum devoted to military history. Lincoln Hall, across the road on the far side of the museum, is the oldest residential building on the grounds, dating from 1929.

Solano Avenue

Return down the hill toward the highway, but just before the entrance ramp, turn right onto Solano Avenue, which has a wide bike lane and parallels Highway 29 for the 7-mile ride back to Napa.

After about 3 miles, you'll pass a beautifully restored home, Vineyard Oaks, at 5129 Solano, that dates from 1871. As you get closer to Napa, the country gives way to suburban development, but there still is an occasional historic building. Just before you reach Salvador Avenue, you can see a two-story Gothic Revival farmhouse on the other side of the highway. It dates from 1870 and is now a bed-and-breakfast establishment.

After crossing busy Redwood Road, continue on Solano another mile to Lincoln Avenue, where you'll turn left on the overpass. Use caution here, watching for traffic entering and leaving the highway. On the other side, take the first right onto California Boulevard. Continue on California past Second Street, and make a left turn at Oak Street. Fuller Park is located on the other side of Jefferson, the end of your tour of the beautiful Napa countryside.

Old Wells Fargo station at 6534 Washington, Yountville. This brick building dates from the 1870s and is now a restaurant.

Additional Information

Vintage 1870: Washington Street, Yountville. Shops open daily 10:00 AM to 5:30 PM.

Yountville Market: 6770 Washington Street. Open Monday through Saturday 7:30 AM to 5:30 PM, Sunday 8:30 AM to 2:30 pm. (707) 944-1393.

Veterans Home of California: West of Highway 29, Yountville. Maps available at the security station at California Drive entrance. (707) 944-4600. Military museum open Wednesday through Friday noon to 2:00 PM, other times by arrangement. (707) 944-4919.

Yountville Chamber of Commerce: 6795 Washington Street. Open Monday through Saturday 10:00 AM to 3:00 PM. (707) 944-0904.

Napa Valley Tourist Bureau: 6488 Washington Street, P.O. Box 3240, Yountville, CA 94599. Information on accommodations or winery tours. Open daily 9:00 AM to 5:00 PM. (707) 258-1957.

Bike Rental: Bryan's Napa Valley Cyclery, 4080 Byway East, Napa. (707) 255-3377.

See Napa Ride, page 40, for more resources.

5. Petaluma

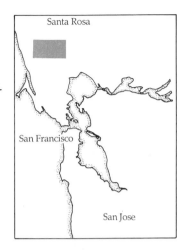

Distance: 21 miles

Rating: *Moderate*, with rolling hills, some narrow roads, and the possibility of city traffic. This ride is especially pleasant when the hills are green after winter rain.

Highlights: Undamaged by the 1906 earthquake, Petaluma has many fine Victorian homes and the West Coast's best collection of ironfront commercial buildings. The ride also takes you into the countryside and to Petaluma Adobe State Historic Park, the rancho home of General Mariano Vallejo.

Location: Petaluma is located along Highway 101, about 35 miles north of San Francisco in southern Sonoma County.

McNear Building on Fourth Street in Petaluma. This ironfront building was constructed in 1886.

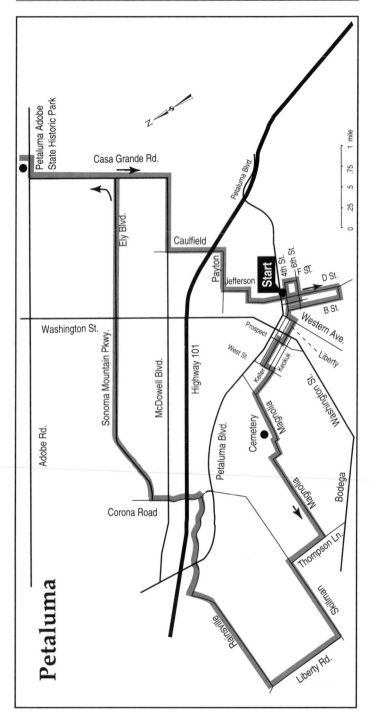

Petaluma

Petaluma Adobe State Historic Park

Casa Grande Rd.

Ely Blvd.

Caulfield

Payton

Jefferson

Start

4th St.

6th St.

F St.

D St.

B St.

Petaluma Blvd.

1 mile

.75

.5

.25

0

Western Ave.

Prospect

Liberty

Washington St.

West St.

Keller

Keokuk

Washington St.

Sonoma Mountain Pkwy.

McDowell Blvd.

Highway 101

Cemetery

Magnolia

Bodega

Adobe Rd.

Petaluma Blvd.

Magnolia

Corona Road

Thompson Ln.

Skillman

Rainsville

Liberty Rd.

Ride through Petaluma

Begin your Petaluma ride at Walnut Park, located at the inter-section of Petaluma Boulevard and D Street. If you are coming from San Francisco on Highway 101, take Petaluma Boulevard South into town. From the north, exit onto East Washington Street, heading to the center of town. Go left at Petaluma Boulevard to D Street and the park. (Restrooms are available here.)

Known as The Plaza when it was originally laid out in 1873, Walnut Park was given its present name in 1896 by the newly formed Ladies' Improvement Club, which created the pleasant landscaped square you see today. The president of the club, Mrs. Henry Atwater, lived across from the park in the attractive 1875 Italianate house at 218 Fourth Street.

From Walnut Park, ride left onto D Street, which passes through one of the finest residential neighborhoods in town. The numerous historic homes here were built from 1865 to 1930 and encompass a wide range of sizes and styles. The large double-turreted duplex at No. 411 was built about 1870. The small cottage in the next block, at No.519, dates from 1865.

The 1925 Spanish Revival dwelling at No. 600 was designed by Julia Morgan, the architect of Hearst Castle at San Simeon. A distinctive Queen Anne home, built in 1890 for H. T. Fairbanks, a successful gold miner, is found at No. 758. Distinguished local architect Brainerd Jones designed the home with the columns and verandas, No. 901, in 1902. On the other side of the street, at No. 920, there is another Queen Anne from the 1870s that once belonged to the Bihn family, who owned of one of the largest hatcheries in the state.

Turn right at the next corner onto Laurel Avenue. Go right on B Street in one block, heading toward the downtown area. Although they are not as grand as the D Street residences, there are several interesting old houses here also, such as the 1870 Queen Anne at No. 827 and the ornate Georgian Revival residence at No. 619 from 1907. In contrast is a modest home at No. 523, built in 1860 in the Greek Revival style.

The Victorian Gothic church at the corner of B and Fifth Street was constructed in 1901. Across Fifth is a 1911 primary school, now the school system administration office, that was designed by Brainerd Jones.

Facing Fourth, at the corner of B Street, is the Carnegie Free Library, built of local sandstone in 1904 with funds donated by Andrew Carnegie. This elegant Classical Revival structure was also designed by Jones and features a beautiful stained glass dome. It served as Petaluma's public library until 1976 and now houses the historical museum.

History of Petaluma

In 1850, the same year California achieved statehood, a hunters' camp was established along the Petaluma River, and a village was soon underway. Two years later, Garrett Keller laid out a town and sold lots. With the river providing a vital link between San Francisco and the North Bay, Petaluma quickly grew into a thriving port. Then, in 1879 Lyman Byce perfected an incubator here that made mass poultry production possible and profitable, creating an industry that would dominate the town's economy for decades.

By the turn of the century, "chicken farming" was widespread, with 90% of the people living near Petaluma raising chickens. Millions of eggs were shipped each year around the globe. In 1923 the world's only chicken pharmacy opened. Giant plaster hens welcomed visitors on the roads into town, and Petaluma became famous as the "Egg Basket of the World." The chicken and egg business began its decline only after World War II, when high labor and feed costs forced thousands of small chicken farms into the hands of a few large producers. Dairying then became the area's prime industry, remaining so until the suburban surge of the 1960s and 1970s.

A history of the town would not be complete without a mention of the McNear family, who played an important role in Petaluma's economy for nearly 100 years. John McNear came to Petaluma with his wife in 1856 and was joined a few years later by his brother George. They established a shipping business together and built grain warehouses along the river. In 1874 George moved to the East Bay to develop the grain trade at Port Costa, while John expanded his interests in Petaluma to banking, railroads, and flour mills. His son, George Plummer McNear, established a feed mill empire that served the emerging egg industry. Over the years, the McNears donated land for a cemetery, a park, a fire station, a school, and a country club.

Beyond Fourth Street, traffic on B is often congested, especially on weekends, so you may want to see this area on foot. The Great Petaluma Mill is located at the end of B Street on the Petaluma River. George P. McNear built this large feed mill in 1902, incorporating some earlier warehouses into the structure, one possibly dating back to 1854. The mill was saved from demolition in 1975 and has been converted into a lively complex of restaurants and specialty shops.

Petaluma Ironfronts

Continue your ride along one-way Fourth Street past the historical museum. On the right you'll see an elaborate ironfront building constructed by John McNear in 1886. Don't miss the moustached faces above each window. This is just one of a number of such decorative ironfront structures still found in Petaluma and unmatched anywhere.

In the 19th century, builders often used cast-iron elements to strengthen and embellish the fronts of brick or wooden buildings. The pieces were cast at a foundry and then bolted onto the underlying structure. Cast-iron façades were thought to be extremely strong and fireproof, but this illusion was dispelled by the 1906 earthquake and fire, which destroyed virtually all of San Francisco's countless ironfronts. Fortunately, Petaluma's buildings were spared by the earthquake and later by urban renewal.

At the end of the block, on the right, you will go by another ironfront, the blue Mutual Relief Building, which was originally the home of a community life insurance cooperative.

For a better view, turn left on Western and stop at the corner. From here you can see the row of ironfronts that are Petaluma's greatest architectural treasure. The smaller structures beyond the 1885 Mutual Relief Building were saloons, 2 of 42 that existed in town in 1886. At the far corner of the block is the three-story Masonic Building, erected in 1882 at the height of Petaluma's river-centered prosperity. The town clock sits on top. Additional ironfronts are located on Petaluma Boulevard and Kentucky Street (the continuation of Fourth). They are best viewed on foot, however, as both of these streets bustle with activity, making cycling difficult. You may have already noticed the I.O.O.F. (International Order of Odd Fellows) Building on Petaluma Boulevard on your way to Walnut Park. It dates from the 1870s.

Historic Homes

Leaving the downtown area, ride on Western for 2 blocks to Liberty and turn right. You will pass two nicely restored 1890s cottages on the left. In the next block, halfway up a short hill, at No. 226, you'll come to an elaborate three-story Queen Anne home built in 1902 for Lyman C. Byce, the inventor of the world's first practical egg incubator.

Movie buffs may recognize the Byce house from the 1986 film *Peggy Sue Got Married*, as the home where Peggy Sue lived. A number of movies have been filmed in Petaluma, including the 1973 classic *American Graffiti*.

Continue along Liberty and make a right turn at the corner onto Prospect Street. At the end of the block, No. 200 is a large Queen Anne constructed in 1892 for Mrs. William Brown, a widow with eight children, shortly after she married the owner of one of the saloons on Western Avenue. As you turn left on Keller Street, note the beautiful stained glass windows. These are from a local funeral home and were added later. More lovely Victorian residences are found on Keller. The Stick style house at No. 311 dates from 1871. The home at No. 343, at the end of the block, was built in 1892 for a dentist from Maine and overlooks the Petaluma River. In between is the 1927 Philip Sweed School, another design by Brainerd Jones.

Continue on Keller to its end at West Street and turn left. In one block, go right on Keokuk and ride down the hill to Magnolia Avenue, where you go left. Although the road has no shoulder, there is generally room for both bicycles and passing automobiles.

Very soon you will come to the entrance of Cypress Hill Cemetery, the final resting place for members of the McNear family. John NcNear donated the land for the cemetery after the death of his 29-year old wife Clara. The circular family plot is located on the highest hill in the far left corner, marked by a white obelisk. Here Clara, John, and their children are buried, along with John's second wife Hattie and other McNears.

Petaluma Countryside

Past the cemetery, you will ride by a mixture of older farm houses and newer residences, as Magnolia, with its gently rolling hills, gradually takes you away from town and into Petaluma's countryside. Some of these country roads have an adequate shoulder, others little or none, but traffic is usually light.

When Magnolia ends, make a right turn on Thompson Lane. Watch for abandoned chicken coops along the route, remnants of the town's chicken-raising heyday. You will also pass numerous tree farms, a mushroom farm, and one that sells pheasants.

Thompson ends at Skillman Lane. Go left on Skillman for a mile, and turn right at the stop sign onto Liberty Road. After another mile, go right again at Rainsville Road, which takes you by more farms and ranches as you head east, back toward town. When you reach Stony Point Road, turn right. This was once the stage road between Santa Rosa and Petaluma and now carries fast-moving automobiles. After crossing Petaluma Boulevard North at the traffic signal, the road becomes Industrial Way, which has a wide shoulder. At its end, turn left onto Corona Road. This takes you over Highway 101 and into east Petaluma, where there will be bike lanes and level riding for most of the remainder of the route.

Continuing on Corona to the second traffic light, turn right onto Sonoma Mountain Road. Petaluma's residential neighborhoods are expanding on this side of town, but there are still

Byce House at 226 Liberty Street, Petaluma. It was built in 1902 for the inventor of the egg incubator that made Petaluma famous as the "Egg Basket of the World."

some open fields protected from development, at least for the time being, by Petaluma's limited-growth policy. Ride along this road, which becomes Ely Boulevard after it crosses East Washington Street, for nearly 4 miles, passing quickly from rural to suburban surroundings.

Petaluma Adobe

At Casa Grande Road, just after the school field, turn left at the stop sign and head toward the rancho home of General Mariano Vallejo.

You will soon see the large structure ahead at the end of Casa Grande. To reach the entrance of Petaluma Adobe State Historic Park, go right on Adobe Road a short distance. If you plan to tour the grounds, be sure to bring a lock, as you must leave your bicycle at the parking lot. Picnic tables and restrooms are located nearby.

The Mexican government sent General Vallejo to Sonoma in 1834 to establish a military garrison. About the same time, he was granted Rancho Petaluma and began building houses and corrals on his 44,000-acre property. Although the main adobe home was never finished, even after ten years of construction, it was once nearly twice as large as it is today and formed a complete quadrangle around a courtyard.

Raising cattle was easy and profitable in this area with its mild climate and rich grasslands. Hides and tallow were traded to foreign merchants for goods manufactured in other parts of the world. Ranch workers also raised horses, sheep, and grain crops.

In 1846 the Bear Flag Revolt in Sonoma brought an end to the rancho's period of prosperity. While General Vallejo was held prisoner by the Americans, his ranch was stripped of its livestock and supplies, and the Indian laborers left. In 1857 Vallejo finally sold the adobe and its surrounding land. A century later, after many years of neglect, the adobe was restored and is now a National Historic Landmark. (For more information on General Vallejo, see Sonoma Ride, page 13.)

When you leave the Petaluma Adobe, return on Casa Grande. At McDowell Boulevard, just over half a mile past Ely, go right. You can still spot an occasional old farmhouse amid all the newer structures.

More Historic Buildings

After less than a mile, turn left onto Caulfield at the traffic signal and ride back over Highway 101. Take the first right on Payran Street, then go left at Jefferson Street, opposite the fair grounds. At the end of the road you'll come to the Sunset Line & Twine Company, housed in an 1892 red brick factory building that resembles an 1870s New England mill. Until 1929, this was the Petaluma Silk Mill, where silk from China was made into thread and hosiery. The left wing and tower, designed by Brainerd Jones, were added in 1922. Today the mill manufactures fishing line.

From the mill, cross Jefferson to Erwin Street and ride to D Street, where you turn left. Go through the intersection with Lakeville Street and over the railroad tracks, through an industrial area and over the 1933 drawbridge that crosses the Petaluma River.

To see a few more historic buildings, turn right onto Fourth Street, one block after Petaluma Boulevard (Walnut Park is on the left). The 1932 post office on the corner is situated where the spacious mansion of John and Hattie McNear once stood. Go left at C Street to St. John's Episcopal Church at the next

Petaluma Adobe State Historic Park on Adobe Road at Casa Grande Road. This rancho home of General Vallejo of Sonoma was constructed in the 1830s to 1840s.

courtesy Redwood Empire Association

intersection. This building, with its tower and spires, was designed by British architect Edward Coxhead in 1870.

After another block, go left onto Sixth Street. Of special interest here is No. 100, a Colonial Revival home built in 1901 for William Lewis, owner of one of the largest dairy ranches in northern California.

Continue on Sixth, crossing D Street. The attractive Eastlake Stick style home with the colorful detail, at No. 312, was built in 1882 by State Senator A. P. Whitney as a wedding gift for his oldest son. The handsome 1862 Victorian farmhouse next door at No. 320 belonged to the senator, who had a very successful grocery business.

At the end of the block, go left on F Street, passing a small 1870 church at Fifth. After another block, a left at Fourth brings you back to Walnut Park and the end of your tour of Petaluma.

Additional Information

Petaluma Historical Library and Museum: 20 Fourth Street. Open Thursday through Monday 1:00 to 4:00 PM. Free admission. (707) 778-4398.

Petaluma Adobe State Historic Park: 3325 Adobe Road. Open daily 10:00 AM to 5:00 PM. Admission fee. (707) 762-4871.

Petaluma Area Chamber of Commerce: 215 Howard Street, Petaluma, CA 94952. Open weekdays 9:00 AM to 5:00 PM (and weekends May to September). (707) 762-2785.

Petaluma Visitor Center: Just south of Highway 101 at the Penngrove exit on Petaluma Boulevard North. Open daily 10:00 AM to 6:00 PM. (707) 769-0429.

Sonoma County Farm Trails Map: Showing the location of local growers and producers, this map is available at the Visitor Center, Chamber of Commerce, and museum.

Bike Rental: Bicycle Factory, 110 Kentucky Street, Petaluma. (707) 763-7515.

6. Petaluma Countryside

Distance: 40 miles

Rating: *Moderately strenuous* because of narrow country roads, rolling hills, and short, stiff climbs. Petaluma's mild climate provides good riding weather any time of year, but this area is at its best in the spring after winter rain has turned the hills lush and green, and the mustard is in bloom.

Highlights: This ride takes you out of the city and into the beautiful countryside with its grassy hills and dairy farms. You will also visit one of California's oldest road-houses, the town of Cotati, and the rancho home of General Vallejo.

Location: Petaluma is located along Highway 101 about 35 miles north of San Francisco in southern Sonoma County.

Charley Martin Ranch, Chileno Valley Road outside Petaluma. The old farmhouse is now delapidated.

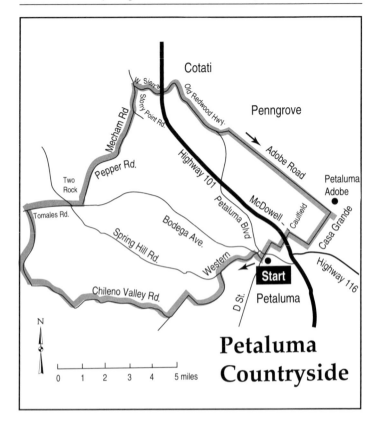

Petaluma was first settled in the 1850s and soon became a thriving river town, shipping food and manufactured goods south along the waterway. In the late 19th century, a new era began when the local economy turned to chickens and eggs, and for four decades thousands of chicken ranches covered the surrounding hills. Today cows have replaced hens, and Petaluma is now a leading dairy center in the North Bay.

Ride through Petaluma Countryside

Begin your ride in Petaluma at Walnut Park, located at the intersection of Petaluma Boulevard and D Street. If you are coming from San Francisco on Highway 101, take Petaluma Boulevard South into town. From the north, exit onto Washington Street, going toward the center of town, and turn left at Petaluma Boulevard until you reach D Street and the park. (Restrooms are available here.)

Walnut Park is in a neighborhood of lovely Victorian homes which you may want to explore later. (See Petaluma Ride, page 51.)

From Walnut Park, ride north on Fourth Street, past the 1932 post office. On the corner of Fourth and B Street is the Carnegie Free Library, built in 1904 with funds donated by steel magnate Andrew Carnegie. This elegant Classical Revival structure now serves as the town historical museum. Farther down the block, on the right, is the McNear Building, an elaborate ironfront constructed in 1886. The ironfronts were a 19th-century attempt to prefabricate and fireproof buildings, and a number of such decorative structures can still be found in Petaluma. You will pass another impressive ironfront at the corner of Western. The blue, three-story Mutual Relief Building dates from 1885.

Make a left turn onto Western Avenue, away from downtown. In 3 blocks you'll pass Markey's Cafe whose healthy food and sidewalk tables are popular with local cyclists. Just ahead you can see the red shingle Five Corners Community Center located in a converted 1910 church building.

After another couple of blocks, you will come to the California Gold cheese factory, home of the California Cooperative Creamery, representing over 500 dairies. It has been making cheese and other dairy products since 1913. The Creamery Store, at the intersection with Baker Street, offers tours and cheese tastings at the gift shop.

A short distance past the cheese factory, you will encounter the first of the numerous hills on this route. This one is not very long, and soon you will have left the city behind.

Chileno Valley Road

A little more than 2 miles from the start of your ride, turn left onto Chileno Valley Road toward Walker Creek Ranch and Putnam Regional Park. (Western becomes Spring Hill Road straight ahead.)

Chileno Valley Road begins with a gradual climb less than a mile long. The shoulder here is narrow but adequate to allow for passing cars. As you start the downhill, you'll pass, on the left, the entrance to Helen Putnam Regional Park, named for a long-time Petaluma mayor and Sonoma County supervisor. (Restrooms are available at the park.) For the next 3 miles of rolling road, you'll ride through some beautiful scenery created by oak-studded hills, peaceful valleys, and old dairy farms.

After crossing the Marin County line and San Antonio Creek, go right toward Tomales to stay on Chileno Valley Road. Here the road has no shoulder, but traffic is very light. The house on the left was once the Laguna Tavern, a 19th-century bar, post office, and store. You'll soon pass a country school where children of ranch families have been educated since 1889. The present building dates from 1906.

The tranquil Chileno Valley was named for a colony of "Chilenos," Chilean-born residents who came to California in the 1860s. Their settlement vanished after an 1890 smallpox epidemic. This whole area was once part of Rancho Laguna de San Antonio, granted to Bartolomeo Bojorques, a soldier who had served under General Vallejo at the San Francisco Presidio. The valley's first settler, however, was John Martin, an illiterate Scottish sailor who did little more than build a hut and plant a few crops. He moved on in 1839 when he was given title to some neighboring land.

This section of Chileno Valley Road is just under 10 miles long. The first half is mostly level, but you'll encounter more hills as you head up the valley, under the watchful gaze of cattle grazing along the way. After about 5 miles, you'll see a dilapidated farmhouse on the left that is the oldest structure in Chileno Valley. The single-story section dates from before 1856, while the large Victorian house was built about 1870 for Charley Martin (no relation to John), a native of Switzerland who came to California in 1852 and started one of the area's first dairy ranches. Eventually he owned eight ranches and thousands of acres of land. He also served as president and director of several early banks. Members of his large family still reside nearby.

In another 2 miles, at No. 6245, is an impressive century-old home and dairy ranch that has been in the Bloom family for over 60 years. After this point there's one more climb before the long, rolling downhill to the junction with Tomales–Petaluma Road.

Two Rock

Turn right on Tomales–Petaluma Road and begin another gradual uphill. You'll pass, on the left, the former Two Rock schoolhouse, now converted to a private residence, and then the entrance to the 800-acre U.S. Coast Guard Training Center, one of the largest such facilities operated by the Coast Guard. During World War II, it served as an Army training station.

Turn right when the road intersects with busy Bodega Avenue. Most of the tiny hamlet of Two Rock, named for two boulders marking an old Indian trail, is located a mile to the left, but the modern Two Rock Presbyterian Church is at the next junction, on Spring Hill Road. Its cemetery has tombstones dating back to the 1860s and is worth exploring. The 1870 grange hall faces Bodega Avenue, on the left, past the church.

Continue east on Bodega Avenue, which has fast-moving traffic but a wide, smooth shoulder. In half a mile, take the first left onto Pepper Road where you'll encounter more rolling hills and dairy ranches.

After riding 2.5 miles, go left on Mecham Road, named for Harrison Mecham who owned much of the land grant called Rancho Roblar de las Miseria. He came to Petaluma in 1853 and became a rancher of enormous wealth, power, and influence. He also earned a reputation for violence after shooting a man who persisted in taking a shortcut across his property. Mecham Road has another short climb.

Washoe House

When Mecham ends, turn left onto Stony Point Road, the old stage road between Santa Rosa and Petaluma. Just ahead, at the intersection with Roblar Road, you'll see the Washoe

Church of the Oak on West Sierra Avenue in Cotati.

House, one of the oldest roadhouses in California and nearly all that is left of a small community once located here. It was built as a stagecoach stop in 1859 and still offers food and drink to travelers.

From the Washoe House, continue on Stony Point Road and take the first right onto West Sierra Avenue. After about a mile, this country lane brings you under Highway 101 and into the town of Cotati.

Cotati

As you ride along, you'll pass the city hall on the left, housed in an old school building. At the intersection with Page Street is the Church of the Oak, a typical small town church building, dating from 1906.

In 1856 this area, called Rancho Cotate after the chief of a nearby Miwok village, was granted to Dr. Thomas Page, a local sheriff. A town was later laid out in a hexagonal pattern, one of only two such designs in the country. (Detroit is the other.) The Plaza is at the center and each of the streets on the rim was named for one of Dr. Page's six sons. Because the railroad to Santa Rosa made a stop here, the town was first called Page's Station. Today students from nearby Sonoma State University make up much of Cotati's population.

Just before you reach the center of the Plaza, follow one-way La Plaza to the right, turning right again in one block onto Old Redwood Highway. There may be some congestion for a few blocks, as this is an active business district with several interesting places for a hungry cyclist to find a snack or meal, but soon you'll be heading out of town in a comfortable bike lane.

Penngrove

Old Redwood Highway was the main road to Petaluma before Highway 101 was completed in the mid-1950s, and it still carries lots of traffic. Follow it for 2.5 miles, passing more old farmhouses, newer structures, and the Green Mill Restaurant, which has been serving travelers since 1930. Turn left when you reach Adobe Road. This takes you by the little town of Penngrove, which was originally a train stop known as Penn's Grove and a prosperous poultry-raising community at the turn of the century.

You will soon cross the intersection of Petaluma Hill Road (on the left) and Main Street (to the right). Main Street is the heart of this peaceful settlement.

As you continue along Adobe Road, a short hill will take you away from Penngrove and back into the countryside toward General Vallejo's rancho. The road here has a narrow but adequate shoulder and some gently rolling hills. The Sonoma Mountains in the distance form a lovely backdrop to the open fields and prosperous-looking ranches. After 2 miles, at the intersection with Corona Road, you'll pass the Waugh School, named for Father Lorenzo Waugh who came to Petaluma in 1852 and devoted himself to encouraging others to "shun the degrading, ruinous habits of using tobacco and intoxicating drink."

Continue riding a few more miles through this beautiful open land. Although Petaluma's suburban growth is expanding on this side of town, it has not yet reached Adobe Road.

Petaluma Adobe

Soon the extensive adobe structure of General Mariano Vallejo's rancho will come into view. The entrance to Petaluma Adobe State Historic Park is located a short distance past the intersection with Casa Grande Road. If you plan to tour the park grounds, be sure to bring a lock, as you must leave your bicycle at the parking lot. Picnic tables and restrooms are located nearby. (For more information about the park, see Petaluma Ride, page 51.)

Petaluma Adobe State Historic Park.

From the Petaluma Adobe, ride down Casa Grande toward the residential developments that began spreading on this side of the river in the 1960s. They are kept in check now, to some extent, by Petaluma's limited-growth policy. After 1.6 miles, go right at the stop sign onto McDowell Boulevard. In less than a mile, turn left at the traffic signal onto Caulfield Lane, which goes over Highway 101. On the other side, take the first right onto Payran Street, and turn left when you reach D Street. This takes you through the intersection with Lakeville Street, across the railroad tracks, over the Petaluma River and back to Walnut Park.

Additional Information

Petaluma Historical Library and Museum: 20 Fourth Street. Open Thursday through Monday 1:00 to 4:00 PM. Free admission. (707) 778-4398.

Markey's Cafe: 316 Western Avenue. Open weekdays 7:30 AM to 10:00 PM, weekends at 8:00 AM. (707) 763-2429.

The Creamery Store: Part of the California Gold cheese plant, 711 Western Avenue. Open Monday through Saturday 10:00 AM to 5:00 PM. Tours hourly 11:00 AM to 3:00 PM. (707) 778-1234.

Helen Putnam Regional Park: Chileno Valley Road. Restrooms, picnic tables, hiking and biking trails. Open sunrise to sunset. Parking fee.

Washoe House: Intersection of Stony Point and Roblar roads. Open daily 11:00 AM to 2:30 PM and 5:30 to 9:30 PM. (707) 795-4544.

Petaluma Adobe State Historic Park: 3325 Adobe Road. Open daily 10:00 AM to 5:00 PM. Admission fee. (707) 762-4871.

Bike Rental: Bicycle Factory, 110 Kentucky Street, Petaluma. (707) 763-7515.

See Petaluma Ride, page 60, for more resources.

7. Point Reyes

Distance: 34 or 42 miles

Rating: *Strenuous*, including lots of climbing and the possibility of a strong wind off the ocean. There is little shoulder much of the way, and you may encounter traffic near the National Seashore Visitor Center and in the town of Inverness.

Highlights: This ride takes you through the multifaceted Point Reyes National Seashore, to either Drake's Beach (34 miles) or all the way to the lighthouse (42 miles). It offers wonderful views of grassy hills, the ocean, and the bay where Sir Francis Drake may have landed in 1579.

Location: Point Reyes is in western Marin County, south of Highway 1, about 35 miles north of San Francisco.

Point Reyes Lighthouse at the end of Sir Francis Drake Blvd. The lighthouse is reached by walking down 300 steps.

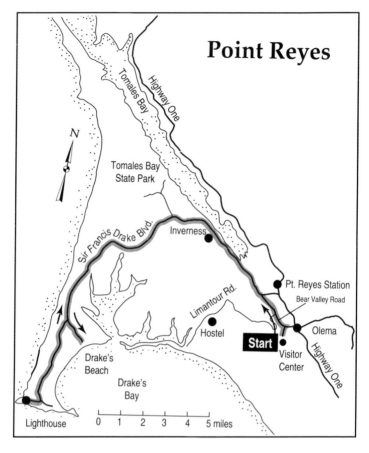

Ride through Point Reyes Peninsula

Begin your ride at the Point Reyes National Seashore Visitor Center on Bear Valley Road off Highway 1, a short distance from Olema. To reach Olema from Highway 101, take the Sir Francis Drake Boulevard exit, heading west through San Anselmo. In Olema go north to the first left turn, which is Bear Valley Road.

At the visitor center you'll find restrooms, maps, and extensive exhibits on the plants, animals, and people of the area. To start your ride, go left (north) on Bear Valley Road. In just over a mile, you will pass Limantour Road, which leads to the Point Reyes Hostel. (That 6-mile route is very strenuous.)

Stay left when Bear Valley Road ends at Sir Francis Drake Boulevard. (The road to the right goes to Point Reyes Station; see West Marin Ride, page 75.)

Inverness

Continue 3 miles on Sir Francis Drake through Inverness Park to the town of Inverness. This charming little resort community was founded in 1889 by James Shafter, part owner of Rancho Punta de los Reyes, who named it for his ancestral home in Scotland. Its early residents were wealthy San Franciscans who built summer homes along Tomales Bay. The old general store from the 1890s is now a picturesque gift shop.

You can stock up on food at the market here or eat at one of the restaurants. As you continue your ride along Tomales Bay, you'll see an interesting assortment of piers and boathouses.

The San Andreas Fault, where the North American plate grinds against the Pacific plate, runs directly under the bay and is responsible for its formation. Point Reyes Peninsula, on the edge the Pacific plate, is actually moving northward at an average rate of two inches a year. However, during the 1906 earthquake, it jumped 20 feet.

History of Point Reyes

For thousands of years before the Spanish arrived, this area was inhabited by the peaceful and spiritual Coast Miwok Indians. They lived in small communities of dome-shaped huts covered with tule rushes or redwood bark. Their diet consisted of shellfish, fresh water fish, venison, and bread made from acorn flour. When Mission San Rafael was established in 1817, the Indians were relocated and nearly all died from smallpox and other European diseases, as well as from the psychological trauma of forced mission life.

Later, the peninsula was a land grant known as Rancho Punta de los Reyes Sobrante, and after the United States annexed the territory in 1846, Point Reyes became the first great dairy center of California. You can see remnants of this period in the remaining historic ranches, including the old Bear Valley Ranch, where the park headquarters is now located.

Point Reyes National Seashore includes nearly all of the Point Reyes Peninsula, about 70,000 acres. The park was created in 1962, just in time to save it from extensive development.

About a mile past Inverness, the flat road ends and the hills begin. The first one over Inverness Ridge is the steepest but is not long. Just over the crest, Pierce Point Road leads to Tomales Bay State Park, about a mile away, where there is camping for cyclists. Sir Francis Drake Boulevard now becomes a narrow road with no shoulder and climbs up and down over the coastal hills and pasturelands of Point Reyes National Seashore.

Traffic is generally light except on clear weekend days in January and March when the gray whales are migrating. Then hundreds of cars create traffic jams as visitors head to the lighthouse to view these gentle giants on their way from the arctic seas to the lagoons of Baja, California, or on their return.

Drake's Bay

After about 2 miles you will begin to have grand views of the Pacific Ocean on your right and the arms of Drake's Estero and Drake's Bay to your left. You'll pass the road to an oyster farm where you can buy the freshly shucked shellfish when they're in season. Several miles farther on, you will come to the road leading to Drake's Beach. You may turn here or continue on to the lighthouse.

The road to the beach is less than 2 miles long, with a short downhill. Along the way you'll pass a historic ranch, dating from 1870, one of the numerous early cattle ranches still in operation. Under the terms of the legislation that established the National Seashore, families may continue to work their ranches under supervision of the Park Service.

At Drake's Bay you will find a snack bar, restrooms, and the Ken Patrick Visitor Center, which has exhibits describing early Spanish exploration and the local marine environment. There is even a minke whale skeleton on display. The beach here is protected from strong ocean winds by the sheltering sea cliffs.

Drake's Bay is named for Sir Francis Drake, the English admiral who circumnavigated the earth from 1577 to 1580. In 1579, having lost four of his five ships in the dangerous waters of the Straits of Magellan, Drake was looking for a sheltered harbor in which to repair his one remaining ship, the *Golden Hinde*. He found a protected spot somewhere along the northern California coast, went ashore, and spent a month resting and making repairs. The actual location of his landing is highly

controversial, although many historians believe it was here at
Drake's Bay.

Point Reyes Lighthouse

To reach the Point Reyes Lighthouse, continue 5 more miles
along Sir Francis Drake after the turnoff to Drake's Bay. You'll
pass several historic dairy ranches along the way, dating from
as early as 1859. There are also cattle grates across the road, so
use caution.

The hills steepen as you get closer to the lighthouse, which
is located past the parking lot on the rocky tip of the peninsula.
This is one of the windiest and foggiest places on the coast and
the site of numerous shipwrecks, but it is a fascinating place
to visit when the weather is clear. There is a small visitor center
here, with restrooms. The lighthouse itself is reached by walking down 300 steps.

Now on the National Register of Historic Places, the lighthouse was in operation from 1870 until 1975, when an
automated light station was built by the Coast Guard just
below the old building. There is also a fog signal, as there are
many days when it is too foggy to see the flashing light. You
may want to picnic here while enjoying the views of the beach
or watching the waves crash against the rocks. Then it is time

*Drake's Beach, Point Reyes National Seashore. It is named for
Sir Francis Drake, who may have landed here in 1579 on his
circumnavigation of the world.*

courtesy Redwood Empire Association

to retrace your route with its last exciting downhill into Inverness. Stay to the right at the junction with Bear Valley Road, and return to the visitor center where you began your explorations of Point Reyes.

Additional Information

Point Reyes National Seashore Bear Valley Visitor Center: Bear Valley Road off Highway 1. Open weekdays 9:00 AM to 5:00 PM, weekends 8:00 AM to 5:00 PM. Bicycles permitted on some trails; check with the ranger. (415) 663-1092.

Ken Patrick Visitor Center: Drake's Beach. Open weekends and holidays 10:00 AM to 5:00 PM. (415) 669-1250. Cafe open daily 10:00 AM to 6:00 PM. (415) 669-1297. Restrooms are always available.

Point Reyes Lighthouse Visitor Center: End of Sir Francis Drake Highway. Open 10:00 AM to 5:00 PM, closed Tuesday and Wednesday. Stairs to the lighthouse close at 4:30 PM. Restrooms always open. (415) 669-1534.

Pierce Point Ranch: One of the oldest and largest historic ranches in Point Reyes National Seashore, 8 miles past Tomales Bay State Park, off Sir Francis Drake Boulevard. Several buildings of this 1858 dairy ranch have been renovated, and the grounds are open from sunrise to sunset. The road to the ranch is narrow and hilly. (415) 669-1534.

Point Reyes Hostel: Just off Limantour Road, about 6 miles from Bear Valley Road. Can accommodate up to 44 guests in the main ranch house and bunkhouse. Hostel office hours are 7:30 to 9:30 AM and 4:30 to 9:30 PM. (415) 663-8811.

Tomales Bay State Park: Pierce Point Road, off Sir Francis Drake Blvd., 4 miles north of Inverness. All camps ites are walk-in (or cycle-in) and available on first-come basis. (415) 669-1140.

Bike Rental: Trailhead Rentals, 88 Bear Valley Road, Olema. (415) 663-1958.

8. West Marin

Distance: 30 miles

Rating: *Moderate*, traveling on country roads through small towns and following a bike path in the state park. The route is generally rolling except for some gradual uphill and one short, steep climb near Olema. Traffic conditions vary from light to moderate. The ride is especially pleasant in the spring when the hillsides are lush and green.

Santa Rosa

San Francisco

San Jose

Highlights: On this ride you will enjoy the peacefulness of open countryside and wooded glens and visit interesting old western towns, Point Reyes National Seashore Visitor Center, and the site of a historic paper mill in Samuel P. Taylor State Park.

Location: Marin County, west of Highway 101, less than an hour north of San Francisco.

Nicasio Schoolhouse. Built in 1871, it is now a private home.

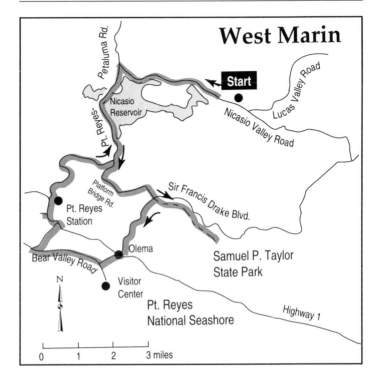

Nicasio

Begin your ride in the tiny village of Nicasio, on Nicasio Valley Road. To reach the start from Highway 101, exit at Sir Francis Drake Boulevard and head west through San Anselmo. At the San Geronimo Golf Club, turn right onto Nicasio Valley Road for just over 4 miles.

Nicasio, originally part of an extensive land grant known as Rancho Nicasio, was once much larger than it is today. In its early years, it was a thriving center for the local cattle and dairy ranches, with numerous businesses and stores, a racetrack, and a three-story hotel whose guests arrived by stagecoach. Nicasio had hopes of becoming the Marin county seat, and in 1863 a large open square was laid out in the center of town as a site for the courthouse. The town lost its bid to San Rafael, however, and now the area is used for baseball games and barbecues.

The most significant turning point in Nicasio's history occurred in 1875 when the railroads came to Marin County but not to Nicasio. From that time on, the town's size and importance dwindled, and today only a few buildings and homes are left. Of special interest is the small, steepled St. Mary's Catholic Church on the east side of the square, dating from 1867. On the west side, next to the 1933 Druids Hall, is a little false-front structure that once housed a pioneer butcher shop.

There is now a restaurant on the site of the old hotel. Food can also be found at the small store next door, and a toilet is located at the ball field.

Leave Nicasio by heading north on Nicasio Valley Road. On the outskirts of town is its most famous landmark, the red Nicasio schoolhouse built in 1871. It served as a school until 1949 but is now a private residence.

The open road beyond has a good shoulder and views of the Nicasio Reservoir and the grassy, rolling hills of the West Marin countryside. When the road ends in just over 3 miles, turn left onto Point Reyes–Petaluma Road, where you'll enjoy 3 miles of gentle downhill. At the stop sign, Point Reyes–Petaluma Road turns right over a bridge, but you'll keep going straight ahead onto Platform Bridge Road. This secluded wooded road is narrow but lightly traveled and parallels Lagunitas Creek, also known as Paper Mill Creek.

St Mary's Catholic Church on Nicaso Valley Road. This church was built in 1867 facing the Nicasio town square.

Samuel P. Taylor State Park

After a little over 2 miles, the road ends at Sir Francis Drake Boulevard. Just before you reach the stop sign, turn right onto a narrow gravel road that takes you over the arched 1933 Platform Bridge. On the other side of the bridge, to your left, is the beginning of the paved, nearly level bike path to Samuel P. Taylor State Park. It is marked as the "Cross Marin Trail."

The bike path follows Paper Mill Creek and takes you into a cool forest of second-growth redwoods, a marked change from the open hills you have just left. At the end of the 2-mile path, go around the gate (restrooms are nearby), and ride on the service road a very short distance to the site of Samuel Taylor's paper mill, the first on the Pacific coast when built in 1856. Originally powered by water and later by steam, it produced newsprint, bags, election ballots, and other paper supplies for San Francisco.

A small town called Taylorville grew up around the mill. In the 1870s, the North Pacific Coast Railroad came through, bringing sightseers to the mill pond and the shady forests. A campground and a three-story hotel were added, and the area became a popular weekend resort. The mill went out of business during the depression of 1893, and all the structures burned in 1915.

Past the mill site are campgrounds, including one for cyclists, restrooms with hot showers, picnic grounds, and hiking trails.

Retrace your route along the bike path, going left at its end to reach Sir Francis Drake Boulevard. Turn right and pedal up the hill over Bolinas Ridge, watching for fast-moving traffic. This is a fairly strenuous climb, but it is only about half a mile long, and you will be rewarded by a fast downhill run into the little town of Olema at the intersection with Highway 1.

Olema

Olema, founded in 1859, was one of Marin's most important early towns, and bustled with activity. But, like Nicasio, its importance began to fade in 1875 when the railroad bypassed it and went through Point Reyes Station instead.

The town's centerpiece today is the old Nelson Hotel, a former stagecoach stop and saloon dating from 1876. Restored as the Olema Inn, it still provides bed and board. This attractive building is of Shaker design, probably the only one of its kind in California. A short distance south on Highway 1, on the left, is a private home that has built in 1881 as the meeting hall of the United Ancient Order of Druids, a fraternal organization. Food is available at the store or restaurants.

Leaving Olema, head north on Highway 1, and at the first turn after the Olema Inn, go left onto Bear Valley Road. Ride to the entrance of Point Reyes National Seashore, a distance of half a mile, and follow the road to the visitor center.

Point Reyes

The triangular Point Reyes Peninsula has a fascinating geological history. It is separated from the rest of Marin County by the Olema Valley, which follows the San Andreas Fault from Bolinas Lagoon in the south to Tomales Bay in the north. It is estimated that this piece of land moves northward approximately two inches per year, sliding ahead each time an earthquake occurs.

The visitor center has a seismograph for monitoring earthquake activity, as well as exhibits and information about the park and its facilities. Nearby is the self-guided Earthquake Trail, a hike of less than a mile, which follows the San Andreas Fault close to the epicenter of the 1906 earthquake. You will

Olema Inn on Highway 1 and Sir Francis Drake Boulevard in Olema. This 1876 hotel was once a stage coach stop.

also find it worthwhile to take the short walk to Kule Loklo, an authentic replica of a Miwok Indian village that includes huts, a sweathouse, and a dance house. Restrooms can be found in the visitor center. (For more information about the park, see Point Reyes Ride, page 69.)

Back at the park entrance, turn left and continue down Bear Valley Road. (You will soon pass Limantour Road, the way to the Point Reyes Hostel.) In less than 2 miles, when Bear Valley Road ends at Sir Francis Drake, turn right. (The road toward the left goes to Inverness and the Point Reyes Lighthouse.)

Point Reyes Station

In less than a mile, make a left turn onto Highway 1 (Shoreline Highway), which will take you over Lagunitas Creek and through the middle of Point Reyes Station along A Street.

Back in 1875, this was called Olema Station and was just a railroad stop connected to the town of Olema by stagecoach. In 1883 the name was changed when the town site was laid out by Dr. Galen Burdell, a dentist and owner of the local hotel and saloon. Purchasers of his town lots were prohibited from selling liquor by a clause in the deeds, a restriction designed not

Kule Loklo, a replica of a Coast Miwok Indian village, Point Reyes National Seashore. The dance house, used for religious ceremonies, was the principal structure in the village.

to keep the town dry but to give Dr. Burdell a monopoly on the sale of alcoholic beverages. When a store across the street rebelled and began offering alcohol for sale, Burdell sued but lost the case in court. His hotel is gone now, but the rival tavern remains, operating as the Western Saloon on the corner of A and Second streets. A or Main Street is the site of the old railroad right-of-way, as the tracks went right through the center of town. (The former depot is now the post office.) The train stopped running in 1933, and Point Reyes Station has changed little since then. Hungry cyclists will appreciate the several restaurants and markets located here.

Leaving Point Reyes Station, follow Highway 1 as it turns right at the other end of town. Take the first left onto Mesa Street for one block to No. 505. The large, brightly painted structure with its twin corner towers was built in 1914 as a meeting place for the Lady Foresters, a local organization.

Return to Highway 1, and go left up the hill. Take a right onto Point Reyes–Petaluma Road, which has more rolling hills and a narrow shoulder. After about 3 miles, at the stop sign, turn left (Platform Bridge Road goes right) and retrace your route past the Nicasio Dam and Reservoir to Nicasio Valley Road. A right turn and 3 miles of pleasant riding will return you to your starting point in the village of Nicasio.

Former railroad depot on Main Street, Point Reyes Station. It now serves as the town post office.

Additional Information

Samuel P. Taylor State Park: Sir Francis Drake Blvd, north of Highway 1, West Marin. Park information, (415) 488-9897. Campsite reservations, MISTIX (800) 444-7275. Camping for cyclists available on a first-come basis.

Camping also available at Olema Ranch Campground, Highway 1 just north of the intersection with Sir Francis Drake Blvd. (415) 663-8001.

Olema Inn: Intersection of Highway 1 and Sir Francis Drake Blvd.. Lunch and dinner daily, except November to April when closed Monday and Tuesday. There are 6 guest rooms. (415) 663-9559.

Point Reyes National Seashore Visitor Center: Bear Valley Road. Open weekdays 9:00 AM to 5:00 PM, weekends 8:00 AM to 5:00 PM. (415) 663-1092.

Marin French Cheese Company: Point Reyes–Petaluma Road, 3.2 miles east of Nicasio Valley Road. Produces Camembert and other soft-style cheeses. Tour the factory, buy cheese and other picnic supplies, and enjoy the lovely grounds. Open daily 9:00 AM to 5:00 PM. Tours 10:00 AM to 4:00 PM. (707) 762-6001.

West Marin Chamber of Commerce: P. O. Box 1045, Point Reyes Station, CA 94956. (415) 663-9232.

Bike Rental: Caesar's Cyclery, 29 San Anselmo Avenue, San Anselmo. (415) 258-9920.

See Point Reyes Ride, page 74, for more resources.

9. Marin Headlands

Distance: 14 miles

Rating: *Strenuous* ride for experienced cyclists only. There are a few sustained climbs, narrow roads, and heavy weekend traffic near the Golden Gate Bridge. As there is little shade, it can be hot in summer on sections away from ocean breezes, and cool, foggy weather is a possibility during any season. An ideal time for this ride is early spring when the Headlands are green and wildflowers are blooming. There are no stores or restaurants on this route.

Highlights: This ride offers the chance to explore remnants of coastal defense fortifications, from Civil War days to the age of nuclear missiles. You will also have spectacular views

View from Battery 129 on Conzelman Road, Golden Gate National Recreational Area. Point Bonita is in the distance.

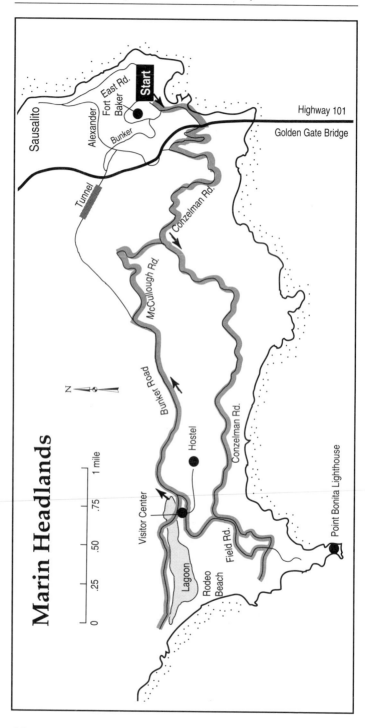

Marin Headlands

of San Francisco, the Headlands, Golden Gate Bridge, and the ocean, especially on a clear day.

Location: The Marin Headlands are located just north of the Golden Gate Bridge off Highway 101 in Marin County.

Ride through Marin Headlands

Begin your ride at East Fort Baker, located beneath the north end of the Golden Gate Bridge. To reach the fort from San Francisco, cross the bridge and take the Alexander Avenue exit. Coming from the north on Highway 101, take the last Sausalito exit. After a short distance, make a left turn, following the signs to GGNRA, East Fort Baker, and the Bay Area Discovery Museum. Immediately before the tunnel, go right on Bunker Road, curving back under Alexander Avenue and down to Fort Baker. Turn right on Murray Circle, and park at the south end of the open parade grounds. (If you miss the turn from Alexander Avenue, continue downhill and make a sharp right onto East Road to reach the fort.) Pit toilets are located near the fishing pier and at several other locations on the route.

Fort Baker, a subpost of the Presidio of San Francisco, began as Lime Point Military Reservation when part of Rancho Saucelito was sold to the United States government in 1866. A permanent fort was established at Horseshoe Bay in 1897 and named for Colonel Edward Dickinson Baker, a Civil War hero

---

History of Marin Headlands

In the latter part of the 19th century, the San Francisco harbor defense system was expanded across the bay to the Marin Headlands. Numerous gun emplacements were embedded into the coastal hillsides as a means of protecting the harbor from foreign naval attack. With the threat of air bombardment after World War I, batteries of anti-aircraft guns were added.

In the 1950s, two Nike ground-to-air missile silos were installed in response to more advanced military technology. Fortunately, none of these fortifications was ever needed to repel enemy attack, but their existence has helped save the land on which they stand from urban sprawl. This grassy, windswept, open space is now part of the Golden Gate National Recreation Area (GGNRA).

and friend of Abraham Lincoln. When the fort was active, several thousand men were stationed here. Today the fort is quiet, though military personnel still reside in the picturesque white houses surrounding the parade grounds.

Army Reserve headquarters and recruiting offices are also located here, and the Bay Area Discovery Museum, an exciting interactive children's museum, is across the road from the parade grounds.

From the parking lot, ride past the Coast Guard Station back to the junction of Murray Circle and the narrow road heading left toward the bay. This is the beginning of Conzelman Road, which will take you along Horseshoe Bay, with its fishing pier and views of the Presidio Yacht Harbor, and beneath the Golden Gate Bridge. The winding road climbs up to the intersection with the main part of Conzelman, where you go left and continue uphill. This section is steep, with narrow shoulders and the possibility of heavy traffic, but it is not long. At the top of the rise, on the left side of the road, is Battery Spencer. Built in 1896, it is one of the earliest Marin military installations. Walk your bicycle off the road to see all of the buildings in the complex and to take in the fine views of the Golden Gate Bridge, Fort Baker, and San Francisco.

Battery 129

The road continues uphill more gradually for another 1.5 miles, passing McCullough Road. At the very top is Battery 129, an unfinished World War II fortification that was to have been armed with two massive, 16-inch–diameter guns with a 25-mile range. The project was terminated in the mid-1940s, however, when it was realized that the guns would be ineffective against the enemy aircraft of the day. It later became the site of a Nike radar station. Today it is also known as Hawk Hill for the numerous species of hawks often sighted soaring overhead.

Ride through the first tunnel of the battery to see one of the gun mounts and to enjoy a view of Point Bonita and the rest of Conzelman Road. Notice, too, the trees here. Battery 129 would have been the highest artillery battery in the Bay Area, and the trees were planted to camouflage it. As you continue your ride, you will see that practically the only trees on the Headlands are those planted at battery sites.

Conzelman becomes one-way past the battery. The downhill is very steep (12% grade) but with good surface, little traffic, and thrilling views of Point Bonita and its lighthouse. After the road flattens out, you will come to Battery Rathbone-McIndoe, completed in 1905. In its early years it was fitted with rapid-fire rifles to protect the entrance to the bay from enemy ships. During World War II, it guarded the mine fields located outside the Golden Gate Bridge. The guns were removed in 1948.

At this point, the road heads down again, though not so steeply. At the bottom of the hill, turn left toward Point Bonita, and climb up to Battery Wallace. Built in 1919 as part of the naval defense system, it was later modified to guard against air attack. The trees originally planted as camouflage now provide shade for the picnic area.

After a downhill, go left at the YMCA Outdoor Conference Center (a former Nike site barracks) and past the road leading to Point Bonita Lighthouse, California's oldest continuously operating lighthouse. The first lighthouse was constructed in 1855 on the cliffs above the present site, but it was rebuilt in 1877 on the rocks below for better visibility in fog.

View from Battery Spencer. Conzelman Road, Golden Gate National Recreation Area. Overlooking Fort Baker, Horseshoe Bay, and the north end of the Golden Gate Bridge, with Angel Island in the background.

Ride on to Battery Mendel, in use from 1905 until 1943 and named for Colonel George Mendel, an engineer who designed many of the military structures in the Bay Area. A short distance beyond the battery is Bird Rock Overlook. From here you can see Rodeo Lagoon, named for the cattle round-ups held there in the mid-1800s when the Headlands were part of Rancho Saucelito, a Mexican land grant.

Return past the lighthouse entrance and ride by the YMCA buildings on Field Road. Beyond Battery Alexander you will see a fenced underground Nike missile site that was in operation from 1954 to 1974. It first housed Ajax missiles, later replaced by the more powerful Hercules missiles. This is the only Nike launch site in the country that has been restored for public viewing.

Marin Headlands Visitor Center

The Marin Headlands Visitor Center is at the bottom of the hill, on the left, in what was once the Fort Barry Chapel. Here you can learn about the natural and cultural history of the area and get information about mountain biking, ranger-led activities, and camping for individuals and groups. (Restrooms are located at the end of the parking lot.) Across from the visitor center, Bodsworth Road leads to the Golden Gate Hostel, located a short distance away in what was once the officers' quarters of Fort Barry. The building dates from 1902 and is a pleasant place to stay if you have made this ride part of an overnight trip.

At the end of Field Road, a left turn onto Bunker Road will take you to Fort Cronkhite and Rodeo Beach. You can also visit the California Marine Mammal Center, located off Bunker Road and housed in another former Nike missile site.

From the beach, ride on Bunker about 2 miles until McCullough Road enters on the right. You must turn here, as bicycles are not allowed in the Bunker Road tunnel ahead. Climb one mile up McCullough and turn left at the top onto Conzelman. A stop here before the mile-long ride downhill will provide one last breathtaking view of San Francisco and the Golden Gate Bridge. Remember the steep hill past Battery Spencer, and use caution. Make the right turn just before the bottom of the hill, following the bike route sign, to return the way you came.

Golden Gate Bridge and Sausalito

From here you may want to ride across the Golden Gate Bridge. The west sidewalk is open for cycling on weekends. You can enter through the parking lot on the left or from a road a short distance down Conzelman. To reach the bay side, where you must ride on weekdays, use the pedestrian walkway under the bridge that leads to Vista Point. (The ride across the Golden Gate Bridge is described in the San Francisco Ride, page 107.)

To end your ride, follow Conzelman Road back under the bridge to Fort Baker.

If you wish to ride to Sausalito, continue past the parade grounds and go right on East Road. Turn right in one mile, just before the subway, following the Pacific Coast bike route sign. This brings you to Alexander Avenue, the busy and narrow road down to Sausalito. Follow Alexander through several turns and soon you will be on Bridgeway, the main street of town. (See Sausalito Ride, page 91.)

Golden Gate Hostel at Fort Barry in the Golden Gate National Recreation Area. It was originally officers' quarters.

courtesy American Youth Hostels, Golden Gate Council.

Additional Information

Bay Area Discovery Museum: 557 East Fort Baker Road.
Open Wednesday through Sunday 10:00 AM to 5:00 PM.
Also open Tuesday during the summer. Admission fee.
(415) 332-7674.

Point Bonita Lighthouse: Field Road. Open weekends
12:30 to 3:30 PM.

Marin Headlands Visitor Center: Near the intersection of
Field and Bunker roads. Open daily 9:30 AM to 4:30 PM.
(415) 331-1540.

Nike missile launch site: Open first Sunday of the month
12:30 to 3:30 PM.

Golden Gate Hostel at Fort Barry: Office open after 4:30
PM. (415) 331-2777.

California Marine Mammal Center: Off Bunker Road at
Fort Cronkhite. Open daily 10:00 AM to 4:00 PM. (415) 289-
7325.

Bike Rental: See San Francisco Ride , page 116, or
Sausalito Ride, page 98.

10. Sausalito

Distance: 10 miles

Rating: *Easy* and mostly flat, but you are likely to encounter a lot of traffic, especially on summer weekends. Much of the route, including the ride to Mill Valley, is along bike paths.

Highlights: Sausalito is known for its impressive bay vistas, elegant shops and galleries, and fine restaurants. A favorite destination for both tourists and cyclists, it is often sunny when San Francisco and the Marin Headlands are shrouded in fog. The ride to Mill Valley goes along Richardson Bay, through peaceful marshland, and has fine views of Mount Tamalpais.

Location: Sausalito is located just north of the Golden Gate Bridge and east of Highway 101 in southern Marin County.

View of foggy San Francisco from Bridgeway in sunny Sausalito.

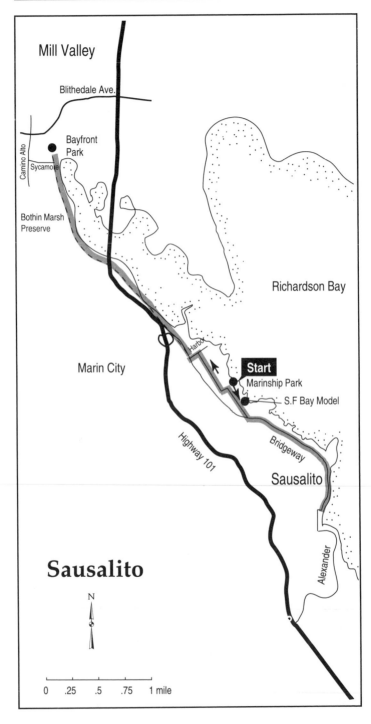

Mill Valley

Blithedale Ave.

Camino Alto

Bayfront
Park

Sycamore

Bothin Marsh
Preserve

Marin City

Richardson Bay

Harbor

Start
Marinship Park

S.F Bay Model

Highway 101

Bridgeway

Sausalito

Alexander

Sausalito

N

0   .25   .5   .75   1 mile

Ride to Downtown Sausalito

Begin your ride at Marinship Park. From Highway 101, take the Sausalito exit to Bridgeway, the main street through town. After 3 blocks, turn left at Harbor Drive and immediately go right on Marinship Way, following the signs to the Bay Model. The park, located across from Marina Plaza, has free parking and public restrooms next to the tennis courts.

This ride consists of two loops: downtown Sausalito (3.5 miles) and the bike path to Mill Valley (6.5 miles). The following description takes you first to see the charms of Sausalito, one place a cyclist will never go hungry.

From the park, go left on Marinship Way, past the Bay Model, which you'll visit on your return. When the road goes up to join Bridgeway, continue straight ahead on the bike path. When the path seems to end, ride across a very short section of gravel and through the parking lot behind an office building to Napa Street. Go right and pick up the bike path again as it parallels the bay side of Bridgeway. The path is narrow here and many cyclists prefer the faster roadway. When the path ends in 6 blocks at Johnson Street, cross Bridgeway at the traffic signal, and continue your ride along the street. The streets of

History of Sausalito

The history of Sausalito goes back to the days of Captain William Richardson, an Englishman who arrived at San Francisco Bay in 1822. He married the daughter of the commander of the Presidio, was appointed captain of the Port of Yerba Buena, and established a civilian settlement that would become the city of San Francisco. In 1838 he moved his family to Rancho Saucelito ("little willows"), a land grant of over 19,000 acres awarded him by the Mexican governor. Richardson operated schooners that carried passengers and freight between Sausalito and Yerba Buena, served as justice of the peace, and built the Sausalito Water Works, which supplied spring water for the city across the bay. For many years he prospered, but eventually he went heavily into debt trying to prove title to his land grant. When he died in 1856, most of his estate went to his lawyer, Samuel Throckmorton.

Sausalito may seem crowded with automobiles today, especially on weekends, but imagine the traffic jams that occurred in the 1920s when ferries provided the only means of reaching San Francisco. Although two ferry companies were in operation, they could not keep up with the huge numbers of travelers. On one summer weekend in 1926, the ferries carried over 70,000 automobiles. The construction of the Golden Gate Bridge in 1937 finally relieved Sausalito's overburdened ferry lines.

As you ride along Bridgeway, you will have the waterfront of Richardson Bay on one side and the hills, crowded with homes and apartments of all sizes and styles, on the other. Soon you'll pass Casa Madrona Hotel and Restaurant. The original structure, located up the hill, was built in 1885 as the private residence of William Barrett, a wealthy lumber baron. Today, with numerous additions extending down to the main street, it is a lovely inn. Next door is Village Fair, a unique, multi-leveled shopping complex, which was once a parking garage for commuter automobiles during the 1920s ferryboat era.

History of Sausalito (continued)

The town began in 1868 with the formation of the Sausalito Land & Ferry Company, a partnership of San Francisco businessmen who purchased three miles of waterfront property from Throckmorton and divided it up into lots. Expanded ferry service and the completion of the North Pacific Coast Railway in 1875 brought new settlers to Sausalito: laborers, merchants, and wealthy entrepreneurs. The town soon became a popular destination for weekend excursions.

By 1900, however, gambling interests had taken over. "Undesirables" from San Francisco arrived by ferry, saloons became the scene of drunken brawls, and city officials collected pay-offs from the gambling houses. The Sausalito Woman's Club attempted to clean up the area and eliminate political corruption, but Prohibition brought even more illicit activity in the form of bootlegging. The picturesque town you see today, with its art galleries, elegant boutiques, upscale restaurants, and yacht clubs, bears little resemblance to the rough-and-tumble place it used to be.

This is the most congested part of the ride, so you may wish to walk your bike along the sidewalk in order to appreciate the sights more easily.

In 2 blocks, on the left, you'll see Plaza Vina del Mar, a small park guarded by two concrete elephants at the intersection of El Portal. The elephant statues once held 100-foot flagpoles at the 1915 Panama Pacific International Exposition in San Francisco. The fountain is also from the exposition. Located behind the park at the end of El Portal is the dock where one can board ferries to San Francisco. To the right of the park is the Sausalito Hotel, which opened in 1915.

To enjoy some of the views for which Sausalito is famous, continue down Bridgeway to the open waterfront. Ahead, on the left, are two buildings that now house popular restaurants. The smaller one was a launch service from 1907 to 1937. The other is the former San Francisco Yacht Club, which helped make Sausalito a major recreation center when the club moved its headquarters to the town in 1878. The present structure dates from 1898. On a clear day, the views of San Francisco, the Bay Bridge, Alcatraz, and Angel Island are spectacular.

At the far end of Bridgeway is the 1902 twin-turreted Castle-by-the-Sea, once a saloon and hotel where Jack London was reputed to have lived. The Chart House–Valhalla Res-

Elephant statues on Bridgeway in downtown Sausalito. They were used in the 1915 Panama Pacific International Exposition in San Francisco.

Betty Johnston

taurant is another block farther on. Built in 1893 as a German beer garden, it was reopened in 1950 by Sally Stanford, the former San Francisco madam who was later elected mayor of Sausalito.

After exploring this end of town, return along Bridgeway. When you reach Princess Street, at the traffic signal, look up to the left. The elegant 1930 Mediterranean style structure on top of the hill is Villa Ladera, once the home of Lorenzo Scatena, one of the founders of Bank of Italy, which is known today as Bank of America. He was president until 1915, when his stepson Amadeo Giannini took over. Princess Street is named for the first ferry that began running from Sausalito to San Francisco in 1868.

When you have finished exploring downtown Sausalito, continue riding along Bridgeway until you reach Johnson Street, where you once again pick up the bike path paralleling the road.

San Francisco Bay Model

When the path ends at Napa, retrace your route behind the building ahead, back to Marinship Way. Soon you'll come to the road that takes you to the entrance of the U.S. Army Corps of Engineers Bay Model, a hydraulic scale model of the entire San Francisco Bay and Delta. The huge model provides a scientific means of analyzing the effects of change on the bay and delta. Docked in front are two historic ships, the 1915 freighter *Wapama*, a steam schooner, and the *Hercules*, an ocean-going steam tugboat. (Restrooms can be found outside the Bay Model entrance.)

The Bay Model is located in what was once the main warehouse of Marinship, where World War II cargo vessels were built. Although boatbuilding has been a continuous activity in Sausalito since Richardson's day, nothing before or after can compare to Marinship, a huge, 200-acre shipyard with thousands of workers. The first Liberty ship, the William A. Richardson, was launched in September 1942, just six months after shipyard construction was begun. In three and a half years of service, Marinship produced 15 Liberty cargo ships, 78 oil tankers, and 20 invasion barges. At the end of the war, Marinship closed its doors, and the former shipyards now house an industrial complex and several marinas.

Bike Path to Mill Valley

Now it is time for the second half of your ride. Returning to Marinship Way, go right, past the park where you started. Turn left when the road ends at Harbor Drive, then immediately go right onto the bike path. (The surface improves in a block.)

After Gate 5 Road, you will see some of the famous Sausalito houseboat colony, which was begun in the 1950s by local artists and writers. In spite of the city's efforts to discourage them, these early bohemians used old boats and ferries as their homes and studios. Today these picturesque floating dwellings, ranging from elegant to derelict, are an established part of Sausalito.

Soon you're following a wide, smooth bike path, constructed on a levee for an old railroad that once connected Sausalito's ferry dock to San Rafael. On the other side of Highway 101 is Marin City, which began as a housing community for Marinship workers during World War II. After passing the heliport, the path swings under the highway, and the roar of traffic quickly becomes a distant rumble. As you ride through peaceful Bothin Marsh Open Space Preserve, where herons, egrets, and numerous other shorebirds make their home, majestic Mount Tamalpais, over 2,500 feet tall, looms in the distance.

Bike path from Sausalito to Mill Valley through Bothin Marsh. Mount Tamalpais. is in the distance.

All too soon, you'll reach your destination at Bayfront Park in Mill Valley. (The path ends in a quarter mile at Blithedale Avenue.) Restrooms can be found across the bridge to the right and next to the fire station at the far edge of the park. After exploring the park, follow the path back to your start at Marinship Park.

Additional Information

U.S. Army Corps of Engineers Bay Model: 2100 Bridgeway. Open Tuesday through Saturday 9:00 AM to 4:00 PM. During the summer, open Tuesday through Friday 9:00 AM to 4:00 PM, weekends 10:00 AM to 6:00 PM. Free admission. A Marinship historical exhibit is located in the visitor center. To borrow a bicycle lock, inquire at the front desk. Tours of the *Wapama* Saturdays at 11:00 AM, of the tugboat *Hercules* Saturday at 12:30 PM. (415) 332-3871.

Red and White Fleet: Ferry service between San Francisco's Fisherman's Wharf and Sausalito. (415) 546-2896.

Golden Gate Ferry Service: Goes to the Ferry Building in San Francisco. (415) 982-8834.

Sausalito Historical Society Museum: 420 Litho Street in the old high school building. Open Wednesday and Saturday 10:00 AM to 2:00 PM. (415) 289-4117.

Sausalito Chamber of Commerce: 333 Caledonia Street, Sausalito, CA 94965. Open weekdays 9:00 AM to 5:00 PM, closed for lunch. (415) 332-0505.

Bike Rental: A Bicycle Odyssey, 1417 Bridgeway, Sausalito. (415) 332-3050. Any Mountain, 71 Tamal Vista Boulevard, Corte Madera. (415) 927-0170.

11. Angel Island

Distance: 7 miles

Rating: *Moderate* because of a few hills and some unpaved roads. The short mileage and absence of automobile traffic, however, make Angel Island a popular excursion for families. Park rangers recommend visiting in spring and fall, when the weather is warm and fog less likely.

Highlights: Few places in the Bay Area combine cycling and history as wonderfully as Angel Island State Park. Here you can explore a Civil War–era camp, see a huge military induction center, and visit a detention station for Chinese immigrants. The island is also known for its natural beauty, and on a clear day you'll have superb vistas of Marin, San Francisco, and the East Bay. Allow a full day to enjoy all that Angel Island has to offer.

Ayala Cove on the northwest side of Angel Island. Cyclists ride past the visitor center, and Tiburon is in the distance.

Surrey Blackburn, Angel Island Association

N

Immigration
Station

Ayala
Cove

Visitor Center
Park Headquarters

Start

Mt.
Livermore

Visitor
Center Fort
McDowell

Camp
Reynolds

Perimeter Rd.

Coast Guard
Station

Angel Island

0   200'   400'   600'

Location: Angel Island sits in San Francisco Bay off the coast
of Marin County, one mile from Tiburon and 3 miles from
San Francisco. It can be reached only by ferry or private boat.

Ride around Angel Island

Your excursion to Angel Island begins with a short ferry ride.
Ferries from Tiburon land at Ayala Cove on the northwest side
of the island, while ferries from San Francisco and Vallejo land
at Fort McDowell's East Garrison. The Tiburon ferry offers
unlimited space for bicycles, so the described route assumes
this is your starting point. To reach the Tiburon ferry dock from
Highway 101 in Marin, follow Tiburon Boulevard to the
downtown area. The dock is located off Main Street.

When you disembark at Ayala Cove, you'll find a snack bar,
picnic grounds, restrooms, and an information booth with
maps. The visitor center has displays depicting the history of
the 740-acre island.

Ayala Cove was first known as Hospital Cove for the U.S.
Public Health Service quarantine station that operated here

from 1892 to the 1950s. Ships and their cargoes were fumigated at this location before they could dock in San Francisco, and passengers suspected of carrying contagious diseases were detained. What is now the visitor center was then the bachelor officers' quarters.

Your tour around Angel Island will be on Perimeter Road, which is just over 5 miles long, and you'll add another couple of miles by exploring various sites along the way. (There is also a 4-mile gravel fire road which parallels Perimeter Road.) Vehicles are not allowed on the island, except for those belonging to park rangers.

History of Angel Island

Angel Island was named in 1775 by Lt. Juan Manuel de Ayala, the first European to sail into San Francisco Bay. He anchored his ship in a sheltered cove on the island he called "Isla de los Angeles" because the day of his arrival fell on that of the Spanish festival of the angels.

The Coast Miwok Indians had lived on the island for thousands of years before the Spanish came. They were expert fisherman and traveled around the bay in simple boats made of tule reeds. They hunted deer and sea otter and gathered acorns and roots for food. But once Mission Dolores was established on the mainland in 1776, their way of life was changed forever, and by 1850 they had all but disappeared.

In those early days the island was heavily forested with oak, bay, and madrone, and was called "Wood Island" by the sailors who cut firewood there. The native trees were decimated as a result; those you see today, such as eucalyptus, cypress, and Monterey pine, were planted later by the army.

In 1839 Angel Island was granted to Antonio Maria Osio by the Mexican governor of California for use as a cattle ranch. When California became a state in 1850, the United States government decided they wanted Angel Island for a military reservation and rejected Osio's claim to his land grant. The army soon took over, beginning a century of military occupation.

Camp Reynolds

To reach Perimeter Road, ride past the visitor center and follow the steep path a quarter mile up the hill to the paved road, where you go right. In a short distance you'll come to a red building, the 1869 hospital for Camp Reynolds, the first army installation on the island. To see the main part of the camp, ride down the gravel road near the hospital.

Construction of Camp Reynolds started in 1863 to protect military installations in the bay from possible Confederate attack during the Civil War. A number of buildings remain, including the bake house and a nicely restored home used for officers' families. Officers' quarters line one side of the parade grounds, but the enlisted men's barracks, which stood on the other side, no longer exist. The 1906 brick quartermaster's storehouse at water's edge is now used for overnight school field trips. When Fort McDowell was established on the eastern side of the island in 1900, this camp was renamed West Garrison.

To continue around the island, follow the gravel road that goes past the white chapel. This brings you back to Perimeter Road, where you go right.

Camp Reynolds on the west side of Angel Island. Former officers' housing dating back to the Civil War era.

Surrey Blackburn, Angel Island Association

Very soon you'll come to a vista point with impressive views of Sausalito, the Golden Gate Bridge, and San Francisco. You can also overlook Battery Ledyard, one of three concrete batteries installed at the turn of the century for harbor defense.

On the south end of the island you'll encounter a section of unpaved road. But you'll also have spectacular views of Alcatraz Island, San Francisco, and the Bay and Golden Gate bridges. A turnoff goes to Battery Drew if you wish to explore this concrete gun emplacement more closely.

Just after a short but rather steep climb, you'll come to an intersection, and the gravel ends. To stay on Perimeter Road, go right. The road to the left leads to the 4-mile fire road that circles the island and goes to the top of Mt. Livermore with its panoramic view. (Bicycles, however, are not allowed on the trail to the summit.) The road straight ahead is off-limits.

Riding along Perimeter Road, you'll pass an old Nike missile site with underground silos, which was deactivated in 1962, the year the army permanently left the island. As you approach a steep downhill, a sign will warn you to walk your bike. Follow the road as it curves left, past the turnoff to Point Blunt and the Coast Guard station, which is closed to the public.

Fort McDowell on the east side of Angel Island. Established in 1909, it became the world's largest induction center for processing overseas military personnel.

Surrey Blackburn, Angel Island Association

Fort McDowell

There's another short stretch of gravel road as you head north, riding downhill toward Quarry Point and the remains of Fort McDowell's massive East Garrison.

Quarry Point was originally a sandstone hill 100 feet high. Quarrying began in the 1850s, and the high-quality stone was used for buildings in San Francisco and around the bay. By the time the quarry ceased operation in 1922, the point had been completely leveled.

The first military use of this area was in 1899, when a detention camp was established to house soldiers who had been exposed to contagious diseases during the Spanish-American War. In 1909 an extensive building program began, and within two years Fort McDowell was the world's largest and most elaborate induction center for processing military personnel for overseas assignments. It served in this capacity until the end of World War II.

To explore the main part of the post, ride past the row of officers' quarters and take the road opposite the Mission Revival style chapel downhill toward the beach. The large structure with the domed roof on your left was the mess hall, where 1,400 men could be fed at one time. Straight ahead you'll see the huge barracks that housed 600 men, the largest barracks on the West Coast. As the road turns left, you will come to the guardhouse, which has been converted into a visitor center. Exhibits here describe the sights at each garrison on the island and include a collection of historic artifacts. Restrooms can also be found at two locations. Ferries from San Francisco and Vallejo land at the East Garrison ferry dock at the end of the road.

When you've finished exploring Fort McDowell and taking in the view of the East Bay, ride back up to Perimeter Road and continue to the right, past the old post hospital.

Immigration Station

After half a mile, on the north side of the island, you'll come to the Immigration Station, the reason Angel Island is often called the "Ellis Island of the West." In operation from 1910 to 1940, the station mainly processed Chinese immigrants to the United States. To see these buildings, ride down the steep gravel road, using caution.

Thousands of Chinese entered the United States in the second half of the 19th century. They provided cheap labor, building railroads, developing fisheries, and doing the work no one else wanted. During the economic recession of the 1870s, however, severe unemployment and a general intolerance of foreigners resulted in various forms of persecution. The Chinese Exclusion Act, passed in 1882, prohibited the immigration of most working-class Asians; only spouses or children of citizens were permitted. When the 1906 earthquake and fire in San Francisco destroyed all civic records, many Chinese living in California falsely declared they were already citizens. Some then sold their family histories to immigrants trying to enter the country by claiming kinship with U.S. citizens.

In an attempt to discover fraudulent claims, officials set up the station on Angel Island to serve as a detention center where immigrants were interrogated about their villages, homes, and families. If their answers did not match those of their sponsor, they were deported. The average period of detention was two weeks; the longest was two years.

The barracks where the immigrants were held is now a museum. There you can see the crowded dormitories and primitive restrooms, as well as a sample of Chinese poetry written on the walls by one of the detainees. A memorial to the Asian immigrants is in front of the museum.

Old post hospital, Fort McDowell. It was built in 1910.

Surrey Blackburn, Angel Island Association

The administration building was destroyed by fire in 1940, and the immigration station was moved to San Francisco. The army took over the buildings, which became Fort McDowell's North Garrison. During World War II, it was used to detain German, Japanese, and Italian prisoners.

To complete your tour of Angel Island, return to Perimeter Road and continue around the island another half mile until you reach the pathway leading down to Ayala Cove and the ferry dock.

Additional Information

Tiburon–Angel Island Ferry: Dock off Main Street, end of Tiburon Boulevard, downtown Tiburon. Parking lot on Tiburon Boulevard, intersection with Mar West. Ferries run daily during summer, and on weekends and holidays rest of the year, starting at 10:00 AM. (415) 435-2131.

Red and White Fleet: Ferry service from San Francisco's Fisherman's Wharf, Pier 43½. Daily during summer, and on weekends and holidays rest of the year. Ferries also run from Vallejo. Limited space for bicycles, accommodated on first-come basis. (800) 229-2784 or (415) 546-2896.

Golden Gate Transit: Ferry service from Larkspur. (415) 453-2100.

Angel Island Association: Docent-led tours at the various forts, garrisons, and museums on weekends during tourist season. Bus tours on summer weekends. (415) 435-3522.

Campsites: Angel Island has nine hike-in campsites, equipped with water, pit toilet, picnic table, and grill. Sites are very popular, especially on weekends. Reservations through MISTIX. (800) 444-7275.

Angel Island State Park: P. O. Box 318, Tiburon, CA 94920. (415) 435-1915.

Bike Rental: Ken's Bike and Sport, 94 Main Street, Tiburon. (415) 435-1683. Planeaway, Cove Shopping Center, 1 Blackfield Drive, Tiburon. (415) 383-2123.

See also San Francisco Ride, page 116.

12. San Francisco

Distance: 21 miles

Rating: *Moderately strenuous* because of numerous short climbs and busy city traffic. However, the route avoids the steepest hills and worst congestion of San Francisco, and some parts of the ride are actually flat and easy, including segments through Golden Gate Park and across the Golden Gate Bridge. Be prepared for cool temperatures if the city is covered with fog, especially common in summer.

Highlights: This exciting ride traces San Francisco's rich heritage from its early days as a barren military outpost through its more recent development as one of the nation's most beautiful cities. Along the way, you will experience

Fort Point, under the Golden Gate Bridge in San Francisco. This red brick fortress was built in 1861.

courtesy Redwood Empire Association

some of its best-known attractions: Golden Gate Park, the Presidio, and Golden Gate Bridge.

Location: San Francisco can be reached from the south by way of Interstate 280 or Highway 101, from the north via 101, and from the east on Interstate 80.

Ride through San Francisco

Begin your ride at Ocean Beach on the Great Highway, located at the west end of Golden Gate Park, between Fulton Street and Lincoln Way. Parking is available along the Esplanade, and restrooms can be found at several locations within the park. To reach the starting point from the Golden Gate Bridge, follow Highway 1 (19th Avenue) onto Park Presidio Boulevard. At Fulton Avenue, on the edge of the park, turn right. From the south via Interstate 280, follow Highway 1 through the park, exiting left onto 25th Avenue. Cross Fulton (a left turn is prohibited here), and in one block make a left onto Cabrillo. From Cabrillo, go left, back to Fulton and turn right. From Interstate 80 from the east and Highway 101 from the south, follow 101 to the Laguna/Fell exit. Take Fell into the east end of the park.

From the Esplanade, enter Golden Gate Park on John F. Kennedy Drive, just south of Fulton Street near the Dutch Windmill. (See the San Francisco – Golden Gate Park Ride, page 117, for a complete description of the park and its attractions.)

At the first stop sign, turn left to stay on Kennedy Drive. After riding less than 3 miles, you'll pass the park museums. At the next stop sign, go left onto Conservatory Drive West, which takes you behind the beautiful Conservatory of Flowers. At the top of the rise, follow the road downhill to exit the park onto Arguello Street.

The ride down Arguello may involve some traffic, but there is usually room for both cars and bicycles. To view one of the least-known treasures of San Francisco, go several blocks and turn right on Anza Street. The second left, onto Loraine Court, brings you to the Neptune Society Columbarium, a repository for urns containing cremated ashes. This elegant neoclassic, green-domed structure was erected in 1898 and is as lovely inside as out. With stained glass windows, marble flooring, and ceiling mosaics, it is definitely worth a visit.

Leaving the columbarium, return to Arguello and continue north. In one block you will cross busy Geary Boulevard,

Ralston Avenue Barracks, Fort Winfield Scott in the San Francisco Presidio. Mission style barracks were built in the 1910s.

Ernest Braun

which was a private toll road leading to the oceanside Cliff House in the 1860s. Just on the other side of Geary is the 1934 brick Roosevelt Middle School, and the domed Temple Emanu-El, built in 1926, is ahead.

Shortly after the temple and before a steep hill, turn left into Presidio Terrace, a collection of large mansions dating from the early 1900s. Perhaps the most unusual is No. 30, immediately on the left, an immense Hansel and Gretel cottage built in 1909. From here, cross Arguello and go straight ahead uphill on Washington Street, which will take you through the lovely residential area known as Presidio Heights. The 1902 Koshland Mansion, at No. 3800 at the intersection with Maple, is particularly impressive.

History of San Francisco

The history of the city of San Francisco dates back to 1776 when the Spanish chose it as the location for a military outpost or presidio, and Franciscan padres established Mission Dolores. For the next quarter century, the only inhabitants were Spanish soldiers and their families, padres, and mission Indians. Although the soldiers suffered from boredom and minimal rations, the Indians fared much worse, succumbing in great numbers to diseases introduced by the Spanish.

After 1800, the harbor at Yerba Buena, as the settlement was then known, began to see increased ship traffic from whalers and Russian sea otter hunters. In 1822, William Richardson, an Englishman, arrived by whaling ship and requested permission to stay. He married the eldest daughter of the commander of the Presidio (by then under Mexican control), and became the first non-Spanish white settler of what would eventually become the city of San Francisco.

American settlers followed, and in 1846 the United States seized control of California. At that time Yerba Buena was still a tiny settlement of only a few hundred people, but the gold rush changed all that. Overnight the sleepy little town turned into a bustling, noisy, dirty tent city. The harbor was crowded with ships, many abandoned when their crews headed for the gold fields. Fortune hunters swarmed into the city from all over the world, and the population swelled to 100,000.

San Francisco Presidio

When you reach Presidio Avenue in another half mile, go left. Soon you will enter the Presidio of San Francisco, a military base since 1776 when Juan Bautista de Anza, commander of the first group of Spanish settlers, chose this site for a military post and built a walled camp on the rocky promontory. After Mexico won its independence from Spain, Mexican soldiers were garrisoned here until the United States took possession in 1846.

The Spaniards considered this a hardship post because of the wind and fog, barren sand dunes and rocky hills, and the scarcity of water. Eucalyptus and pine trees were planted in the 1880s, however, and today this is one of San Francisco's prettiest spots. Now the Presidio's long career as a military base is drawing to an end, and it is being taken over by the National Park Service as part of the Golden Gate National Recreation Area (GGNRA).

As you enter the Presidio grounds, you will begin a long downhill. Be careful here, as the road is narrow, though traffic is not heavy. On the way down, you will have a great view of

---

History of San Francisco (continued)

As the supply of gold ran out, the city's importance and population suddenly declined. But San Francisco was not destined for obscurity. It became the headquarters for the operations of the Comstock silver mines in Virginia City, Nevada, and for the transcontinental railroad, completed in 1869. Despite periods of boom and bust, the city grew; by 1900 it had over 300,000 inhabitants.

Now millionaires and multi-millionaires vied with each other to see who could spend their money in the most ostentatious ways. Fantastic mansions were built by Crocker, Flood, Hopkins, and Stanford on Nob Hill. A wonderful assortment of Victorian homes was constructed by the less affluent in other parts of the city.

Then the most famous event in San Francisco's history occurred. On April 18, 1906, a major earthquake shook the city. The fire that ensued destroyed dwellings of the wealthy and poor alike and left more than 200,000 homeless. San Francisco was quickly rebuilt, however, and since that time has become "everybody's favorite city."

the Palace of Fine Arts below, built for the 1915 Panama-Pacific Exposition, and the ocean beyond.

Traffic increases at the bottom of the hill, when Lombard Street joins from the right at the stop sign. Continue straight ahead onto busy Lincoln Boulevard, and turn left when you reach Funston Avenue, following the 49-Mile Scenic Drive sign. The building on the corner, dating from 1864, was used as a hospital and dispensary for over 100 years and currently houses the army museum. Farther along Funston there is a fine collection of early Victorian style officers' quarters, some constructed as early as 1862. Follow the road right onto Moraga Avenue. The Officers' Club on the left is built around a section of adobe wall from the original Spanish headquarters, probably the first building erected in San Francisco.

Turn right onto Montgomery Street. The row of Georgian style, red brick buildings, dating from 1895, were the first permanent barracks constructed by the army here. At Sheridan (following the 49-Mile Drive sign), a left turn will bring you back to Lincoln Boulevard, where you go left by the National Cemetery. In use since 1852, it contains over 24,000 graves, including those for Colonel Edwin Baker, General Frederick Funston, and General Hunter Ligget, as well as Pauline Fryer, an actress and Union spy, and "Two Bits," an Indian scout for the army. Congressman Philip Burton, founder of the GGNRA, is also buried here.

Continue on Lincoln Boulevard for less than a mile. You'll pass a small view area that overlooks Crissy Field, which was created by landfill to hold exhibits of the Panama-Pacific International Exposition. After the fair closed, it was used by the army as an airfield until 1936. Now it is a popular park for picnicking and kite flying.

Fort Point

Just after the stop sign, as Lincoln starts to climb left to the Golden Gate Bridge, angle right on the narrow, downhill road leading to Fort Point. As you ride along the bay, be aware that waves sometimes wash over the road!

This strategic location has been used to guard the harbor of San Francisco since the Spanish first erected an adobe fort here in the late 18th century. In 1861, the U.S. Army replaced the ruins of that building with the massive, red brick fortress you see today. Fort Point was designed to house 600 soldiers and to mount 126 cannon. Three interesting granite spiral stair-cases open onto the courtyard, and a lighthouse, built in 1864, sits on top of one of them. The walls are 5 to 12 feet thick.

The fort is now a National Historic Site administered by the National Park Service. You may wander through its three tiers on your own or join a ranger-led tour. Be sure to climb to the roof for grand views of the ocean and bay.

Golden Gate Bridge

Return up the steep road, and go right, back onto Lincoln Boulevard. To reach the Golden Gate Bridge, make a right turn into the View Area parking lot just before the Highway 101 underpass. (If you wish to skip the ride across the bridge, continue straight ahead on Lincoln.)

The Golden Gate Bridge, completed in 1937 to connect San Francisco and Marin counties, is one of the city's most endur-ing landmarks. In the View Area is a statue of Joseph B. Straus, chief engineer of the bridge, a cross section of bridge cable, and a colorful flower garden. (Restrooms are located nearby.) To ride across the bridge, go up the slight incline by the visitor center to the sign at the beginning of the bridge that informs you where to ride. On weekdays you will use the sidewalk on the bay (east) side; on weekends you will be directed to a path under the bridge to reach the ocean (west) side.

Montgomery Street Barracks in the Presidio, San Francisco. These Georgian style red brick barracks were built in 1895.

The 2-mile ride across the bridge offers splendid views of the Marin Headlands ahead, and Angel Island, Alcatraz, and San Francisco to the right. At the far end, on the bay side of the bridge, is Vista Point. (Restrooms are also located here.) If you are riding on the ocean side and want to reach this view area, you will have to use the pedestrian underpass at the end of the bridge, which necessitates carrying your bike down and up the stairs. When you have taken in the views of the city, bridge, and Fort Baker below, retrace your route for an exhilarating ride back across the bridge to the View Area on the San Francisco side. (Or, if you want to add more miles, you may connect with the Marin Headlands route, page 83.)

From the San Francisco View Area, ride to the right on the road that goes under the bridge approach, following the bike route markings. Turn left and then right onto Merchant Road, toward Golden Gate NRA. As you ride up the hill to rejoin Lincoln Boulevard, you will pass a reinforced concrete battery on your right. This was one of several military fortifications built at the turn of the century to protect the city's harbor.

At Lincoln, make a right turn. You will have the ocean on your right and the Presidio grounds to your left. Traffic may be heavy here, and the shoulder is often narrow. After a short climb, there is a mile-long downhill. Two parking areas along the way provide places to stop and again appreciate views of the bridge and Marin Headlands.

Palace of the Legion of Honor

As the road levels out, Lincoln becomes El Camino del Mar Road and passes some fine San Francisco homes. Continue to follow the 49-Mile Scenic Drive signs, which will, after a half-mile strenuous climb, direct you left onto Legion of Honor Drive and to the California Palace of the Legion of Honor. This splendid art museum, built by a donation from Adolph and Alma Spreckels, was dedicated in 1924 to the "youth of our land who died to make men free" during World War I. It is a replica of the Palace of Legion of Honor in Paris. The views of the Golden Gate Bridge and Marin Headlands from the plaza in front of the museum are breathtaking.

Nearby you can also see the Lincoln Park Municipal Golf Course, the location of Golden Gate Cemetery until 1900, when interment within the city limits was no longer allowed.

A few years later the cemetery was turned into a park and many of the graves were left undisturbed and unmarked.

Ride down the hill past the museum to Clement and turn right. Clement has more climbing and, after passing the Veterans Administration Medical Center, becomes Seal Rock Drive. At its end, a right turn on El Camino Del Mar brings you to the USS *San Francisco* Memorial. This is the actual bridge of the ship, which lost 107 crew members in the Battle of Guadalcanal in 1942. From here you will also have an excellent view of the Point Bonita Lighthouse across the Golden Gate.

Cliff House

To continue your ride, turn around, and take the first right on Point Lobos Avenue. This is a fast downhill which soon becomes the Great Highway and takes you by the Cliff House. Traffic is often congested at this popular tourist attraction, so be sure to use caution.

The original 1863 Cliff House was purchased by Adolph Sutro in 1882. When it burned down in 1894, he rebuilt it as a fantastic Victorian hotel and added the famous Sutro Baths, with five saltwater pools of different temperatures and one freshwater plunge.

Sutro, who had made his fortune as an engineer in the Comstock silver mines, was a mayor of San Francisco, donated land for the University of California medical school, gained protection for the sea lions that occupied Seal Rocks, and left his fine collection of books and Egyptian art to the public. His estate, Sutro Heights, was located on the bluff across from Cliff House and is now a city park. The imaginative 1894 hotel was destroyed by fire in 1907 and replaced by the present utilitarian building, which has been remodeled several times. The baths burned in 1966, leaving only ruins to be seen today.

Walk down the stairs to the view area for dramatic vistas of the coast and to watch the sea lions offshore on Seal Rocks. On the lowest level is the National Park Service Visitor Center. Restrooms are available here, as well as in the Cliff House restaurant.

From Cliff House, it is only a short distance back to your starting point at the beach and the completion of your ride through San Francisco.

Additional Information

Neptune Society Columbarium: 1 Loraine Court, off Anza Street. Open to the public daily 9:00 AM to 1:00 PM. Free admission. Tours given Saturdays, 10:00 AM to 1:00 PM. (415) 221-1838.

Presidio Army Museum: Funston Avenue at Lincoln Boulevard. Open Tuesday through Sunday 10:00 AM to 4:00 PM. Free admission. (415) 561-4115.

Fort Point National Historic Site: Off Lincoln Boulevard under the Golden Gate Bridge. Open daily except holidays 10:00 AM to 5:00 PM. Free admission. (415) 556-1693.

California Palace of the Legion of Honor Museum: Legion of Honor Drive. Presently closed for renovation, but scheduled to reopen in 1994. Open Wednesday through Sunday 10:00 AM to 5:00 PM. Admission fee except Saturday morning and first Wednesday of the month. (415) 863-3330.

Visitor Center at the Cliff House: On the Great Highway. Open daily 10:00 AM to 4:30 PM. (415) 556-8642.

Golden Gate National Recreation Area Headquarters: Fort Mason, Building 201, San Francisco, CA 94123. Open weekdays. (415) 556-0560.

San Francisco International Hostel: Building 240, Fort Mason, San Francisco, CA 94123. Open for registration 7:00 AM to 2:00 PM and 4:30 PM to midnight. (415) 771-7277.

Hostel at Union Square: 312 Mason Street, San Francisco, CA 94102. (415) 788-5604.

San Francisco Visitor Information Center: 900 Market Street, San Francisco, CA 94102. Open weekdays 9:00 AM to 5:30 PM, Saturday 9:00 AM to 3:00 PM, Sunday 10:00 AM to 2:00 PM. (415) 391-2000.

Bike Rental: Golden Bike, 407 O'Farrell Street, (415) 771-8009. Lincoln Cyclery, 772 Stanyan Street, (415) 221-2415. Marina Cyclery, 3330 Steiner Street, (415) 929-7135. Park Cyclery, 1865 Haight Street, (415) 221-3777. Velo City, 638 Stanyan Street, (415) 221-2453.

13. San Francisco – Golden Gate Park

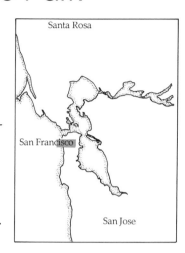

Distance: 7.5 miles plus 4-mile bike path

Rating: *Easy*, taking place on nearly level roads and a flat bike path. Traffic may be heavy in the east end of Golden Gate Park near the museums, but it tends to move slowly. Fog frequently covers San Francisco, especially in summer months, and brings cool temperatures.

Highlights: Golden Gate Park, one of the largest man-made parks in the world, offers a wealth of inviting sights and attractions, while the ride along the Great Highway has wonderful views of the ocean. The whole family will enjoy this outing.

McLaren Lodge on the east side of Golden Gate Park. It served as home and office to John McLaren from 1894 to 1943.

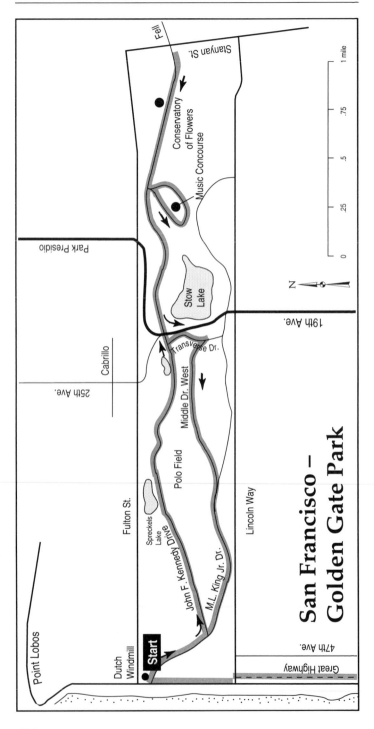

San Francisco –
Golden Gate Park

Location: Golden Gate Park is located on the west side of San Francisco. All major highways—1, 101, 80, and 280—converge in the city.

Ride through Golden Gate Park

Begin your tour of Golden Gate Park at its west end, across from Ocean Beach on the Great Highway, between Fulton Street and Lincoln Way. Parking is available along the Esplanade. Restrooms can be found at several locations within the park. Although you can buy food at snack bars, you may wish to bring a picnic lunch.

To reach the starting location from the Golden Gate Bridge, follow Highway 1 (19th Avenue) onto Park Presidio Boulevard. Turn right at Fulton Avenue, on the edge of the park. From the south via Interstate 280, follow Highway 1 through the park, exiting left onto 25th Avenue. Cross Fulton (a left turn is prohibited here), and in one block make a left onto Cabrillo. From Cabrillo, go left, back to Fulton and turn right. From Interstate 80 from the east and Highway 101 from the south, follow 101 to the Laguna/Fell exit. Take Fell into the east end of the park.

History of Golden Gate Park

Back in 1870, when the 1,017-acre site for Golden Gate Park was selected, this area was on the outskirts of town and consisted mostly of windblown sand dunes. The initial park design was created by William Hammond Hall, the first superintendent, who applied innovative sand reclamation techniques and began planting trees. But it was John McLaren, a Scottish landscape gardener, who turned the park into the verdant forest you see today.

Appointed superintendent in 1887, McLaren made Golden Gate Park his life's work and devoted the next 55 years to its development. Under his guidance, thousands of trees were planted (mostly Monterey cypress, Monterey pine, and eucalyptus), as well as a variety of rhododendron, turning the park into a monument to his skill and love of nature.

Golden Gate Park is crisscrossed with numerous roads, bike paths, and foot paths. Wooded glens, grassy meadows, and hidden gardens are just waiting to be discovered. The following route was designed for easy riding with the least amount of traffic but will still allow you to see the park's major attractions.

Enter the park on John F. Kennedy Drive near Fulton Street, between the Beach Chalet and Dutch Windmill. The windmill was built in 1902 to pump the thousands of gallons of water needed to irrigate the plantings in the park. After electric pumps were installed in the 1920s, the windmill fell into disrepair until it was renovated in 1981. The Queen Wilhelmina Garden here is especially beautiful in the spring when the tulips bloom. A second windmill, built in 1905 at the south corner of the park, has not been restored.

The Beach Chalet, on the Great Highway, is a Spanish Revival style building which opened as a municipal restaurant in 1925. It was the last work of the great architect Willis Polk.

Since most of the tourist sites are located on the eastern side of the park, the west end is more peaceful and less traveled. As you ride along, try to imagine what it looked like before 1870 when it consisted of sand dunes, or just after the 1906 earthquake when thousands of refugee shacks were erected in the park for those who had lost their homes.

At the first stop sign, turn left to stay on Kennedy Drive. (Martin Luther King Jr. Drive goes straight ahead.) You will have gentle uphill cycling for about 2 miles.

Soon you will pass the Buffalo Paddock, Rhododendron Island (where the road divides), and Spreckels Lake. (Restrooms are located to the left of the lake.) In just over half a mile you'll come to Lloyd Lake on your left. Across the pond is the structure called "Portals of the Past." This doorway is all that was left of the A. N. Towne residence, located on Nob Hill, after the 1906 fire. (If you are cycling on a Sunday, you will be happy to find that JFK Drive is closed to automobile traffic shortly after this point. Of course, you will have to share the road with pedestrians, other cyclists, and roller skaters.)

Park Museums

Less than a mile past Lloyd Lake, and after the turn to Stow Lake, go to the right to reach the museums. Here you will be greeted by a statue of Padre Junipero Serra, founder of the

California missions. The large depression beyond is the Music Concourse, the site of the 1894 Midwinter International Exposition. A 266-foot high Tower of Electricity was a central feature of the fair, which also included more than 100 temporary buildings and a lively midway. At the far end of the concourse stands the Spreckels Temple of Music, an ornate band shell constructed in 1900 and the home of the Golden Gate Park Band, one of the oldest municipal bands in the country. Free music programs of all kinds are held here. Follow the one-way street right past the M. H. de Young Memorial Museum, which opened in 1919, replacing the fine arts building from the Midwinter Fair. The Asian Art Museum is next door.

Beyond the museums you'll come to the Japanese Tea Garden, the only survivor from the 1894 exposition and the oldest Japanese-style garden in the United States. The fortune cookie, now traditionally offered in Chinese restaurants, is said to have been invented here by the Hagiwara family, who ran the concession from 1907 until 1942 when they were sent to a World War II detention camp. Today tea and cookies are served in the open-air pavilion overlooking the garden.

To cross to the other side of the concourse, walk your bike behind the Music Temple (restrooms can be found here). Ride

Conservatory of Flowers on JFK Drive. The oldest building in Golden Gate Park, it was installed in 1879.

Betty Johnston

Additional Information

M. H. de Young Memorial Museum: Off John F. Kennedy Drive in Golden Gate Park . Open Wednesday through Sunday 10:00 AM to 5:00 PM. Admission fee also covers the Asian Art Museum, (415) 668-8921, next door. Free admission first Wednesday and first Saturday morning of the month. (415) 863-3330.

Japanese Tea Garden: Near the de Young Museum. Open daily 8:30 AM to 6:30 PM. Tea House open daily 10:15 AM to 5:15 PM. Admission fee except on major holidays and first Wednesday of the month. (415) 752-1171.

California Academy of Sciences: Off Kennedy Drive in Golden Gate Park. Open daily 10:00 AM to 5:00 PM, with longer hours during the summer. Admission fee except first Wednesday of the month. (415) 750-7145.

Conservatory of Flowers: Kennedy Drive in Golden Gate Park. Open daily 9:00 AM to 5:00 PM, with longer hours during the summer. Admission fee except on major holidays and first Wednesday of the month. (415) 666-7017.

McLaren Lodge: Kennedy Drive at Stanyan Street. Office of the San Francisco Recreation and Park Department. Building open weekdays during regular business hours. (415) 666-7200.

Strybing Arboretum and Botanical Gardens: Martin Luther King Jr. Drive, near 9th Street and Lincoln Way. Open daily. Free admission. (415) 661-1316.

San Francisco Zoo: Sloat Boulevard just west of the ocean. Open daily 10:00 AM to 5:00 PM. Admission fee. (415) 753-7083.

See San Francisco Ride, page 116, for bike rental information and more resources.

14. Half Moon Bay

Distance: 7 miles plus 6-mile bike path

Rating: *Easy*, taking place on flat, quiet streets with light to moderate traffic. The ride is most pleasant during the off-season, without the summer beach goers. Also, be sure to avoid the annual Pumpkin Festival, held the third weekend in October, when the town is crowded with tourists. Fog and cool temperatures may greet you during the summer, but the weather usually clears by midday.

Highlights: Half Moon Bay has retained much of its small farming town charm despite recent growth and development. This tour includes an excursion to the beach and visits to sites that exemplify the town's rural history.

San Benito House, 365 Main St. in Half Moon Bay. Built as the Mosconi Hotel in 1905, it still houses a restaurant and hotel.

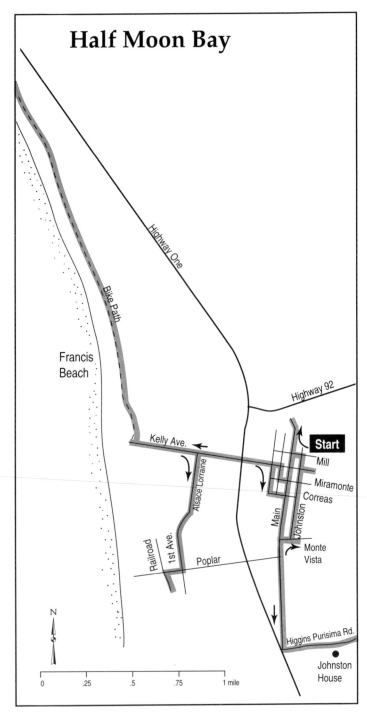

Half Moon Bay

Highway One

Bike Path

Francis
Beach

Kelly Ave.

Highway 92

Start

Mill

Alsace Lorraine

Miramonte

Correas

Main

Johnston

Railroad

1st Ave.

Poplar

Monte
Vista

N

Higgins Purisima Rd.

Johnston
House

| 0 | .25 | .5 | .75 | 1 mile |

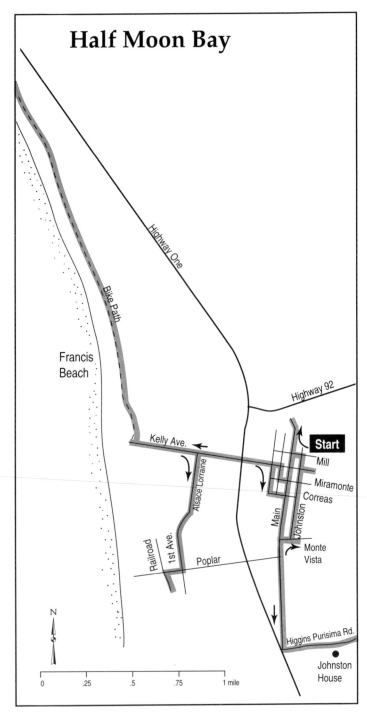

Location: Half Moon Bay is located at the intersection of Highways 1 and 92 in San Mateo County.

Ride through Half Moon Bay

Begin your ride at the parking lot at Johnston and Mill streets, one block off Main Street, south of Highway 92. The Miramontes adobe ranch house was originally located here but has long since disappeared.

Go right on Mill and right again on Main Street, heading north toward Highway 92. Soon you will cross over Pilarcitos

---

History of Half Moon Bay

When Gaspar de Portola camped at Half Moon Bay in 1769 in search for the bay at Monterey (discovering instead San Francisco Bay), this was the home of the peaceful and hospitable Costanoan Indians. When Mission Dolores was founded in San Francisco nine years later, the area became its grazing land and all the Indians were sent to work at the San Pedro ranch, which supplied food for the mission and presidio. With the secularization of the mission system after Mexico achieved its independence from Spain, the pastures were divided into ranchos. Part of Rancho El Corral de Tierra, north of Pilarcitos Creek, was granted to Tiburcio Vasquez in 1839. Rancho Arroyo de los Pilarcitos, south of the creek and also known as Rancho San Benito, was granted to Candelario Miramontes in 1841. These two large families were the earliest settlers of what was to become the town of Half Moon Bay.

Originally the settlement was known as San Benito, after the Miramontes rancho, but during the 1850s the newly arrived Yankees began calling it Spanishtown. The next 20 years brought rapid growth, with immigration from a variety of European countries, and in the 1870s the town was renamed Half Moon Bay, a term that had been used for the farming district around the crescent-shaped beach.

Half Moon Bay's early economy was based on cattle and sheep, which are still important, along with vegetable crops, such as Brussels sprouts, artichokes and, of course, pumpkins. Today the main industry is growing flowers, including chrysanthemums, carnations, and roses. Tourism is also a major activity.

Creek, the dividing line between the two land grants. The bridge, constructed of steel-reinforced concrete, was an engineering marvel at the time it was built in 1900. It replaced an earlier wooden wagon bridge, part of a precarious wagon road over the mountains to San Mateo. A toll gate was located several miles up the canyon.

The first house on the left, No. 270, was built in 1869 by Tiburcio Vasquez' youngest son next to his father's adobe, which no longer exists. The Vasquez descendents were prominent in the community well into the 20th century, but Tiburcio was gunned down in a Half Moon Bay saloon in 1863.

Cross back over the bridge. The charming Zaballa house, at 326 Main, was built in 1859. Zaballa, who married one of Miramontes' daughters, was the owner of the general store and was responsible for the plotting of Half Moon Bay in 1863. His home is now one of several bed-and-breakfast inns in town.

The old Mosconi Hotel, dating from 1905, is on the corner ahead. It is now the San Benito House and Saloon, a hotel and gourmet restaurant and deli.

As you ride down Main Street, you will see a variety of commercial and residential buildings from the late 19th and early 20th centuries. Most of the old adobe and brick buildings were destroyed by the earthquake of 1906, but many frame structures survived.

At the corner of Main and Kelly Avenue is Cunha's Country Store, which has been operating at this location since 1924. The building was constructed in 1900 by Joseph Debenedetti, a pioneer merchant. Across the street is Mac Dutra Park, a small plaza with picnic tables and restrooms. A bakery, popular with cyclists, can be found just beyond. On the other side of Main is the City Hall, housed in a 1922 bank building.

The false-front structure farther down the street, on the left at No. 527, is the oldest place of continuous business in town. It was built in 1873 as a general store and saloon. Turn right at the next corner onto Miramontes Street and right again on Purissima Street. The 1872 structure on the corner, at No. 546, was the home and office of an early country doctor.

Before turning left at Kelly Avenue, the next cross street, look to the right to see the 1928 Dutra Funeral Home, an outstanding example of Art Nouveau architecture. Proceeding down Kelly, you will soon come to Our Lady of the Pillar Catholic Church. The bronze bell on the front lawn dates from

1867, when it was part of the chapel at Pilarcitos Cemetery on Highway 92. The stained glass windows in the sanctuary are from an 1883 church building.

Across the street and farther along, at No. 520, there is an elegant Eastlake style house built in 1908 by Ben Cunha. Today it is home to the chamber of commerce and Coastal Art League.

Francis Beach

Continue along Kelly and cross Highway 1. At the end of the road, you'll come to the entrance to the Francis Beach section of Half Moon Bay State Beach. From here you will have a good view of the four-mile crescent of sandy beaches that gave the town its name. Pillar Point is at the far end. The park has restrooms and camping facilities, including sites for cyclists, should you plan to stay overnight.

There is also a flat, scenic bike path that begins at the Francis Beach entrance, heads north along coastal dunes and ends at Mirada Road in Miramar, less than 3 miles away. The path is paved except for a short stretch in about a half mile, where you angle right to the crossing of Pilarcitos Creek and may have to walk your bike in the soft sand.

From Francis Beach, return on Kelly, but before Highway 1, go right on Alsace-Lorraine Avenue, which eventually becomes First Avenue. In about half a mile, just after the road narrows, turn right on Poplar Street, and at the next corner, take a left onto Railroad Avenue, a gravel street.

The building before you dates from 1908 and was once a station for the Ocean Shore Railway, a railroad project that was originally designed to run along the beach from San Francisco to Santa Cruz. It was never completed and went out of business in 1920 when the automobile provided a more popular means of transportation. Notice the station's second-story dormer which allowed the stationmaster a clear view of the tracks located along Railroad Avenue. The building is now a private residence.

Main Street

Return the way you came, and at Kelly turn right, back toward town. After crossing Highway 1, take the first right onto Church Street and, when the road ends, go left onto Correas Street. Turn right when you reach Main Street again.

laid around the property in 1911. Half a block farther down Johnston is the former Half Moon Bay jail, at No. 505. This small, solid concrete building has barred windows and two cells. It is now the Spanishtown Historical Society Museum.

Turn right on Kelly at the next intersection. The Simmons House, on the corner at No. 751, was built in 1865 by the town's first undertaker, who was also a carpenter. One block farther along, at 505 San Benito, you will come upon a pretty little Queen Anne Victorian dating from 1892. The two-story building behind it with the false front was once a bakery.

Return to Johnston Street, and turn right. Soon you will reach your starting point and the end of your tour of Half Moon Bay.

Additional Information

San Benito House: 356 Main Street. Open Thursday through Sunday for dinner and Sunday brunch. Deli open daily for lunch. (415) 726-3425.

Francis Beach: This is a section of Half Moon Bay State Beach, entrance at end of Kelly Avenue off Highway 1. Camping is on first-come basis. (415) 726-8820.

Johnston House Foundation: P.O. Box 789, Half Moon Bay, CA 94019.

Spanishtown Historical Society Museum: 505 Johnston Street. Open Friday through Sunday noon to 3:00 PM. (415) 726-7084.

Half Moon Bay Chamber of Commerce: 520 Kelly Avenue. Open weekdays 9:00 AM to 5:00 PM, closed for lunch. (415) 726-5202.

Montara Lighthouse Hostel: Highway 1 at 16th Street in Montara, about 10 miles north of Half Moon Bay. Provides inexpensive lodging in a former coast guard facility. Office open daily 7:30 to 9:30 AM and 4:30 to 9:30 PM. (415) 728-7177.

Bike Rental: The Bicyclery, 432 Main Street, Half Moon Bay. (415) 726-6000.

15. Half Moon Bay Countryside

Distance: 14 miles

Rating: *Strenuous*, including a steep uphill on a narrow, winding road and, perhaps, a coastal headwind on the return segment. You can combine this route with the Pescadero–San Gregorio Ride (see page 137), which starts about 10 miles south on Highway 1.

Highlights: This ride through inland canyons takes you past old ranch buildings and two parks and offers the chance to enjoy peaceful country roads and ocean vistas. While the coastal lowlands are often covered with fog during the summer, the inland hills may be sunny and warm.

Location: Half Moon Bay is located at the intersection of Highways 1 and 92 in San Mateo County.

Higgins Purisima Road, southeast of Half Moon Bay.

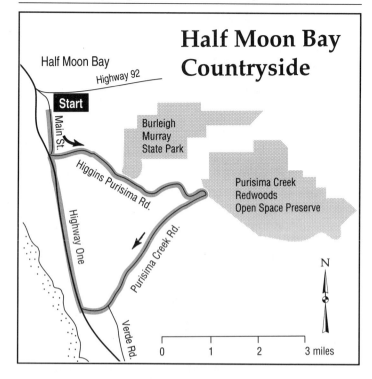

Half Moon Bay
Countryside

Half Moon Bay
Highway 92

Start

Main St.

Burleigh
Murray
State Park

Higgins Purisima Rd.

Highway One

Purisima Creek Rd.

Purisima Creek
Redwoods
Open Space Preserve

Verde Rd.

N

0   1   2   3 miles

Ride through the Countryside

Begin your ride on Main Street in Half Moon Bay, off Highway
92, and head south through town, where you will see a variety
of old commercial buildings and historic homes, as well as
numerous shops and eating establishments. On weekends, especially during summer months, you are likely to encounter many
visitors, but in a few blocks you'll leave the crowds behind.

After a little more than a mile, just before Main Street
intersects with Highway 1, make a left turn on Higgins
Purisima Road. You'll ride by the White House of Half Moon
Bay, the earliest frame home still standing along coastside San
Mateo County. It was built by James Johnston, who came to
this area in 1853, and for years the house was a center of social
activity for his well-to-do family. Then James' wife and
daughter died and he lost most of his money in the panic of
1873. The house was abandoned for many years and nearly
collapsed from neglect. Fortunately, it has been restored by the
Johnston House Foundation and is now on the National
Register of Historic Places.

Burleigh Murray State Park

About a mile past the Johnston house, the narrow road along Arroyo Leon begins to climb, and you will soon come to the entrance of Burleigh Murray State Park on the left. Once a dairy ranch, this newly established park includes 1,300 acres of coastal hills. Some of the old buildings remain and can be reached by walking or cycling one mile along the mostly level dirt road which follows Mill Creek. Just before you get to the employee residence (a former farmhouse), go left a short distance to see a large redwood barn dating from the 1890s. This is California's only example of an English style "bank barn"— a barn built into the side of a hill. Hay was brought in at the upper level and moved through drop boxes to feed cattle on the downhill side. Past the barn, the road deteriorates into a bumpy trail and ends in another mile.

Continuing along Higgins Purisima, you will catch glimpses of more old ranch buildings and have views of the ocean as you ride higher. The last uphill mile is very steep (8.5% grade), but you will also experience a sense of what the area must have been like in quieter times. The mile-long downhill on the other side is narrow and winding, but there is little traffic.

"Bank Barn," Burleigh Murray State Park, Higgins Puisima Road. This 1890s building is California's only example of an English style barn built into the side of a hill.

Purisima Creek Preserve

At the bottom of the hill, just after the creek crossing, is the entrance to Purisima Creek Redwoods Open Space Preserve, which was once the site of the longest-running logging operation in Peninsula history. From the 1850s to 1920, the Hatch family harvested timber and ran a sawmill in Purisima Canyon. Today the steep fire roads offer a challenging ride to mountain bikers.

Follow rolling Purisima Creek Road 4 miles back out to the coast. Just before you get to Highway 1, Verde Road intersects from the left and you will pass a stand of eucalyptus trees. This is the site of the once-flourishing town of Purisima. A lively place in the 1860s, it had a hotel, saloon, store, post office, and school, as well as the 17-room Dobbel house, the finest in the area. Now only the trees remain.

When you reach Highway 1, go right to return to Half Moon Bay 3 miles away. (To connect with the Pescadero–San Gregorio Ride, go left for about 7 miles.) As you approach town, you will see the Johnston House on the hill. Turn right at Higgins Purisima Road and left onto Main Street for the mile ride back to your starting point. On the way, you may wish to make a stop at the Half Moon Bay Bakery at No. 514. Although the original 1926 ovens are still in use, most cyclists are more interested in the goodies that come out of them.

Additional Information

Burleigh Murray State Park: Higgins Purisima Road, 1.75 miles from Highway 1. Open 8:00 AM to sunset. Free admission. Bicycles and horses are allowed on the trail. Pit toilets are located about a block from the road.

Purisima Creek Redwoods Open Space Preserve: 4 miles from Highway 1 on Purisima Creek Road. Mountain bikes permitted on some trails.

Half Moon Bay Bakery: 514 Main Street. Open Tuesday through Saturday 6:00 AM to 6:00 PM, Sunday 6:00 AM to 4:00 PM. (415) 726-4841.

Bike Rental: The Bicyclery, 432 Main Street, Half Moon Bay. (415) 726-6000.

See Half Moon Bay Ride, page 132, for more resources.

---

16. Pescadero – San Gregorio

Distance: 28 miles

Rating: *Strenuous*, with several significant hills. Traffic can be heavy, especially on summer weekends, and morning fog is common during summer months. The route takes advantage of the prevailing winds, generally from north to south.

Highlights: This ride takes you to the little coastal villages of Pescadero and San Gregorio, once major resort areas, and to historic Pigeon Point Lighthouse. You will ride alongside miles of beaches and pounding surf and on quiet country roads.

Location: Coast of San Mateo County, along Highway 1, south of Highway 84 and about 35 miles from San Francisco.

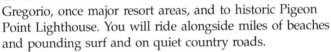

Pigeon Point Lighthouse, south of Pescadero Road on Highway 1. This former Coast Guard station is now a youth hostel.

In 1894 Coburn built a three-story, 200-room luxury resort hotel overlooking the beach, but it remained vacant while court battles continued. When it finally began operation in 1904, few guests were willing to make the long and uncomfortable trip by carriage, and within a few years the hotel closed and was torn down.

In another mile is Bean Hollow Beach, which has restrooms but no drinking water. You'll ride past fields of artichokes and Brussels sprouts, old farm buildings, a nursery, and an occasional modern beach home. In 3.5 miles, you will come to Pigeon Point Lighthouse. There are two entrances to Pigeon Point Road; the first takes you off Highway 1 and closer to the beach for a half mile before coming to the lighthouse. The second entrance is marked by a sign directing you to the hostel.

Pigeon Point Lighthouse

Standing 115 feet tall, Pigeon Point Lighthouse has been guiding mariners since 1871. It was built after several ships were wrecked off the coast, including the clipper ship *Carrier Pigeon*, which ran aground in 1853 near what was then called Whale Point for the Portuguese whaling community located there. Later the point was renamed in memory of the ill-fated vessel.

Pigeon Point is currently operated by the American Youth Hostels. The individual bungalows, originally built as Coast Guard family residences, provide inexpensive lodging for travelers of all ages from all over the world. The 1902 fog signal building has been converted to a recreation room for guests.

From the lighthouse, go back north along Highway 1. You may encounter headwinds going this direction, but in 2 miles you'll angle to the right to get off the highway and onto Bean Hollow Road. (A blue sign reading "disposal site" also marks the turn.) The road climbs about one mile past open fields of artichokes. Be careful on the downhill as the road is quite narrow. Turn right at the intersection with Pescadero Road.

Ride through Pescadero

The Ohlone Indians lived in this area for centuries, finding abundant food in the creeks and ocean, but the Indian population virtually disappeared during the Spanish mission period. In 1833 the land became part of Rancho El Pescadero ("the fishing place") when it was granted to Juan Jose Gonzales, majordomo at the Santa Cruz Mission.

The town of Pescadero was established in 1856 and first inhabited by farmers, ranchers, and lumbermen. By the 1860s, Pescadero had a population of several hundred and resembled a neat New England village. Many of the early residents came from Maine and constructed homes in the style of that area.

Pescadero's period of greatest activity occurred in the late 19th century when it was a popular resort community. Visitors came for the excellent hunting and fishing, to search for the pretty stones at Pebble Beach, or just to appreciate the natural beauty of the redwood forests and ocean beaches. Millionaires such as the Floods and Crockers often drove their carriages over the mountains to enjoy these unspoiled surroundings. By the late 1800s there were two good hotels in town, which were booked months in advance.

But Pescadero's prominence soon faded. The advent of the automobile in the early 1900s gave travelers greater access to places farther away. Fires destroyed much of the business district in the 1920s. When the coast highway was built, traffic bypassed the town, and Pescadero reverted to the quiet little village you see today.

The intersection of Pescadero Road and Stage Road, where the flagpole is located, was once the heart of the business district. Go right to start your tour of some of the town's historic structures.

First, on the left, is the former Methodist-Episcopal Church, built in 1890 after the original structure north of Pescadero Road burned down. By 1905 the local Methodist membership could no longer support a pastor and sold the building. It was used as a community social center and then a Japanese cultural center until December 1941, when it became a movie theater. Today it is owned by the Native Sons and Daughters of the Golden West.

Next door, at No. 110, is the former I.O.O.F. Hall. The International Order of Odd Fellows constructed the back part in 1878, while a front section, including the veranda and porch, was added later. It is now a private residence.

The house at No. 80 was built by Thomas Moore, the younger brother of the town's first settler, Alexander Moore, and probably dates from 1863. It has pierced columns on the porch and a single-story kitchen wing at the back.

At the end of the block you'll see the buildings of the I.D.E.S. (Irmandade do Dovino Espirito Santo), the Brotherhood of the Divine Holy Spirit. Each spring this Portuguese religious society sponsors the Festival of the Holy Ghost with a parade and barbecue.

Ride back toward the flagpole, cross Pescadero Road, and you will see the most famous establishment in town straight ahead. Duarte's Tavern was started in 1895 when Frank Duarte had a barrel of whiskey brought from Santa Cruz. Since then, business has thrived through four generations of the Duarte family. The restaurant, noted for its artichoke soup and olallieberry pie, is a favorite stop for cyclists.

Across the street from Duarte's is the site of a hotel that burned to the ground in the late 1920s. All that remains is the large magnolia tree behind the service station. There are several other businesses located on Stage Road, but perhaps the most important for cyclists is Arcangeli Grocery, founded in 1929. Fresh baked bread, as well as other food and picnic supplies, can be found here.

At the end of the block is the 1867 Pescadero Community Church, the oldest surviving Protestant church on the peninsula still on its original site. When built, it had just a square bell tower above the entry, but in 1890 the steeple was added, making it the tallest building in Pescadero. Although constructed of redwood, the siding is scored to simulate stone.

Across the street from the church, nearly hidden by trees, is the house James McCormick built in the late 1860s. McCormick, a native of Ireland, owned several businesses in town, including a hotel.

Turn right onto North Street, toward the residential part of town. Go right again at Goulson to the attractive home at No. 172. Built by Bartlett Weeks in 1885, it is occupied by the third generation of the Weeks family. The log cabin across the street is a Boy Scout project of more recent vintage.

Return to North Street, go right, and continue past St. Anthony's Catholic Church, which was built after the 1906 earthquake destroyed an earlier structure. Down the street on the right you'll see the old Pescadero High School, used from 1925 until 1960.

When North Street intersects Pescadero Road, you may wish to go left a short distance to Phipps Ranch, where you can find all sorts of produce, dried beans, and herbs. Picnickers are welcome, and there are many farm animals to see. This was also the site of the 1855 Alexander Moore house, the first

American home built in Pescadero. The 14-room house was destroyed by fire in 1975.

On the mile-long ride back into town, Cloverdale Road intersects from the left. If you plan to camp in the area, Butano State Park is 4.5 miles up this road. The park rangers will always find space for those who arrive by bicycle.

When you reach the flagpole, turn right onto Stage Road and, once again, ride down the main street. As you leave Pescadero, make one last stop at Mt. Hope Cemetery, located on the hill past North Street, where many of Pescadero's pioneer settlers are buried. The cemetery was founded in 1875 by the I.O.O.F. Today half of it is owned by the Community Church and half by St. Anthony's. Although it seems dry and barren much of the year, the cemetery is beautiful when the pink lilies called "naked ladies" bloom in late summer.

Ride to San Gregorio

Before Highway 1 was constructed along the coast, Stage Road was the main connection between Pescadero and San Gregorio. The 7-mile ride is hilly but also provides some wonderful views unless fog obscures the coast. You will have two significant climbs of one mile each, but that means you will also have two very welcome downhills. As you near the bottom of the second one, you will see what is left of the little town of San Gregorio. Don't miss the old one-room Seaside School on the knoll to your right. Dating from the 1870s, it is one of the oldest surviving elementary schools on the peninsula.

San Gregorio was once a well-known resort community but has since shrunk to a population of less than 200. Remaining from this earlier time is the San Gregorio House, an old hotel with full-length balcony, located between San Gregorio Creek and Highway 84. It was built in 1866 by George Washington Carter on what was then the stage road to Pescadero. It was enlarged in 1875 by a new owner and for many years was filled with tourists who came for hunting, fishing, or just relaxing. The hotel finally closed in the 1930s, after the town was bypassed by the new coast highway. Today it is a private residence. The empty, dilapidated service station on the corner in front of the hotel was a saloon before Prohibition.

Across Highway 84 is the Peterson & Alsford General Store, commonly called the San Gregorio Store, the main attraction in town. You can find almost anything you want here: food, beverages, clothes, books, kitchen equipment, hardware, and more. Cyclists are welcome, but please use the bike rack; don't lean your bicycle against the building.

After browsing through the general store, it is time to return to your starting point, less than a mile away. Ride toward the ocean on Highway 84, and when you reach Highway 1, go left to the San Gregorio State Beach parking lot to complete your exploration of the San Mateo County coast.

Additional Information

Pigeon Point Lighthouse Hostel: Highway 1, south of Pescadero. Office hours 7:30 to 9:30 AM and 4:30 to 9:30 PM. Hostel closed during the day, but lighthouse grounds, are open to visitors. Lighthouse tours on Sundays for a small fee. Call hostel for reservations. (415) 879-0633.

Duarte's Restaurant: 202 Stage Road, Pescadero. Open daily for breakfast, lunch, and dinner, except major holidays. (415) 879-0464.

Arcangeli Market: 287 Stage Road, Pescadero. Open weekdays 10:00 AM to 7:00 PM, Saturday 9:00 AM to 7:00 PM, and Sunday 10:00 AM to 6:00 PM.

Phipps Ranch: 2700 Pescadero Road. Open daily, summer 10:00 AM to 7:00 PM, winter 10:00 AM to 6:00 PM. (415) 879-0787.

Butano State Park: Cloverdale Road, Pescadero. Camping facilities, miles of hiking trails through the redwoods. (415) 879-0173. Advance campsite reservations through MISTIX. (800) 444-7275.

San Gregorio Store: Intersection of Stage Road and Highway 84. Open daily 9:00 AM to 6:00 PM Restroom.

Año Nuevo State Reserve: 7 miles south of Pigeon Point Lighthouse on Highway 1. A large colony of elephant seals gather here each winter to breed. December through March, reservations required for docent-led tours. Call MISTIX at (800)444-7275. Park open from 8:00 AM to sunset. Admission fee. (415) 879-0227.

Bike Rental: See Half Moon Bay Ride, page 132, or Woodside–Portola Valley Ride, page 226.

17. Benicia

Distance: 12 miles plus 4-mile option

Rating: *Moderate*, mostly flat to rolling with some short climbs along lightly traveled city streets. This a pleasant excursion any time of year, as the westerly winds off the Carquinez Strait bring cooling breezes even on hot summer days. The optional route to Dillon Point is flat and easy.

Highlights: Benicia is a delightful small town with lots of history to explore, including a former state capitol and the pre–Civil War-era federal arsenal. Part of the ride follows peaceful Carquinez Strait and offers views of tankers and freighters on their way to Port Benicia.

Location: Near the intersection of Interstates 680 and 780 in southern Solano County.

Bachelor Officers' Quarters on Grant Street, Benicia Arsenal.

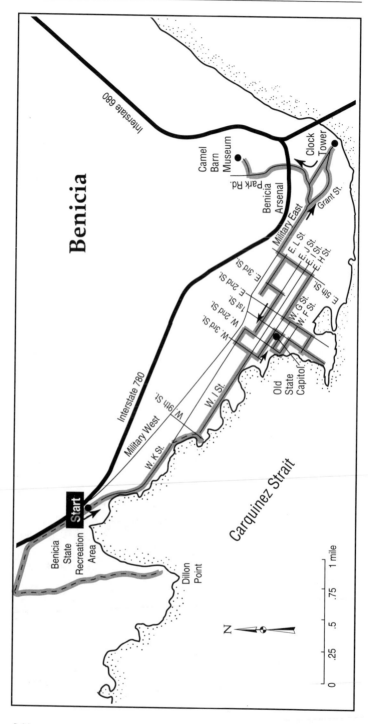

Ride through Benicia

Begin your ride at the Benicia State Recreation Area east side parking lot, next to Carquinez Strait. It is located off Interstate 780 at the Military West exit.

From the parking lot, turn right on West K Street, and follow the Bay Trail Bike Route along Carquinez Strait. The city of Benicia has constructed a series of attractive waterfront parks, the first of which you'll pass at the foot of West Twelfth Street.

At West Tenth Street, turn right to find the entrance to a bike path that leads to the larger Ninth Street Park at Jones Point. The park has a swimming beach, a boat-launching ramp,

History of Benicia

When Benicia was established in 1847, it was expected to become California's leading city, the commercial and maritime rival of nearby San Francisco. The chief founders were Dr. Robert Semple and his partner Thomas O. Larkin. Impressed with the beautiful Carquinez Strait as a possible site for a city, Semple negotiated with General Mariano Vallejo, who was imprisoned during the Bear Flag rebellion, for donation of the land, part of the General's vast estate.

Semple suggested the new town be named Francisca, after Vallejo's wife, but when the town of Yerba Buena across the bay changed its name to San Francisco, Semple renamed the new city Benicia, one of Mrs. Vallejo's other names.

Located in a position to command both ocean and interior waterway navigation, the town quickly attracted a number of settlers. Its population had grown to 1,000 by 1850, when Benicia, along with Monterey, became the first cities to be incorporated in the newly formed state of California.

Benicia, however, never reached the expectations of its founders. By World War I, its growth had slowed, as San Francisco became the major city of northern California. Today, despite recent commercial development, the central part of Benicia still looks much as it did in the early part of the century.

restrooms, picnic grounds, and a monument to Commodore Jones for whom the point is named.

Leave the park by way of West I Street, following the Bike Route signs. You will see a number of early Benicia homes as you ride along, many of which have been beautifully restored. The bike route takes you right on West Third, then left on West H Street, past the site of the 1849 Peabody Hospital, the first hospital to be established in the West.

Old State Capitol

Continue on the H Street Bike Route to First Street, the main street of Benicia, where you will find several restaurants, stores, and antique shops, many located in buildings from the early 1900s. Turn right and then right again in one block. On the corner with West G Street you'll see the Old State Capitol, the most noteworthy structure from Benicia's pioneer days.

This two-story brick building was constructed in 1852 and offered to the state for use as a capitol. The offer was accepted, and in 1853 Benicia became the third capital of the state of California after San Jose and Vallejo. Just one year later, however, the capital made its final move to Sacramento.

In the years since, this dignified building, designed to resemble a Greek temple, has been used for a variety of purposes. It has housed a school, library, church, police station, fire department, and city hall. Now, as the Benicia Capitol State Historic Park, it has been restored and furnished as it appeared during the period of legislative use.

The Fischer-Hanlon House next door started as a hotel on First Street. It was purchased by Joseph Fischer in 1856 and moved to this site. After renovations and additions, this handsome residence was occupied by generations of the Fischer family until donated to the state in 1969.

Continue on G Street and turn left on West Second, back on the Bay Trail Bike Route, and then onto the bike path. At the end there is another tiny park with excellent views across the strait to the rolling hillsides beyond.

Follow the bike route on West F Street to First Street and turn right. In the next block, at No. 401, is the Union Hotel, dating from 1882, which is still an inn and restaurant. Across D Street you'll see the Washington House, an 1850 wharf building that was moved to this site and remodeled as a hotel. At various times in the past, it served as a bordello, a speakeasy, and a Chinese lottery, but now accommodates more conventional tenants.

Turn right on West D Street to reach two pioneer saltbox houses at No. 123 and No. 145. They were prefabricated in the East and shipped to California to be reassembled at this location during the gold rush days.

Waterfront

Return to First Street again, going right. As you continue riding toward the water, the number of buildings dwindle, but this area once teemed with activity. The first ferry across the strait was established nearby in 1847 by Dr. Semple. Ferry service between Benicia and Martinez was in continuous operation for 115 years until the highway bridge was completed in 1962.

The end of First Street was the location of the transcontinental train-ferry dock. These ferries were the largest in the world, carrying an average of 30 Southern Pacific trains across the water daily. They ran between Benicia and Port Costa from 1879 until 1929 when the railroad bridge was constructed.

Benicia was also a relay station for the Pony Express during the short time it operated from 1860 to 1861. A sign marking the site can be found at the corner of First and A streets. The

Old State Capitol, Benicia Capitol State Historic Park, West G Street at First Street. It was constructed in 1852 and used when Benicia served briefly as the capital of California.

waterfront was the site of the first canneries in Solano County, and several tanneries were located here as well. At one time Benicia was the principal leather-processing center of the Pacific Coast.

Little remains today to evoke the past. Point Benicia is now just a fishing pier, and the only buildings left are the 1900 railroad depot and dilapidated Jurgensen's Saloon, a favorite haunt of author Jack London when he lived on a houseboat along the waterfront. Restoration of these structures is part of the proposed waterfront improvement plan.

Return up First and go right on East D Street, which has several well-preserved early residences. At the end you'll see the yacht club and 309-berth marina. Almost deserted during the week, it's a busy place on summer weekends.

Turn left on East Second Street, away from the waterfront, and then go right on East H Street. In 3 blocks, turn left onto East Fifth. At the next corner, to the left, you can see St. Dominic's Catholic Church with its twin steeples. The first church was built on this site in 1852, and the present structure dates from 1890.

Benicia Arsenal

Continue along East Fifth Street to the traffic signal and turn right onto Military East. This thoroughfare becomes Grant Street in half a mile as you enter the Benicia Arsenal, now the Benicia Industrial Park.

The Benicia Barracks, established in 1849, became the first arsenal on the Pacific Coast two years later. Although the importance of the Benicia military post was superseded in later years by the San Francisco Presidio, it served the needs of the U.S. military until it closed in 1964. Gunpowder, cannon-balls and, later, high explosives were stored here. Among its most famous soldiers were the young lieutenants Ulysses S. Grant and William Tecumseh Sherman.

During the Civil War, the arsenal was a staging area for western troops. The last of its garrisoned soldiers were sent to the Philippines at the time of the Spanish-American War, but the arsenal remained important. During both world wars and the Korean War, it served as ordnance headquarters for the Pacific coast

Much of the arsenal property has been converted to commercial and industrial use, including studios for artists and

craftspeople, but most of the principal historic military structures have been preserved. As you enter the Industrial Park,
you will see the large Mission style arsenal headquarters building dating from World War II. It now houses the park offices.

Continue on Grant, staying to the right when the road
divides, and you will soon arrive at the Bachelor Officers'
Quarters, located on the left at No. 983, just after the road
crosses a short bridge. This two-story stone building with its
columned porch dates from 1872. A short distance up the road,
at No. 1060, is the old Command Post, built in 1870.

Clock Tower

Turn right onto Adams Street, then immediately go left up the
short hill on Washington Street, leading to Johansen Square
and Commandant's Lane. Stay to the right to visit the Clock
Tower Fortress, built in 1859 to command Carquinez Strait and
protect the post from Indian attack. The sandstone building
originally had a third story and a second tower, but both were
destroyed by an accidental explosion in 1912. When the
fortress was rebuilt, the clock was added as a memorial to
Colonel Julian McAllister, commander of the arsenal for 25
years. Before leaving, take time to enjoy the fine views of the
Port of Benicia and the bridge over the strait.

Across the parking lot from the Clock Tower, you'll see the
imposing Commandant's Home. This 20-room mansion of
classic Georgian design dates from 1860 and was once a social
center for Bay Area society. From 1906 to 1911, poet Stephen
Vincent Benet lived here while his father was commanding
officer of the post.

Ride through the parking lot on the left side of the house,
past the barricade, and straight ahead on the rough roadway
which becomes Jefferson Street. The large structure at No. 1063
was once an officers' home and was built about the same time
as the commandant's mansion. At Park Road make a right
turn, following the road uphill and under Interstate 780 as you
head toward other historic arsenal buildings.

Camel Barn Museum

After a short distance, go right on Camel Road, following the
signs to the Camel Barn Museum. There you will see two long
sandstone buildings, constructed in 1853 and 1854 for use as

warehouses. They are more popularly known as the Camel Barns, however, for the brief period in 1863 when they were used to stable a herd of camels. The animals had been imported by the government in 1856 as an experiment in the transportation of military supplies across the southwest desert. When the camels proved unsatisfactory, they were driven to Benicia and sold at auction. The last of these unfortunate beasts died in 1934 at Griffith Park in Los Angeles. The Benicia Historical Museum is now located in the first building.

Retrace your route on Park Road, going past Jefferson to the bottom of the hill, and turn right on Adams. Adams rejoins Grant, which soon becomes Military East again, as you leave the arsenal. A left turn at the traffic light will bring you back onto East Fifth Street.

In one block, go right on East L Street. Across from City Hall, No. 235, is Captain John Walsh's Home, built in 1849. His house, now a bed-and-breakfast inn, was one of three identical dwellings built in Boston, dismantled, shipped around the Horn, and reassembled in the Bay Area. A second house was sold in San Francisco and no longer exists. The third became Lachryma Montis, the residence of General Mariano Vallejo in Sonoma.

St. Paul's Church and Rectory

Turn around here and go right at the corner onto East Third Street, which takes you past the old Benicia Primary School. Turn right at the next corner onto East J Street. In the next block, at No. 120 on the left, you'll see St. Paul's Rectory. This typical New England saltbox house was originally built in Connecticut in 1790. It was purchased in 1868 by Captain Julian McAllister, who had the house disassembled and shipped around the Horn to be rebuilt at its present site. Two rooms were added the following year.

The Gothic style St. Paul's Episcopal Church is next to the rectory, on the corner of East J and First streets. Dating from 1859, it is the oldest Episcopal church in California. Work on the building was done by shipwrights, and the arched ceiling resembles the inverted hull of a ship. The bell tower was added in 1863. You may see the beautiful redwood interior and stained glass windows during services on Sunday and Wednesday by asking at the church office in the rectory.

Continue on J Street across First Street. At 110 West J Street you'll pass the first Masonic Temple built in California, dating from 1850. On the other side of the street is an old Congregational church building, and at the end of the block, on the left, is a former Methodist church.

Turn right on West Second Street to West K Street. To the right is the City Park, site of the first Protestant church in California in 1849. On the far side of the park, at 160 Military West, is the Fire Museum, where antique fire extinguishers and fire engines, including California's first, are on display.

A left turn onto West K Street will bring you to the 1891 Ridell-Fish house at No. 245, one of the largest and most impressive residences in Benicia. At the next intersection, go left at West Third, then right onto West I Street. You are now back on the Bay Trail Bike Route.

At the end of I Street, in less than a mile, is the Ninth Street Park and the beginning of the bike path. From here, retrace your route back to the starting point to conclude your tour of this historic waterfront town.

Dillon Point

If you want to do more riding, take the flat bike path from the other side of the parking lot. In less than a mile you will come

Captain John Walsh's Home at 235 East L Street, Benicia. Built in 1849 and identical to General Vallejo's home in Sonoma, it is now a bed-and-breakfast inn.

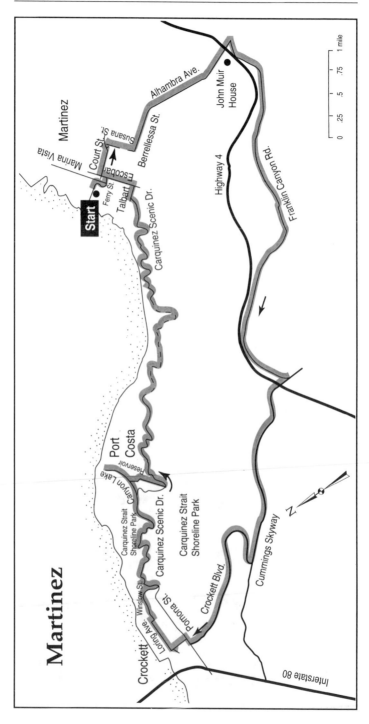

Martinez

Ride through Martinez

Begin your ride at Martinez Regional Shoreline, a popular recreational area that bears little resemblance to the time when ferries, ships, and fishing boats lined its waterfront. To reach the park from Interstate 680, take the Marina Vista exit, going left about 1.5 miles to Ferry Street. Turn right to the park entrance. The park has miles of nature trails, an exercise course, a horse arena, soccer fields, picnic areas, even bocce ball courts that harken back to the predominantly Sicilian population of the shoreline's early days. The softball complex is named for Martinez native Joe DiMaggio, who played for the New York Yankees. A marina and fishing pier are located at the end of the road. With all this activity, the park is likely to be a busy place, especially on summer weekends. Try parking in the first lot on the left. (Restrooms can be found nearby.)

Leaving the park, you will ride by the Amtrak Railroad Station, the same depot, with some alterations, built by the Northern Railway Company in 1877. As you cross the tracks, imagine the congestion in the days when shipping grain by rail and boat was a million-dollar industry. Now only a few trains pass through town each day.

Continue on Ferry Street, crossing Marina Vista into the downtown area. Fires in 1894 and 1904 destroyed many structures, so the oldest commercial buildings here date from the early 20th century.

Martinez Historical Museum

Turn left in one block onto Escobar to reach the Martinez Historical Society Museum at the corner of Escobar and Court streets. It is housed in a two-story cottage built in 1890 for Dr. J. S. Moore as his residence and dental office and has a fine collection of local memorabilia.

From the museum, go up Court Street past the County Finance Building, which was originally the courthouse when built in 1901. This area was once the city's elite residential district, but the fine homes and mansions have since been replaced by the county buildings you see today.

After a short distance, just as the road curves left and becomes Pine Street, turn right to stay on Court, which takes you into a neighborhood of older homes. When you reach Susana Street, named for Susana Martinez Smith, wife of the founder of the city, go right. Just on the other side of Alhambra Creek you'll see a small, tree-shaded park with restrooms.

Susana ends at the plaza, donated to the city by the Martinez family in 1849. To the left is the Boys and Girls Club, housed in a much-altered 1909 grammar school. To the right is the Martinez City Hall and Police Department, built in 1916 as the grammar school annex. Ride through the park and cross

---

History of Martinez

Carquinez Strait, the waterway connecting the Sacramento River with San Francisco Bay, became a major route of commercial shipping during the second half of the 19th century. Grain from the Central Valley was brought by boat and railroad to ports along the strait to be shipped to markets in San Francisco and Europe. Ferries carried both passengers and trains across the strait to the northern part of the state. Later, sugar and oil refineries were built. The bustling waterfront was crowded with warehouses and wharfs, ships and railroads, hotels and saloons.

The town of Martinez, named for the original Spanish land grantee, was laid out in 1849 and designated the county seat of Contra Costa County the following year. With its location on the strait and the railroad reaching Martinez in 1878, shipping became the town's major industry. Warehouses lined the waterfront all the way to Port Costa, and the area swarmed with thousands of railroad men, sailors, teamsters, and stevedores.

By 1885 the railroad and wharves of Port Costa carried most of the grain crops to market, and, although local orchards continued to load their crops at Martinez docks, shipping at Martinez fell into decline, and other industries gradually took its place. The first oil company arrived in 1895, followed by the Royal Dutch Shell Oil Company in 1914, Shell's first refinery in the United States. The Alhambra Water Company started bottling pure mineral water in Martinez in 1903.

Martinez remained an important business and cultural center until the 1930s, when transportation to the larger cities of Oakland and San Francisco improved. Today many people think of the city only in terms of the oil refineries that they see from Highway 680, but Martinez and its surrounding countryside has much more to offer.

one-way Alhambra Avenue. At the next corner, turn left onto one-way Berrellessa Street. Although there is often heavy traffic, this street is wide enough for both cars and bicycles.

John Muir Historic Site

Soon Berrellessa merges with Alhambra. You will pass the grounds of the Merrithew Memorial County Hospital on the right. The oldest of the hospital buildings dates from 1910. Ride along Alhambra for a little over a mile to the John Muir National Historic Site.

John Muir was born in Scotland in 1838 and came to the United States in 1849, eventually making his way to California. Most of his life was spent exploring, studying, and writing about the great mountains of California and Alaska, their valleys, glaciers, and wildlife. Many of the mountain peaks and glaciers along the Pacific coast were discovered and named by him.

In 1880 Muir met and married Louie Strenzel of Martinez. The large Victorian home you see here on the hill was built in 1882 for Dr. John Strenzel, Muir's father-in-law. Strenzel was a colorful figure in his own right, having been a Polish revolutionary, medical doctor, Texas frontiersman, and forty-niner before settling down as a successful fruit rancher in the Alhambra Valley. Muir, who lived about a mile away with Louie and their two daughters, joined his father-in-law in the orchard business. When Dr. Strenzel died in 1890, the Muirs moved into this home.

Soon afterward, John Muir retired as an orchardist and returned to his travels, especially to his beloved High Sierra, and devoted the rest of his life to saving America's vanishing wilderness. His prolific writings were highly influential in establishing the conservation of natural resources as a national policy. He was also one of the founders of the Sierra Club in 1892 and served as its president until his death in 1914. Muir felt his greatest accomplishment was the part he played in the creation of Yosemite National Park in 1906. His most bitter disappointment came in 1913 when he was unable to save the beautiful Hetch Hetchy valley from being dammed for use as a reservoir.

To visit the John Muir home and grounds, enter through the visitor center (restrooms are located here) and ask a ranger to open the locked gate so you can safely leave your bicycle on the other side of the fence. Of special interest in the house is Muir's study and the displays highlighting the history of the Sierra Club. From the bell tower, you will see that the view of Martinez has changed dramatically since Muir's day. After touring the house, take the orchard walk past the carriage house to the Martinez Adobe.

Martinez Adobe

In 1824 Ignacio Martinez, the Commandante of the San Francisco Presidio, was granted Rancho El Pinole, a large parcel of land stretching from Alhambra Creek in present-day Martinez west to Point Pinole. At his death in 1848, the land was divided among his children. Vincente Martinez built this adobe in 1849 on his portion of the inheritance. The house was sold a few years later to Edward Franklin, for whom Franklin Canyon is named.

Dr. Strenzel bought the adobe and surrounding land in 1874 and planted fruit and nut trees. The structure then became a storehouse and a residence for ranch employees. Many years later, it served as the home of Muir's daughter Wanda and her husband.

When you have finished exploring the Muir site, go right on Alhambra and beneath Highway 4. Just on the other side, turn right onto Franklin Canyon Road. This takes you away from the traffic of the city and into the quiet countryside. The first part of the road is narrow and mostly level, and you will ride by a variety of homes, farms, and ranches. Gradually, as you climb higher, the trees disappear and the shoulder widens. After 3.5 miles, McEwen Road to Port Costa intersects on the right. The section past this point is steeper but less than a mile long. When you reach the top of Franklin Canyon Road, go right on Cummings Skyway over Highway 4 and enjoy the views of the open grassy hills as you climb for another 1.5 miles. To the left you can see San Francisco Bay and, if the day is clear, Mt. Tamalpais beyond. As you start down the other side, watch for a right turn in half a mile onto Crockett Boulevard. This is an exhilarating 2-mile downhill ride with little traffic.

Crockett and C & H Sugar Refinery

Crockett Boulevard ends at Pomona Street and the town of Crockett. To your left is the red brick John Swett High School, named for the man who developed the state's public school system. His ranch was located in nearby Alhambra Valley. The Carquinez Bridge (Interstate 80) dominates your view past the school. Its southbound span dates from 1927.

Go right on Pomona and immediately turn left on Rolph Avenue. At the end of the street you'll see the massive C & H Sugar Refining Plant, the center of Crockett's economy since 1906 and the largest sugar mill in the world. Here also is the Crockett Historical Museum, located in the former railroad depot.

In 1865 a lawyer named John B. Crockett received a strip of land along Carquinez Strait in payment of legal fees. He offered a partnership in the land to Thomas Edwards, who became the first settler. In 1880 Edwards purchased part of Crockett's share and Dr. John Strenzel of Martinez bought the remainder. Edwards laid out a town on his land and named it Crockett. Strenzel laid out another town to the west that he called Valona. Both towns grew and prospered during the heyday of shipping, but only Crockett remains today.

The Old Homestead, the Edwards family residence, can be found under the tall palm trees in the far corner of the parking lot across from the museum. Dating from 1867, it is the oldest home in Crockett. It is now the Women's Community House.

The first factory in Crockett was located on the present site of the C & H plant, where John Heald began manufacturing farm machinery in 1881. The following year Abraham Starr constructed a huge flour mill next to Heald's plant. In 1897 Starr's mill was converted to sugar beet refining by George McNear, but this venture was not successful. The mill was then leased to the Spreckel's sugar company and in 1906 the plant became the California and Hawaiian Sugar Refinery. Ships brought sugar cane from Hawaii and docked directly beside the mill. Once refined, the sugar was distributed throughout the country by the railroad whose tracks were next to the factory.

In the first quarter century, business at C & H was brisk, and Crockett thrived as the company provided many services for the town, including sewers, road improvements, a public library, a men's club, parks, and a swimming pool. Most of the town's residents were C & H employees. Even during the Depression, all C & H workers who were heads of households kept their jobs. But times changed. The first of several strikes by the refinery workers' union was called in 1935, and World War II and automation brought further modifications in the work force and working conditions. And, as new highways

Riding down the hill from the cemeteries, you'll end up on Talbart Street. In a few blocks, at the corner of Escobar, is a large 1888 Queen Anne that belonged to Dr. John Tennent, a Martinez descendent. Up Escobar, to the right at No. 110, is Captain Tucker's house, one of the most handsome in town.

From the Tucker house, ride down the hill, continuing on Escobar through the downtown area. At Ferry Street, go left, back to Shoreline Park.

Additional Information

Martinez Regional Shoreline: At the foot of Ferry Street in downtown Martinez. Open daily. Bicycles permitted on all trails. (510) 228-0112.

Martinez Historical Museum: 1005 Escobar. Open Tuesday and Thursday 11:30 AM to 3:00 PM, and first and third Sunday each month 1:00 to 4:00 PM. Free admission. (510) 228-8160.

John Muir National Historic Site: 4202 Alhambra Avenue, Martinez. Open Wednesday through Sunday 10:00 AM to 4:30 PM. Admission fee. (510) 228-8860.

Crockett Historical Museum: Intersection of Rolph and Loring. Open Wednesday and Saturday 10:00 AM to 4:00 PM. Free admission. (510) 787-2178.

Carquinez Strait Regional Shoreline: Two entrances along Carquinez Strait Scenic Drive. Open sunrise to sunset. Bicycles allowed on some trails. (510) 228-0112.

Warehouse Cafe and Burlington Hotel: Port Costa (510) 787-1827.

Martinez Area Chamber of Commerce: 620 Las Juntas, Martinez, CA 94553. Open weekdays 9:00 AM to 4:00 PM. (510) 228-2345.

Crockett Chamber of Commerce: P.O. Box 191, Crockett, CA 94525. (510) 787-1155.

Bike Rental: Martinez Cyclery, 4990 Pacheco Boulevard, Martinez. (510) 228-9050. Any Mountain, 1975 Diamond Boulevard, Concord. (510) 674-0174.

19. Berkeley

Distance: 40 miles plus 8-mile bike path

Rating: *Strenuous*, for experienced cyclists only. There are many hills, some quite steep, and narrow roads that often have no shoulder. Nimitz Way, however, is a gently rolling, paved recreation path and is rated easy. There is no place to buy food along the route.

Highlights: Those who attempt this challenging route through the Berkeley-Oakland hills will be rewarded with spectacular views of Berkeley, San Francisco Bay, and inland hills and canyons. It offers a wonderful escape from the crowded city, as you ride through several parks and preserves and along some lightly traveled roads.

Cyclists stop to rest along Grizzly Peak Blvd. in the Berkeley hills overlooking San Francisco Bay.

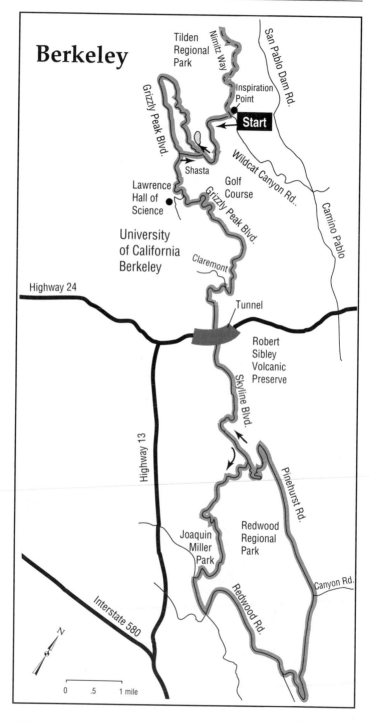

Berkeley

Tilden Regional Park

Nimitz Way

San Pablo Dam Rd.

Inspiration Point

Start

Grizzly Peak Blvd.

Shasta

Wildcat Canyon Rd.

Camino Pablo

Lawrence Hall of Science

Golf Course

Grizzly Peak Blvd.

University of California Berkeley

Claremont

Highway 24

Tunnel

Robert Sibley Volcanic Preserve

Skyline Blvd.

Highway 13

Pinehurst Rd.

Joaquin Miller Park

Redwood Regional Park

Canyon Rd.

Redwood Rd.

Interstate 580

N

0   .5   1 mile

Location: East of Interstate 80 and west of Interstate 680 in the hills above Berkeley and Oakland, along the border of Alamada and Contra Costa counties.

Ride through Tilden Park

Begin your ride at Inspiration Point in Tilden Regional Park. The easiest way to get there is to take the Orinda exit from Highway 24, about halfway between Interstates 880 and 680, east of the Caldecott Tunnel. Go north, through Orinda Village on Camino Pablo, and after about 2 miles turn left at the traffic signal onto Wildcat Canyon Road. The Inspiration Point parking lot is located 2.5 miles uphill on the right; if the lot is full, try parking along the road. There are no facilities here except for picnic tables, although water and restrooms are available in various parks along the route.

Established in 1937, Tilden Park is the oldest of 46 parks that comprise the East Bay Regional Park District. It was named for Major Charles Lee Tilden, founder and first president of the park district. Tilden believed so strongly in preserving the parkland, he lent his own money for the purchase of the original 60 acres. Today Tilden Park has over 2,000 acres of forested hills and open meadows. There are hiking and

View from Lawrence Hall of Science, Centennial Drive, University of California, in the hills above Berkeley.

equestrian trails, as well as a lake, golf course, carousel, nature center, and other attractions. There is also a popular 4-mile paved hiking and cycling path called Nimitz Way heading north from Inspiration Point, which you may want to explore later.

From Inspiration Point, ride to the right, downhill through the eucalyptus groves along narrow and winding Wildcat Canyon Road. After 1.3 miles, you'll come to the Botanic Garden, a large collection of California's native plants displayed by geographic region. (Water and restrooms are located next to the parking lot on the left.)

You will next ride by the Brazil Building, a lovely stone structure whose interior is paneled with tropical hardwoods

---

History of Berkeley

For thousands of years, the area that is now known as Berkeley was home to the Hutchiun tribe of the Ohlone Indians. In 1820 it became part of Rancho San Antonio, a vast land grant given to Luis Maria Peralta. By the mid-1850s, a small community called Ocean View was growing along the east shore of the San Francisco Bay. Its residents were merchants and farmers who were looking for cheap land, plentiful water, and close proximity to the booming gold rush markets of San Francisco.

But what has made Berkeley unique is the university, which had its beginning in 1855 as the College of California, a private liberal arts institution. The college was originally chartered in the frontier town of Oakland, but the founders wanted a more secluded environment for their students and chose another location on the slopes above the settlement of Ocean View. After setting aside land for a campus, they laid out and sold lots for a town that they named for Bishop George Berkeley, an 18th-century English philosopher who believed in the westward movement of civilization. They ran out of money, however, before the college could be moved to the new site.

In 1867 the state of California decided to open a university, so the trustees of the struggling college suggested that the state take over their holdings. The following year, the University of California was chartered in Oakland, and in 1873 it moved to the Berkeley campus. There were two buildings and 191 students, including 22 women.

used in the 1939 World's Fair on Treasure Island. This is one of the East Bay's most popular wedding sites and is usually booked a year in advance. (More restrooms are available at the Island picnic area just beyond.)

Less than a mile from the Botanic Garden is the junction with Central Park Drive, the road down to Lake Anza and the antique merry-go-round. The 1911 carousel, which is listed on the National Register of Historic Places, has an interesting variety of hand-carved animals, including frogs, dragons, pigs, and tigers. (A snack bar is located next to the carousel.)

Berkeley-Oakland Hills

As you ride out of the park, you can see Wildcat Canyon and open hills, the first of many beautiful views you'll enjoy on this route. Go left at the stop sign onto Grizzly Peak Boulevard, the beginning of a 4-mile climb with an elevation gain of more than 800 feet. You will first ride through a residential neighborhood, and then, after a couple of miles, you'll come to the intersection with Centennial Drive on the right, the way to the upper part of the University of California campus. The Lawrence Hall of Science is located about a half mile down this

---

History of Berkeley (continued)

Today the university has 32,000 students and more than 100 buildings on its 1,200-acre campus. It has earned a reputation for academic excellence, an outstanding faculty, and an active, progressive student body, famous for the Free Speech Movement and anti-war protests of the 1960s. Things may seem quieter on campus these days, but the university and the surrounding community are still known for their lively, outspoken opinions about intolerance and social injustice. (To mark the 500-year anniversary of Columbus' arrival in the New World, the Berkeley City Council voted to rename Columbus Day as Indigenous People's Day.)

Berkeley has hundreds of historic buildings, from Victorian homes and churches to extensive university structures, but narrow streets and heavy automobile and pedestrian traffic can make it difficult to explore the city by bicycle. So, do what the locals do, and head for the hills.

---

road. Named for Ernest O. Lawrence, developer of the cyclotron and winner of the university's first Nobel Prize, the museum has hands-on exhibits ranging from earthquake simulations to life-size dinosaur models.

As you continue climbing along Grizzly Peak, you can see the city of Berkeley and the Bay Bridge below, with San Francisco and the Golden Gate Bridge in the distance. Your ascent is followed by a mile-long fast downhill, but after crossing Claremont/Fish Camp Road, there's another climb. You'll ride up and down along Grizzly Peak about 8 miles, passing parks and regional preserves with more views of both the bay and inland hills. You'll also ride through part of the area burned in the Oakland hills fire of 1991.

At Skyline Boulevard, turn left and start downhill. This takes you through the shady parklands of Robert Sibley Volcanic Regional Preserve and Redwood Regional Park and provides more spectacular panoramic vistas. (At two places along the way, you'll need to angle to the left to stay on Skyline.) After 5 miles and a mile-long, curving downhill, turn left at the stop sign to stay on Skyline, which is now a divided road. (Joaquin Miller Road goes to the right.) In half a mile, go left at the traffic signal onto Redwood Road for a long descent along a narrow wooded road that follows a little creek and passes Anthony Chabot Regional Park (on the right) and Redwood Regional Park (on the left). After 2.5 miles, turn left onto Pinehurst Road for a strenuous, mile-long ascent. As you climb higher, you'll come out of the trees to scenes of open hills and Upper San Leandro Reservoir below. Then a winding downhill takes you back into the shady redwood forest. These trees are all that remain of the great forests that were felled to supply the gold rush building boom. A second growth of redwoods was cut after the San Francisco earthquake and fire of 1906.

After passing Canyon Road, which goes to Moraga 2 miles away, Pinehurst begins a 4-mile climb, quite gently at first. This is probably the prettiest part of the ride, taking you through a deep redwood canyon along San Leandro Creek. There is little traffic as you ride by the school and post office of the tiny hamlet of Canyon, a former logging camp that became a counterculture enclave in the 1960s. The road gets steeper, and the last 1.5 miles are very challenging, with an 8% grade near the top. Pinehurst finally brings you back to Skyline

Boulevard, where you turn right and retrace your route to Tilden Park.

After 1.7 miles, turn right on Grizzly Peak Boulevard for 6 more miles of up and down, including a climb past Fish Camp Road/Claremont followed by a wonderful descent of nearly 2.5 miles. Just after the stop sign at Shasta Road, make a right turn into the Shasta entrance to Tilden Park. From here you'll have a short, steep downhill with some rough pavement that ends at Wildcat Canyon Drive. Go to the right, and in 1.5 miles you'll be back at Inspiration Point.

Nimitz Way Bike Path

For an easy, relaxing ride to end the day, you can take Nimitz Way, a wide, paved recreation trail that starts at Inspiration Point. This popular path was named for Chester Nimitz, a navy fleet admiral. It was formerly a service road to Nike missile sites, but now it is part of the Bay Area Ridge Trail that will eventually circle the entire bay.

The trail follows San Pablo Ridge, offering splendid views of the San Francisco Bay, Angel Island and Marin, San Pablo Bay, and San Pablo Reservoir. The open, grassy hills are especially pretty in the winter and spring. After 4 miles, the paved section ends, though a gravel trail continues. Be sure to climb up the hill to see the former location of the missiles.

View of Berkeley, the Bay, and San Francisco from Grizzly Peak Blvd. in the Berkeley hills.

Retrace your route back to Inspiration Point to complete your tour of the Berkeley hills.

Additional Information

Tilden Regional Park: Open dawn to dusk. Mountain bikes allowed on some trails; see park brochure available at Inspiration Point parking lot. (510) 843-2137.

Botanic Garden: In Tilden Park. Open daily 8:30 AM to 5:00 PM. Free admission. (510) 841-8732.

Carousel: In Tilden Park. Open daily during summer and weekends all year 10:00 AM to 5:00 PM. Admission fee. (510) 848-7373.

Lawrence Hall of Science: Centennial Drive, University of California at Berkeley. Open daily 10:00 AM to 4:30 PM. Admission fee. (510) 642-5132.

University of California Visitor Center: University Hall, 2200 University Ave., Berkeley. Guided tours. (510) 642-5215.

Anthony Chabot Regional Park: Has a lake, hiking trails, paved bike paths, and family and group camping sites. For camping reservations, call (510) 562-2267.

Bike Rental: Backroads Bike Shop, 801 Cedar, Berkeley. (510) 527-1888. Berkeley Cycle, 2020 Center Street, Berkeley. (510) 845-7560. Karim Cyclery, 2801 Telegraph Avenue, Berkeley. (510) 841-2181. Encina Bicycle Center, 2891 Ygnacio Valley Road, Walnut Creek. (510) 944-9200.

---

20. Alameda

Distance: 10 miles

Rating: *Easy*, taking place on bike paths, bike lanes, and quiet city streets. There are a few busy intersections, however, and the possibility of congestion along the Shore Line Drive bike path on summer weekends.

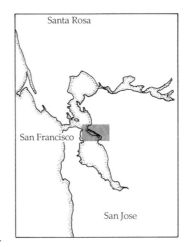

Highlights: Alameda is known for its Victorian architecture and you will see a wonderful variety here, ranging from small cottages to "Gold Coast" mansions. Riding along the shore, you will also enjoy spectacular views of San Francisco Bay.

Location: Alameda is an island located west of Interstate 880 near Oakland in Alameda County.

Queen Anne house at 893 Union Street in Alameda. It was built in 1891 and designed by architect J. A. Leonard.

Betty Johnston

"Coney Island of the West" was enormously popular, but it finally went bankrupt in 1939.

Nothing is left from that era except Croll's Bar, at the intersection of Webster and Central. Built in 1879 as a hotel, the mansard-roofed structure is one of Alameda's most interesting commercial buildings. The first saloon was installed in 1883, and the original bar, brass railings, and beveled mirrors remain intact. At the turn of the century, several boxers who trained in a camp across the street lived upstairs. Perhaps the most famous of these fighters was heavyweight champion James "Gentleman Jim" Corbett. During World War II, the military took over the beach area and turned it into a maritime training center. The structure that now houses the visitor center was a military hospital, and the brown maintenance building beyond was the training center itself. The beach became a state park in 1959 and is now managed by the East Bay Regional Park District.

Shore Line Drive

From the visitor center, go left along the bike trail that follows Crab Cove, a marine reserve. The path soon brings you to the main part of Crown Beach. At the bath house, the path turns inland toward a large parking lot. When the path divides, continue to the right; this will bring you back to the bay and along Shore Line Drive. Here you will have great views across San Francisco Bay and of Bay Farm Island ahead. This whole section of Alameda was underwater until the 1950s, when it was filled in by the Utah Construction Company in a controversial project. More recently, sand has been trucked in to create the beach you see today.

When Shore Line ends, stay on the paved path that curves left along Broadway. Turn right at the first corner, and ride along Bayview Drive until you reach Otis Drive at the traffic signal. Turn right and immediately get on the sidewalk, which soon becomes a wide, paved path leading to the Bay Farm Island Bridge. If you want to combine this ride with a trip to Bay Farm Island (see page 181), ride along the path toward the left, up to the bridge. To continue your tour of Alameda, go to the right, following the path under the bridge.

Stay on the path, riding past the historic Aeolian Yacht Club, until you can safely exit onto Fernside Boulevard. Soon you will have a bike lane.

At the stop sign about half a mile farther, turn left onto Central Avenue, where you will see some of the many Victorians for which Alameda is known. The land to the right was once part of a great estate known as Fernside, which belonged to A. A. Cohen, a lawyer who also owned railroads and a ferry service to San Francisco. His palatial three-story, 50-room mansion had an art gallery and huge library. It burned to the ground in 1897.

Webster House

Go left when you reach Versailles Avenue in several blocks. In the block past Encinal, at No. 1238, you'll find the oldest house still standing in Alameda. Built in 1854 for J. N. Webster, a San Francisco money broker, it probably was prefabricated in the East and shipped around Cape Horn. Its charming Carpenter Gothic style with "icicle" trim is unaltered except for the exterior shingles. It is now a bed-and-breakfast inn.

Continue on Versailles to the corner and turn right on San Jose Avenue. In a few blocks you'll ride through Jackson Park, surrounded by a number of well-preserved Victorian homes.

Gold Coast mansion at 2070 San Jose Avenue, Alameda. Built 1893, this is one of Alameda's finest homes.

Betty Johnston

You'll then cross Park Street, which was the central business district of the town of Encinal and has been the heart of Alameda since the 1890s.

Central Alameda

Just past Park, turn right onto Oak Street. To visit the Alameda Historical Museum, turn right onto Alameda Avenue in 3 blocks. The museum is in the 1926 Masonic Building and has memorabilia from the city's past.

Continue on Oak and turn left at Central Avenue. You'll see the impressive Twin Towers Methodist Church on the corner. Constructed in 1909, it was designed by Henry Meyers, the principal architect for Alameda County in the 1910s and 1920s. Alameda High School, on the left, dates from 1926.

Two other notable structures are located one block off the route on Santa Clara Avenue, at the intersection with Oak. The brick and sandstone City Hall, built in 1896, originally had a 60-foot central clock tower, but it was damaged in the 1906 earthquake and eventually removed. Plans have been approved to reconstruct it, but the project lacks funding. The Alameda Free Library, built in 1902 with money donated by Andrew Carnegie, is across the street.

Continue riding along Central. At the next corner is the 1929 Veterans Memorial building, one of ten that Henry Meyers designed in Alameda County. In another block make a left turn onto Willow, and soon you will come to San Jose Avenue again.

Gold Coast Mansions

This side of town was known as the "Gold Coast" during Alameda's most prosperous decades, from 1870 to 1900, because of the many large and lavishly decorated homes constructed here.

Two elaborate structures are located at the intersection of Willow and San Jose. The one on the left, 2103 San Jose, was built in 1891 for George Brown, who made his money in San Francisco real estate. The larger one, at 2070 San Jose, dates from 1893 and was the home of David Brehaut, a contractor. This incredible residence used every ornamental motif popular at that time. Each of these Queen Anne style homes cost about $4,000 to build.

Go right on San Jose, turning left in 3 blocks onto Union Street to see more impressive homes from the 1890s. At the very end of the street, at No. 891, is an 1896 shingled dwelling with two turrets. This was the home of John Leonard, one of Alameda's most productive architect-builders. Constructed at a cost of $20,000, no expense was spared on its interior detail, and it was one of the earliest houses wired for incandescent lighting.

Originally these lots were located directly on the bay, but Alameda's south shoreline has changed drastically since the Victorian era. The land you see on the other side of the estuary was created by bayfill when South Shore was developed in the 1950s, depriving these homes of their wonderful views.

Return up Union, and at the corner go left onto Clinton for one block, then right at Grand Avenue. Ride along Grand for 2 blocks and make a left at San Antonio Avenue. Don't miss the superb detail of the 1889 house at the next corner on the left. There are several other well-preserved Victorian structures here surrounding Franklin Park.

Tilden House

Another residence of note is located several blocks farther along San Antonio at No. 1031. Built in 1896, this was the home of Major Charles Lee Tilden, one of Alameda's most prominent citizens and a founder of the East Bay Regional Park District. The Classical Revival design was copied from one in San Francisco that was later destroyed in the 1906 fire. In Tilden's day, the grounds included tennis and croquet courts, a stable and horse paddock, gardens, and a conservatory.

At the next corner, turn right onto Caroline Street, and turn left when you reach Santa Clara Avenue. Cross Webster Street, and ride on Santa Clara for another 3 blocks. This end of Alameda has more modest homes, but you can still see many of the same elaborate decorations found on the larger Victorians.

Turn left at Fourth Street, cross Central, and ride straight ahead, through the Ballena Bay complex, to the yacht club. This development was also constructed on bayfill. From here you may see the profile of a massive aircraft carrier based at the U.S. Naval Air Station, which incorporated both an early Army field and the municipal airport. In 1935, when the airport was the base for Pan American Airlines, this was where the China Clipper began the first transpacific flight by a commercial airline. Across the bay you'll have views of the San Francisco skyline.

Leaving Ballena, go right on Central for a short distance. Watch for the bike path entrance on the right at the sign "Beach Access," just before Crown Drive. Follow this path along the water back to your starting point at the Crab Cove Visitor Center. This route has taken you by only a fraction of the many fascinating buildings in Alameda, so you may want to continue exploring the residential streets on your own. You might also want to stop at Croll's for a cool drink before leaving town.

Additional Information

Alameda Ferry Terminal: 2990 Main Street. In Oakland, the terminal is at Jack London Square. In San Francisco, stops are at the Ferry Building and Pier 39. (510) 522-3300.

Crab Cove Visitor Center: 1252 McKay Avenue off Central. Open Wednesday through Sunday 10:00 AM to 4:30 PM, March through November. Closed during the winter. Restrooms located behind the building are open year-round. Fee parking on summer weekends, but street parking often available. (510) 521-6887.

Croll's Bar & Grill: 1400 Webster at Central Avenue. Open daily 10:00 AM to 2:00 AM. (510) 522-8439.

Webster House Bed and Breakfast Inn: 1238 Versailles Avenue. Also serves brunch, afternoon tea, and dinner by reservation only. (510) 523-9697.

Alameda Historical Museum: 2324 Alameda Avenue. Open Wednesday through Sunday 1:30 to 4:00 PM, Saturday 11:00 AM to 4:00 PM. Free admission. (510) 521-1233.

Alameda Chamber of Commerce: 909 Marina Village Parkway, No. 348, Alameda, CA 94501. Open weekdays 9:00 AM to 5:00 PM. (510) 522-0414.

Bike Rental: Cycle Sports, 2238A South Shore Center, Alameda. (510) 521-2872.

21. Alameda – Bay Farm Island

Distance: 6 miles

Rating: *Easy*, taking place entirely on paved bike paths. This is an excursion the whole family will enjoy.

Highlights: The route around Bay Farm Island offers spectacular bay vistas, uncrowded paths, and even a bit of solitude, as you explore new developments and former farmlands.

Location: Bay Farm Island is located just south of the main part of Alameda, west of Interstate 880, in Alameda County.

Harbor Bay Maritime ferry terminal on the west side of Bay Farm Island offers ferry service to San Francisco.

Ride around Bay Farm Island

The ride along the Shoreline Park bike path begins at the end of Veterans Court on Bay Farm Island. To reach the starting place by car from Alameda, cross the drawbridge located at the end of Otis Drive. On the other side, go right onto Island Drive, and immediately make a sharp right turn onto Veterans Court, and park along the street. (If there is no parking available here, continue along Island to the next intersection, go right on Bridgeway Road, right again on Packet Landing Road and park at the end of the street. You can reach the bike path by going in front of the Harbor Bay Club.)

You can also get directly to Bay Farm Island from Interstate 880 by taking the Hegenberger Road exit west to Doolittle Drive (Highway 61), where you turn right. When Doolittle ends at Island Drive, just before the bridge, go left and immediately make a sharp right turn onto Veterans Court. If you're cycling to Bay Farm Island, ride on the bike path along Otis Drive. (See Alameda Ride, page 173.) Cross Peach, and continue along the path toward the left, up and over the bridge.

On the other side of the channel, take the first right turn onto Veterans Court.

The bike path begins at the end of Veterans Court. Ride to the left, and in just over a half a mile, you will come to the first of several picnic areas and restrooms situated along the route. This is the most congested part of the path due to its proximity to Bay Farm Island's extensive housing developments.

Thirty years ago, this land did not exist. But in 1966, after receiving an exemption from the state law prohibiting bayfill, the Utah Construction Company (also responsible for Alameda's South Shore bayfill) filled in 908 acres of tideland around Bay Farm Island. Various plans for development were rejected by the city and delayed by litigation, but in 1977 the Harbor Bay project began construction of the first of 3,000 residential units built around a series of lagoons that are bordered by bicycle and pedestrian paths.

Shoreline Park

As you ride along Shoreline Park, you will have wonderful vistas of the city of Alameda, the naval air station, the Oakland hills, the Bay Bridge, and San Francisco. Property owners here pay dearly for the view, but you can enjoy it for free. The path

Shoreline Park bike path on the east side of Bay Farm Island.

curves around the end of the island and eventually brings you to the Harbor Bay ferry landing. (Restrooms are located near the parking lot.) This side of the island is especially peaceful, and you'll have new views of San Francisco and the peninsula.

Past the ferry dock, the path parallels Harbor Bay Parkway. After another mile, at South Loop Road, cross the street to continue on the bike path. This area, also part of the Harbor Bay project, is a business park with little weekend traffic.

Once you cross Maitland Drive, you'll have the Alameda Municipal Golf Course on your left and the Oakland airport on the right, one of the Bay Area's first airports. The Oakland Municipal Airport was formally dedicated by Charles Lindbergh in 1927. It was from here that Amelia Earhart, the

History of Bay Farm Island

What you see of Bay Farm Island today gives little hint of its natural history or early development. Prior to the 1850s, the island was a scant spit of treeless land half its present size, consisting of 230 acres of upland surrounded by an extensive salt marsh, meandering sloughs, and mudflats. The marsh, part of the greatest bird habitat on the west coast of North America, was filled with tens of thousands of native and migratory shorebirds, including egrets, avocets, pelicans, great blue herons, and flocks of ducks and geese. The earliest human visitors were Ohlone Indians who lived on the east end of the Alameda peninsula. The Indians fished the island waters from tule reed boats and gathered shellfish along its shore.

Development of Alameda began in 1851 after a Spanish land-grant rancho was purchased by Gideon Aughinbaugh and William Chipman. When the township of Alameda was formed, its boundary was drawn to include roughly half of Bay Farm Island, and the remainder became part of Oakland. By this time a few settlers were already farming the upland's rich soil, giving Bay Farm Island its name.

The 1870s saw an increase in the island's population after the first of many marshland reclamation projects and the completion of a permanent bridge to Alameda. The most prominent of the new residents was Amos Mecartney, a wealthy land owner whose two-story, octagonal mansion was built on reclaimed land and surrounded by a dike. By the 1880s, sixty people lived on the island.

first woman to fly solo across the Atlantic Ocean and America's most famous female aviator, took off in 1937 on her first attempt at a round-the-world flight. Later that same year, on her second attempt, she and her navigator disappeared in the South Pacific. Neither the fliers nor the plane was ever seen again. A duplicate of Earhart's twin engine Lockheed airplane is housed in the Western Aerospace Museum off Earhart Drive.

An expanded Oakland International Airport was built in 1963 on 600 acres of new land created by additional bayfill.

When you come to Doolittle Drive, cross at the traffic light and continue on the bike path straight ahead. This takes you past the model airplane field on the left and San Leandro Bay on the right. You are now riding around what was, until 1980, the Alameda garbage dump (called "Mt. Trashmore" by the locals), and the hilly mounds represent many years' accumulation of trash. Soon you'll see the drawbridge ahead and the historic Aeolian Yacht Club on the other side of the channel.

History of Bay Farm Island (continued)

Separated from the growing city of Alameda, the close-knit island community endured continual lowland flooding and washed-out roads. Nevertheless, the farms prospered with crops of hops, asparagus, and other vegetables and fruit, which were transported by ferry to the booming markets in San Francisco. The early settlers gradually sold their land to new immigrants, and by the 1920s Portuguese and Italian families owned all the upland farms.

The 1920s was a pivotal decade for the island. There was another land reclamation project and the first subdivision; the main road was paved; a major airport and golf course were established. Farming continued unchanged, however, until 1957, when the first of the upland was sold for residential development. Population grew from 400 in 1950 to 3,000 in 1970, and the last of the old farms succumbed to subdivision in 1985.

The late 1960s brought a massive bayfill project that dramatically altered the character of the island. Subsequent development has resulted in a shopping center, a business complex, and thousands of new homes, bringing today's population to nearly 8,000. A waterfront park has also been constructed, where much of this route takes place.

To complete your tour of Bay Farm Island, ride across the wooden bridge beneath the Otis Street drawbridge, past a fishing pier and back to Veterans Court.

Additional Information

Harbor Bay Maritime: Daily ferry from the west side of the island to Ferry Plaza in San Francisco. (510) 769-5500.

Harbor Bay Landing: Intersection of Island Drive and Mecartney Road, about a half mile from the bridge. A large shopping complex, including a bike shop, as well as several places to buy food.

Western Aerospace Museum: Off Earhart Drive opposite Hangar 7 at Oakland Airport. Open weekends 10:00 AM to 5:00 PM. Admission fee for adults. (510) 638-7100.

Bike Rental: Cycle Sports, 2238A South Shore Center, Alameda. (510) 521-2872.

See Alameda Ride, page 180, for more resources.

22. Pleasanton

Distance: 6 miles

Rating: *Easy*, short, and flat, though traffic can be heavy on Main Street.

Highlights: Pleasanton is one of the fastest-growing communities in the East Bay, but you can still see its small-town origins when you cycle down Main Street and through surrounding neighborhoods. This ride includes a Victorian hotel, an old adobe, and several early cottages and commercial buildings.

Location: Pleasanton is located east of Interstate 680 and south of Interstate 580 in eastern Alameda County.

Pleasanton Hotel at 855 Main Street, Pleasanton. Rebuilt in the 1890s after fire destroyed the original hotel, it is now a restaurant.

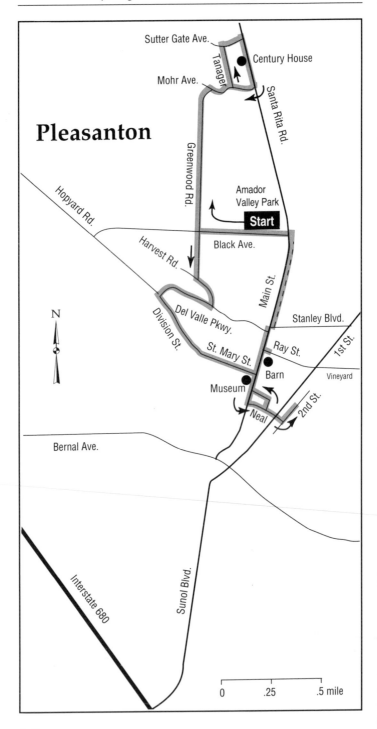

Ride through Pleasanton

Begin your ride at the Amador Valley Community Park, located at Santa Rita Road and Black Avenue. (Restrooms are located near the playground behind the Aquatic Center.) To reach the park from Interstate 680, take the Sunol Boulevard or Bernal Avenue exit and continue through downtown Pleasanton. Santa Rita is the continuation of Main Street. From Interstate 580, go south on Hopyard Road to Black Avenue and turn left.

From the park, ride west on Black Avenue (away from Santa Rita) and take the first right on Greenwood Road. In just over half a mile, Greenwood ends at Mohr, where you go right for one block, then turn left on Tanager Drive. This takes you behind Century House and Bicentennial Park, your destination. To reach the entrance, turn right on Sutter Gate Avenue and right again on Santa Rita. Since traffic is usually heavy here, you may want to use the sidewalk.

History of Pleasanton

When the Amador-Livermore Valley was divided into ranchos after Mission San José was disbanded in 1834, the area around what is now Pleasanton was granted to members of the Bernal family and was known as Rancho El Valle de San José. In 1850 Agostin Bernal became the first settler and built an adobe house which still stands on Foothill Road.

John Kottinger, the man who was to become founder of Pleasanton, arrived in Alisal, as the town was first known, in 1851. After marrying into the Bernal family, he established the first store and served as justice of the peace. He also mapped the town in 1867 and renamed it in honor of his good friend Alfred Pleasonton, a Civil War general. The name became Pleasanton due to a clerical error.

The small town grew rapidly with the introduction of the railroad in 1869. By the time of incorporation in 1894, Pleasanton was the thriving center of an agricultural community of ranches, dairy farms, hop fields, and vineyards. Today most of the farmland has given way to suburban homes, shopping center development, and huge office and industrial buildings.

Century House

Century House was built in 1878 by George Atkinson as a secluded hunting lodge, but it is now surrounded by modern subdivisions. In 1976 the Gothic Revival style house was restored and dedicated as part of Bicentennial Park and is operated by the city of Pleasanton as a rental facility.

After viewing the house and grounds, continue along Santa Rita, using the sidewalk if traffic is heavy. At the corner, go right on Mohr, then left on Greenwood, retracing your route. Continue past Black and make a left turn at Harvest Road. Go right at Del Valle Parkway, which ends at Hopyard Road, named for the area north of town that once had the largest hop fields in California. Most of the crop was exported to London for ale-brewing. Turn left on Hopyard, using the sidewalk bike path to cross over the arroyo.

Hopyard immediately becomes Division Street as you enter one of Pleasanton's early residential neighborhoods. Division soon angles left onto St. Mary. The house at No. 443, across the railroad tracks, was constructed around 1880 by local architect Charles Bruce, who often chose floor plans from East Coast pattern books and modified them to fit the small town's simpler style. This building was home to Charles Graham, a mortician, and his descendents from 1900 to 1967. The charming little Queen Anne home next door, No. 431, dates from 1895.

Main Street

Turn right when you reach Main Street, which still retains much of its small-town ambiance. The metal "Pleasanton" sign over the street has been welcoming visitors since 1932.

At the far end of the block, on the right, is the Amador-Livermore Valley Historical Society Museum. The 1914 building was first used by the Women's Improvement Club and later became the town hall, public library, and police department. The house next door, which is now a restaurant, was built in the 1890s for Jerome Arendt, a well-to-do businessman.

Across the street you'll see the 1890 Kolln Hardware building with its white corner tower, probably the most recognizable landmark in town. One of the small attached structures facing Division Street was built in 1869. Continue riding on Main Street for another block and stop to see a pair of two-story brick commercial buildings in the Italianate style, both dating from 1896. The Johnston Building on the right, at the corner of Rose, was originally a saddle shop and later a candy store. Currently, it houses an antique store. The structure across the street, on the corner of Neal at No. 450, was Pleasanton's first mercantile establishment, a general supply and dry goods store owned by the Arendt family. Later it became a feed and grain business.

On the other corner of Neal and Main you'll see the 1900 Arendt Building, formerly the location of a bank, post office, and telephone exchange. You may have noticed the turret of a Victorian style structure farther down Main. Although it looks old, it was actually built fairly recently to blend in with the rest of Main Street's architecture.

Turn left on Neal Street. Half a block down, on the right, you'll pass a white brick commercial building dating from the 1880s. Originally constructed as a family-run market with living quarters on the second floor, it has also housed a bank, the justice court and, for many years, law offices.

Just beyond is the renovated 1901 railroad station painted mustard yellow, the characteristic color of Southern Pacific properties. It has been converted to an office building and coffee house.

Century House at 2401 Santa Rita Road, Pleasanton. It was built in the 1870s as a hunting lodge.

After crossing busy First Street, you'll come to another residential neighborhood. At the next corner is the picturesque Amador Valley Baptist Church, originally a Presbyterian church. It was built in 1876 on land purchased from Joshua Neal who, like Kottinger, acquired property when he married one of the Bernal daughters.

Second Street Homes

Turn left on Second Street to see more early homes. The Gothic Revival house at No. 4466 was once owned by the superintendent of the Southern Pacific Railroad. It dates from 1874, but the one-story wings on either side were added later. On the next corner, at No. 4397, you'll see one of the largest older homes in Pleasanton. It was built around 1890 for Joseph Arendt, a wealthy downtown property owner. A little farther on, at No. 4362, is a small cottage that still has an old barn in back.

Turn around here, ride back to Neal Street, and turn right, re-crossing First Street. Just after the railroad tracks, go right on Railroad Street to the brick fire station, part of which dates from the 1920s. Turn left onto one-way Division Street which takes you by Kolln Hardware, back to Main Street.

Amador-Livermore Historical Society Museum, 603 Main Street, Pleasanton. This 1914 building was once the town hall.

Kottinger's Barn

Go right on Main, then take the second right onto Ray Street to see Kottinger's Barn, an adobe built in 1851. Now restored as an antique store, it is located in the shopping center parking lot on the right. When Kottinger was a judge, there were no funds for public buildings, so his home on Main Street was used as the courtroom, a corner of his barn served as the jail, and an underground passage connected the two. Kottinger was evidently kept quite busy during the 1850s when Alisal was known as "the most desperate town in the west." It often served as a refuge for bandits who had ambushed prospectors returning from the gold fields, and Main Street shoot-outs were not uncommon.

Return to Main Street and go right to the Pleasanton Hotel, rebuilt after the original establishment burned in 1898. Although it no longer offers rooms, this attractive building houses an excellent restaurant. Across the street is the Pleasanton Cheese Factory, a popular destination of cyclists who come here for the large deli sandwiches.

To complete your ride, continue on Main Street over Arroyo del Valle. Just past Stanley Boulevard, use the sidewalk bike path to cross the railroad tracks, then ride down to the frontage

Kottinger's Barn on Ray Street, off Main Street, in Pleasanton. The adobe was built in 1851 by the founder of Pleasanton.

road paralleling Santa Rita Road, the extension of Main Street. In .75 miles, at the stop sign after Nevis Street, go left on Black and cross Santa Rita at the traffic light. This brings to back to Amador Valley Park, where you started your tour of Pleasanton.

Additional Information

Amador-Livermore Valley Historical Society Museum: 603 Main Street. Open Wednesday through Friday 11:00 AM to 4:00 PM, weekends 1:00 to 4:00 PM. Free admission. (510) 462-2766.

Pleasanton Cheese Factory: 830 Main Street. Open daily 9:00 AM to 5:00 PM. (510) 846-2577.

Shadow Cliffs Regional Recreation Area: Stanley Boulevard, about one mile east of Pleasanton. Formerly a gravel quarry, it has a lake with swimming beach and boat launch, waterslides, and picnic grounds. (510) 846-3000.

Pleasanton Chamber of Commerce: 450 Main Street, Suite 202, Pleasanton, CA 94566. Open weekdays 8:00 AM to 5:00 PM. (510) 846-5858.

Bike Rental: Paquette's Cycle, 1991L Santa Rita Road, Pleasanton. (510) 846-4788. Dublin Cyclery, 7001 Dublin Boulevard, Dublin. (510) 828-8676.

---

23. Livermore

Distance: 26 miles

Rating: *Moderate* because of the rolling country roads, although the ride through the city is flat. It is especially enjoyable in springtime, when the hills are green, or during the fall grape harvest.

Highlights: On this ride you'll see some of Livermore's Victorian-era homes and explore its still undeveloped countryside. You will also visit the Ravenswood estate and several historic wineries.

Location: Livermore is located south of Interstate 580 in eastern Alameda County.

Ride through Livermore

Begin your ride at Carnegie Park at Third and J streets in central Livermore. To reach the park, take the North Livermore

Ravenswood Historic Site at 2647 Arroyo Road, Livermore.

courtesy Livermore Area Recreation and Park District

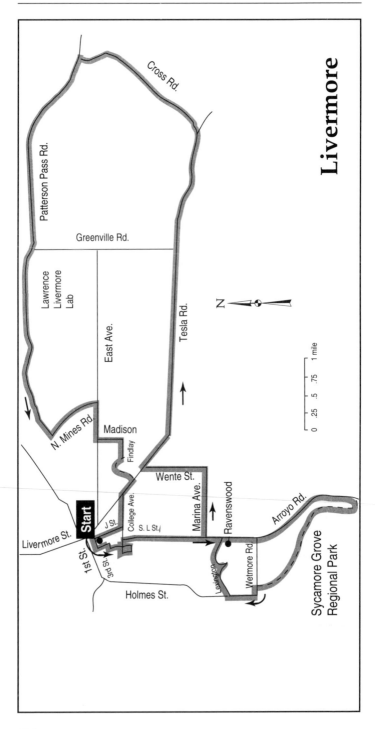

Livermore

Avenue exit from Interstate 580, heading south. As you go through town, you'll see a number of interesting commercial buildings from the early part of the century. At the intersection with First Street, on the left, is the imposing former Bank of Italy, constructed in 1921. On the opposite corner is the three-story Masonic Temple. When built in 1909, the lower level housed a bank, a pool hall, and other businesses. The building next door, 2211 First Street, dates from 1914.

Continue past First, and go right on Third Street to the park. Here you'll see the Carnegie Building, constructed in 1911 with a grant from steel magnate Andrew Carnegie and used as the Livermore Public Library until 1966. Designed by William Weeks, a well-known Bay Area architect, it now houses Livermore's History Center and Art Gallery.

Restrooms are located in the lower level of the building. Unrestricted parking is available along J and K streets.

History of Livermore

Robert Livermore was a young English sailor who came to California by trading ship in 1821. He applied to the Mexican governor for a large spread of land in the remote inland valley that would later bear his name, and in 1839 he was granted Rancho Las Positas. Here he and his wife, Josefa Higuera Molina, raised cattle, horses, and sheep. Ranching made Livermore a wealthy man, but he was more interested in horticulture and viticulture, planting the first vineyards and orchards in this part of California. Livermore died in 1858, before the birth of the town that was named for him.

After the Central Pacific Railroad laid tracks through the valley in 1869, William Mendenhall, who had come from Pennsylvania in 1845, decided to found a town that he called Livermore in memory of his old friend. Mendenhall also donated land for the first railroad depot, a school, a church, and parks. The town of Livermore was incorporated in 1876.

From the 1880s to the turn of the century, Livermore grew rapidly as the center of commerce for the ranches and farms of the surrounding countryside. In recent years the town's expansion is due to suburban residential development, which now covers much of the fertile farmland.

Leaving the park, ride west on Third, away from Livermore Avenue, to South L Street and turn left. In two blocks you'll pass the 1930s Veterans Memorial Building, designed by Henry Meyers, who grew up in Livermore and was the principal architect for Alameda County for many years.

Historic Neighborhood

This is one of Livermore's historic residential neighborhoods. Down the block on the right, at No. 567, is the first stucco house in town, built in 1898 for Thomas Knox, a cement contractor and politician. Will and Lillie Taylor's home next door, No. 565, was designed by Henry Meyers, her brother. Another brother, Oscar Meyers, lived directly across the street at No. 580, the 1892 Queen Anne style home.

Turn right at Sixth Street, then left at South M Street. The property on the corner, 1881 Sixth Street, has one of the last carriage houses in Livermore. The house was built sometime before 1886.

Farther down the block on the right, at No. 737, is another Queen Anne home, the only one in Livermore with a tower. When constructed in 1895, most of the land behind it was cow pasture.

When South M ends at College Avenue, cross the street, and ride straight onto Mendenhall Drive. This takes you through what was once the grounds of the Livermore Sanitarium, a private health facility for the treatment of "nervous dyspeptics, neurasthenics, and general disease." Established in 1895 by Dr. John W. Robertson, typical therapy included diet, exercise, and water massage.

Turn right on Old Tower Road to one of the few structures remaining from that era, a four-story tower that has been turned into an unusual residence. The circular water storage tank is now a garage.

Return to College on Kingsbury Drive, named for the founders of the Livermore Collegiate Institute which was located here in 1870. It closed in 1893 when the first public high school opened. Go right on College, and at the corner turn right again onto South L Street. Here you'll pass one of the sanitarium cottages with its white pillars at No. 989.

Ravenswood

Once you cross over Arroyo Mocho, L Street becomes Arroyo Road and, in less than 1.5 miles, brings you to the entrance of Ravenswood Historic Site. This was once the country vineyard estate of San Francisco politician Christopher Buckley. The smaller Queen Anne style cottage was built in 1885 as living quarters for the Buckleys and their guests. The stable, carriage house, and tank house also date from that time. The larger building dates from 1891 and was used for parties and social gatherings.

Buckley, an influential figure in the San Francisco Democratic party in the 1870s and 1880s, was totally blind by the time he was 30 as result of either a neurological disorder or excessive alcohol consumption as a youth. After his death in 1922, Ravenswood was sold to a Catholic order that intended to build a college on the site. The college was never realized, however, and in 1971 the property went to a developer who turned most of the estate into a housing subdivision. The land where the buildings stand was given to the public and is maintained by the Livermore Area Recreation and Park District. Ravenswood is now listed in the National Register of Historic Places and is a favorite site for weddings.

Continue on Arroyo for another 1.5 miles. At the intersection with Wetmore Road you'll see a stone entrance gate marked "Olivina," a remnant of the once-great estate of Julius P. Smith. Smith and his brother had a claim in Nevada where they mined borax for the product that eventually became Twenty Mule Team Borax. In 1884 he took the money from the sale of his stock and established a large winery in the Livermore Valley. Part of the estate is now Sycamore Grove Park.

Wente Bros. Cellars

From here it is less than 2 miles to the Wente Bros. Sparkling Wine Cellars. The road is narrow and there may be some traffic, but the rolling hills are spectacular, especially in the fall when the grapevines turn red and gold. Before Prohibition, 15,000 acres of vineyards carpeted the valley floor. Although only 3,000 acres remain, this is one of California's oldest and finest wine-producing regions.

The Wente Bros. Cellars are located at what was the Cresta Blanca Winery, established in 1882 by Charles Wetmore and named for the white cliff above the vineyards. In 1889 a Cresta

Blanca vintage was the first American wine to win an international gold medal, proving California could produce wines to compete with the best in the world. Since 1981 the property has been owned by Wente Bros., whose original winery, which you'll see later on your ride, is located a few miles away. Several Cresta Blanca buildings are still in use, including the tasting room and sandstone caves. A gourmet restaurant is also on the grounds.

Sycamore Grove Park

Leaving the winery, go left to reach the entrance to Veterans Park across the road. Here you will pick up a pleasant 2.5-mile bike path that starts at the far end of the parking lot. (Restrooms are located nearby.) The path goes under the approach to the 1925 Veterans Administration Medical Center and then parallels Arroyo Road a short distance before turning left toward Sycamore Grove Park. As you ride through the park, you will pass an old almond orchard and several tree-lined avenues left from the former Olivina estate. Part of the multi-story winery building can be seen across the field to your left about 1.5 miles along, just before you go under the lines of the electrical towers. The park also has one of California's largest and oldest stands of native Western sycamore trees.

The bike path ends at the park's main entrance. Exit the park, turn left onto Wetmore Road, then right on Holmes. You will ride only a short distance on this busy roadway. Just past Independence Park, turn right onto Lexington Way, then left onto Superior Drive. This will bring you back to Arroyo Road, where you go left. Turn right at Marina Avenue, which becomes Wente Street when it curves left.

When Wente ends, go to the right onto Livermore Avenue, which becomes Tesla Road. Although there may be some fast-moving traffic, the shoulder is wide as you ride by acres of vineyards and open fields. You will soon see a large 1886 Queen Anne home with a square central tower, seeming a bit out of place on this country road. The house was moved from town to this location, but it has not yet been restored.

Historic Wineries

Just beyond the house you'll come to the Concannon Vineyard, established in 1883 by James Concannon, a native of Ireland.

When Prohibition closed all the other local wineries from 1920 to 1932, Concannon's was allowed to remain open to make sacramental wines for church services.

Continue on Tesla less than a mile to another historic winery, the original Wente Bros., the oldest family-owned, continuously operating winery in California. Carl H. Wente came from Germany and planted the first vineyards here in 1883. Since then the Wente family has continued to make the Livermore Valley one of the premier wine-growing areas of California.

Traffic diminishes as you ride along Tesla and escape farther into the countryside with its peaceful farms and ranches. Less than a mile after passing Greenville Road, turn left onto Cross Road, where you will have a gradual climb of about a mile, followed by a short, steep downhill to the junction with Patterson Pass Road. Turn left for a fast, 2-mile run back toward town.

Lawrence Livermore Laboratory

The city suddenly reappears as you cross Greenville Road once again. To the left you can see the Lawrence Livermore National Laboratory, established by the University of California in 1952 for nuclear weapons research under the auspices of the U.S. Department of Energy. It was named for Ernest O. Lawrence, a Berkeley professor who won a Nobel Prize for his work in nuclear physics. This huge facility, often the scene of anti-nuclear demonstrations, has also become an important center for electrical engineering and electronics research. For those who wish to learn more, a visitor center is located at the east gate, off Greenville Road.

Continue on Patterson Pass Road through new housing developments until it ends at North Mines Road, and turn left. At East Street, a right turn will take you back toward the more established part of the city.

After half a mile, go left at the traffic signal onto Madison Avenue, and when you reach Findlay Way in 6 blocks, go right. When Findlay ends, cross Hillcrest and pick up the bike path at the Bike Route sign. You'll ride by empty fields and then the century-old home belonging to the owners of Retzlaff Vineyards. At Livermore Avenue, turn right. (The bike path continues on the other side of the road and ends in just over 2 miles at Murietta Boulevard, south of Stanley Boulevard.)

You'll soon see Civic Center Park. Make a left turn opposite the modern City Hall onto College Avenue. The house at 2211

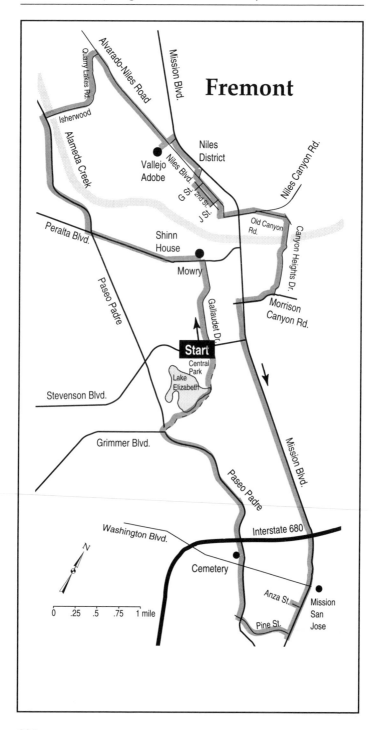

Ride through Fremont

The city of Fremeont was created in 1956, incorporating the former towns of Niles, Centerville, Mission San José, Irvington, and Warm Springs.

Begin your ride at Central Park near the intersection of Stevenson Boulevard and Paseo Padre Parkway. This popular park has numerous picnic areas and playgrounds, a boat launch and swimming pool, and a two-mile bike path around Lake Elizabeth. To reach the starting point from Interstate 880, take Stevenson Boulevard about 3 miles, passing Paseo Padre Parkway, the library, and the civic center, to the parking lot opposite Gallaudet Drive and next to the tennis courts. Restrooms can be found nearby.

From the parking lot, ride across Stevenson onto Gallaudet, which becomes Cherry Lane after crossing Walnut. Turn left at busy Mowry Avenue, and when Mowry angles left, stay to the right, moving onto Peralta Boulevard (Highway 84).

Shinn Historic Park

Take the first right on Sidney, and then immediately go right again. Although the sign here says "Youth and Family Counseling Services," you have come to Shinn Historic Park.

The small, white private residence you see first is the cottage built around 1848 by Captain William Sim from lumber salvaged from ships abandoned in San Francisco Bay. It was purchased by pioneer nurseryman James Shinn when he and his wife Lucy first came to California from Texas in 1856. It has been moved here from its original location along Alameda Creek.

Beyond the cottage is the Shinn House, a stylish redwood Victorian ranch home built by the Shinns in 1876. Shinn was noted for his ornamental plants and fruit and nut trees, some of which were newly introduced from Japan. The house contains late 19th-century furnishings, including some memorabilia of the Shinn family.

There is also a foreman's house from about 1910 (now the counseling center) on the property, as well as barns, antique farm equipment, and formal gardens containing a number of Shinn's specimen trees from his early ranch and nursery business. Bicycles are not allowed in the park, but you may lock them just inside the fence.

Leaving the park, return to Peralta, and turn right. In less than a mile, go right onto Paseo Padre Parkway, where there is a bike lane. After 1.5 miles, as the road draws close to Alameda Creek, turn right at Isherwood Way.

At this point you can connect with the Alameda Creek Regional Trail (see page 211), a paved path that follows the south side of the creek 12 miles from Niles Canyon to San Francisco Bay.

To continue the main route, follow Isherwood Way over Alameda Creek. The trail on the other side is unpaved and used for horseback riding and mountain bikes. There are also picnic tables and a pit toilet beyond the parking lot. As you continue on Isherwood, you'll ride by Alameda Creek Quarries Recreation Area, an old gravel quarry.

Niles District

Soon Isherwood becomes Quarry Lakes Road, turns left and heads through open fields and farmlands. At the end of Quarry Lakes, go right on Osprey, and then right onto Alvarado–Niles Road toward the Niles district of Fremont.

After 1.25 miles you will come to the Mission Adobe Nursery, originally known as the California Nursery Company when it was founded in 1865 by John Rock. It was owned by the Roeding family from 1917 to the early 1970s and played a major role in the development of the fruit industry in California.

Turn right into the driveway, and ride through the parking lot behind the nursery. There you will find, nearly hidden in the eucalyptus, a small adobe built about 1845, probably for the use of overseers and workmen. This was part of Rancho Arroyo de la Alameda, which was granted to José de Jesus Vallejo in 1842. Vallejo, elder brother of General Mariano Vallejo of Sonoma, was the first administrator of the secularized Mission San José and owned 17,000 acres of former mission land. Today the adobe is owned by the city of Fremont and is available for rental..

Leave the nursery, cross Niles Boulevard, and take Nursery Avenue straight ahead to Mission Boulevard. Turn to the right, and soon you will see the old 1904 Southern Pacific railroad station which has been restored as a museum.

At the next corner, make a right turn at the Sullivan Underpass. The road is very narrow here, so you may want to use the sidewalk. At Niles Boulevard, go left into the oldest part of Niles.

Although the town of Niles grew up around Vallejo's flour mills and was first called Vallejo Mills, its real development was associated with the coming of the railroad in 1869. It was renamed for state supreme court judge and railroad official Addison Niles and became an important rail center for both the Central Pacific and Western Pacific, which is why you cross so many railroad tracks on this ride. But Niles' greatest claim to fame comes from its brief heyday as a motion picture center during the silent film era.

In 1912 Chicago producer George Spoor and his partner, "Bronco Billy" Anderson, brought their Essenay Film Company to Niles. During the next few years, the streets of Niles and the hills of Niles Canyon were the setting for nearly 400 one-reel westerns starring Bronco Billy. The most famous movie made here, however, was Charlie Chaplin's *The Tramp* in 1915, the last of five he filmed during his three-month stay in Niles. It was the first time Chaplin appeared in the baggy pants, black coat, and dapper hat that became his trademark. In 1916 the movie company moved to southern California, and the excitement was over.

Today Niles looks much the same as it did then, except that main street stores are now occupied by antique shops. Nothing remains of the block-long Essenay studio, but several small cottages built to house studio staff can still be found on G Street and along Second Street, one block from Niles Boulevard.

As you ride down Niles Boulevard, notice the false-front at No. 37364; it is one of the oldest structures in town, dating from about 1875. The turn-of-the-century building on the corner of H Street was once the Wesley Hotel, where a number of actors stayed while filming in Niles. The I.O.O.F. Hall on the corner of J Street now houses a market and liquor store. Turn right on J, past the earlier 1890 Odd Fellows Hall, and go right onto Second Street, which will take you past a number of older homes and cottages. Don't miss the old courthouse and jail at the corner of I Street. When you're done exploring, return to the main street.

Follow Niles Boulevard as it leaves downtown, turns left and crosses busy Mission Boulevard. On the left, after the intersection, is Vallejo Mill Historical Park, the site of Vallejo's flour mills. All that remains today are the ruins of the stone foundation.

You are now riding on Niles Canyon Road, a popular cycling route to Sunol, despite the fast-moving traffic. Take the first right onto Old Canyon Road and, as you cross Alameda Creek, you will see beautiful Niles Canyon ahead, the site of many Bronco Billy westerns. You will also pass the beginning of the Alameda Creek Regional Trail (See Fremont–Alameda Creek Trail Ride, page 211.) Turn right on Clarke Drive, then right again onto Canyon Heights Drive. At Maar Avenue, jog right and then left, back onto Canyon Heights. Turn right at Morrison Canyon Road, and when you reach Mission Boulevard, go left.

Mission San José

Ride south on Mission Boulevard for just over 3 miles. You will have a bike lane most of the way and a gradual uphill as you head toward Mission San José. Amid all the newer homes, shopping centers, and the freeway interchange, you can still see an occasional old farmhouse, barn, and water tank that have not yet succumbed to Fremont's rapid growth.

Just before the mission, you will pass the old Beard estate on the right, hidden behind ivy-covered walls and towering palms. Palmdale, built on former mission land, is now the home of the Sisters of the Holy Family, a Catholic order established in San Francisco in 1872.

At the next intersection is Mission San José, founded by Father Lasuen in 1797. Although conversion went slowly at first, eventually the mission had nearly 2,000 native Indians under its control. This was probably the most productive and prosperous of all the California missions and was noted for its 30-piece Indian orchestra, organized by Father Duran, who served at the mission from 1806 to 1833. After the Secularization Order of 1834 liquidated mission lands, the buildings were used as a tavern, hotel, and trading post before being returned to the church in 1858.

A section of a remaining 1809 monastery wing contains an interesting museum. The main church, however, was destroyed by the earthquake of 1868, one of the largest in California's recorded history. A wooden church called St. Joseph's was built on the site the next year and used until 1965 when a new St. Joseph's was completed nearby. The old building was sold to an Episcopalian congregation and moved to San Mateo to make way for a replica of the original mission

church. The large church you see today is a historically ac-
curate reconstruction completed in 1985 at a cost of $5 million.
The inside has also been beautifully decorated, as befitting the
mission's status as one of California's richest.

Under the floor of the church is the grave of Robert Livermore, the wealthy rancher for whom the town of Livermore
was named. This site was only recently discovered during the
archaeological dig that took place prior to the restoration of
the mission. Livermore was among the most prominent
citizens of the area, so he had been awarded the honor of
interment in the mission itself. You can find the tombstones of
many of the county's other pioneers by exploring the cemetery
next door.

Behind the mission is the Sisters of St. Dominic Convent.
The south wing, now covered with stucco, is an impressive
three-story, mansard-roofed structure dating from about 1880.
The Mater Dei shrine, located in the gardens, was built in 1922
and has a very ornate gilded chapel inside.

Continue south on Mission Boulevard for a view of the
town that grew up around the mission. During the gold rush,
it became a boisterous provision center for the forty-niners
heading to the southern mines.

The bed-and-breakfast inn next to the mission was once the
Washington Hotel, built in 1856. (The house with the tower is
new.) Note the red brick building on the right at No. 43363. It
was built in 1893 as the Ehrman General Store and later became
the Wells Fargo office. Two doors down, there is a flower shop
that was once an old saloon.

St. Joseph's Rectory

Turn right at Anza Street to No. 152, a beautifully restored
Victorian, built in 1890 as the rectory for the old St. Joseph's
Church. It was moved to this location in 1979 to make room
for the mission reconstruction.

Return to Mission Boulevard, and go right. In the next
block, at No. 43551, is a 1913 school building that has been used
as Fremont's city hall and as classrooms for Ohlone College,
the community college located across the street and up the hill
where mission vineyards once flourished.

Ohlone Cemetery

Ride on Mission for 2 more blocks, and turn right on Pine Street. When you reach Paseo Padre Parkway at the bottom of the hill, go right. In just over half a mile you will cross Washington Boulevard. To the left, beyond the eucalyptus trees, is the Ohlone Cemetery, where 4,000 Indians who built and worked at Mission San José are buried. This is sacred ground, and trespassing is forbidden. There is little to see but a sign declaring this to be an American Indian Historic Site.

Continue along Paseo Padre for about 2 miles. At the edge of Central Park, just past the traffic signal for Grimmer Boulevard, turn right into the driveway, and ride through the parking lot to the right of the swim lagoon. From here you'll go right on the path that circles the lake. On the far side, when the path follows the lake to the left, ride straight ahead, then through the soccer fields, as you head toward the tennis courts and the end of your tour of Fremont.

Additional Information

Shinn Historic Park: 1251 Peralta Boulevard. Grounds open daily dawn to 10:00 PM. House tours on the first Wednesday and third Sunday of each month 1:00 to 3:00 PM. Fee for tours.

Niles Depot Museum: Mission Boulevard, north of the intersection with Niles Canyon Road. Open first weekend and the third Sunday of each month 10:00 AM to 4:00 PM. Free admission. (510) 797-4449.

Mission San José: 43330 Mission Boulevard, at the intersection with Washington Boulevard. Church and museum open daily 10:00 AM to 5:00 PM, closed major holidays. Admission by donation. (510) 657-1797.

Fremont Chamber of Commerce: 2201 Walnut, Suite 110, Fremont, CA 94538. Open weekdays 8:00 AM to 5:00 PM. (510) 795-2244.

Bike Rental: Niles Ski and Bike, 37469 Niles Boulevard, Fremont. (510) 793-9141.

25. Fremont – Alameda Creek Trail

Santa Rosa

San Francisco

San Jose

Distance: 19 miles or less (The Alameda Creek Trail is 12 miles one way.)

Rating: *Easy*, along a wide, smooth, and mostly level bike path. On weekends, you may encounter many walkers and other cyclists. Mornings are an especially good time to ride, before the afternoon westerly winds begin. The route to Ardenwood Historic Farm involves a small hill and some traffic.

Highlights: Once home to Ohlone Indians, Alameda Creek now offers cyclists a tranquil, leisurely ride along its banks away from city traffic. In the spring, when the creek is high, you may see great blue herons standing silently at water's edge. Children and adults alike will enjoy the visit to Ardenwood Park to see what life was like on a late 19th century farm.

Alameda Creek Trail goes from Fremont to the bay.

courtesy East Bay Regional Park District

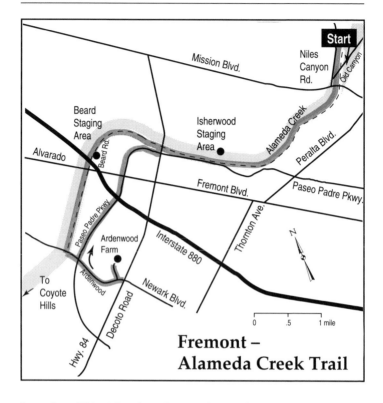

Fremont –
Alameda Creek Trail

Location: This ride takes place at the northern edge of
Fremont, roughly paralleling Highway 84, in Alameda County.

Ride along Alameda Creek

For centuries before the Spanish arrived, the Ohlone Indians
lived in camps and villages along the banks of AlamedaCreek.
Much of their time was spent gathering food, including mus-
sels, clams, fish, geese, and edible roots. They made gruel and
bread from ground acorns. Because the Ohlones didn't have
pottery, they used tightly woven baskets for cooking by ad-
ding heated stones to the food placed inside. When Mission
San Jose was established, the Indians were forced to give up
their way of life and to reside and work at the mission.

The Alameda Creek Regional Trail is a paved cy-
cling/hiking trail that follows the flood control channel from
the mouth of Niles Canyon westward to San Francisco Bay, a
distance of 12 miles. Begin your ride at the tiny park at the
Niles Canyon end of the trail. To reach the starting point from

Interstate 880, take the Thornton Avenue exit and follow State 84 west, through town to Mission Boulevard and turn left. From Interstate 680, exit onto Mission Boulevard (Highway 238) and head north. From Mission Boulevard, go right (east) just after crossing Alameda Creek onto Niles Canyon Road, and take the first right onto Old Canyon Road. The entrance to the park is a short distance on the left. Here you'll find a trail brochure and water. Pit toilets are located here and at several other locations along the way.

To shorten your ride you may wish to begin closer to Ardenwood. There are parking lots at Isherwood Way (which cuts 7 miles from your route), Decoto Road off Paseo Padre Parkway (which cuts 8.6 miles), and at the end of Beard Road off Fremont Boulevard (which cuts 10.8 miles). Mileage markers on the pavement let you know your distance as you ride along.

Begin riding west, which takes you under Mission Boulevard, the first of several underpasses. The trail winds and curves along the now-channeled Alameda Creek, as you pass neighborhood backyards, old quarries, and open fields. At Isherwood Way (3.5 miles from your start), you can leave the bike path to cross over the creek to the small park on the other side, where you'll find a pit toilet and picnic tables beyond the parking lot.

Ardenwood Farm

To visit Ardenwood Historic Farm, exit onto Ardenwood/Newark Boulevard by riding underneath the overpass at the 7.25-mile marker on the pavement and turning left on the gravel road leading to the street. Here you will have to share the wide road with fast-moving traffic as you go right, toward Ardenwood Farm.

(If you are riding with children or are inexperienced in traffic, you may wish to exit onto Ardenwood on the gravel pathway before the overpass and ride along the sidewalk on the north side of Ardenwood Boulevard.)

The entrance to Ardenwood Regional Preserve is a little more than a mile away on the left, after an overpass and just before the entrance to Highway 84. From a distance, you can see the grove of eucalyptus and other trees that cover much of the farm, now nearly surrounded by residential development.

Ardenwood was named after the woods in Shakespeare's play *As You Like It*, by George Patterson, who settled here in 1851 after failing as a gold miner in the Sierra. He was successful in agriculture, however, and eventually owned 3,000 acres of rich and fertile land and one of the most prosperous farms in the Bay Area. Today only 205 acres of Patterson's property remain as part of the farm; the rest lies under tract homes and industrial parks. The farm, with its walnut orchards, fields of vegetable crops, eucalyptus grove, farm animals, and restored antique farm machinery, has been re-created to give visitors a living picture of farm life in the period between 1870 and 1920.

Ride half a mile to the admissions gate which is located in the railroad station. (Restrooms are available here.) Bicycles are not allowed past this point, so lock your bike along the fence. Allow plenty of time for your visit, as there is much to see. There is also a picnic area and food service on the grounds.

The centerpiece of the park is the stately Patterson House. The rear section was built in 1856, while the large Queen Anne section in front was added around 1883 after Patterson married Clara Hawley. Since then, three generations of Pattersons have lived here, and the house still contains original family furnishings. The farm also has barns, animal pens, horse corrals, a blacksmith shop, a pool house, and a gazebo. You may

Patterson House, Ardenwood Historic Farm, 34600 Ardenwood Blvd., Fremont.

courtesy East Bay Regional Park District

even see an antique penny-farthing (high-wheeled bicycle) being ridden near the house.

After exploring the park, retrace your route on Ardenwood Boulevard back to the creek trail. From here you will have a very gradual incline on your return to Niles Canyon, but the wind will be at your back.

An alternative return route cuts one mile from the distance but follows city streets and has two overpasses with slight inclines. Ride on Ardenwood Boulevard less than a mile to Paseo Padre Parkway and turn right. There may be some traffic, but the street is wide and eventually has a bike lane. Follow Paseo Padre 3.5 miles to Isherwood Way, where you rejoin the bike path heading east.

When you return to Niles Canyon, be sure to explore the old town of Niles where Charlie Chaplin made several films in the 1910s. (See Fremont chapter, page 206.)

Additional Information

Ardenwood Historic Farm: 34600 Ardenwood Boulevard. Open Thursday through Sunday, 10:00 AM to 4:00 PM, April through November, with special Christmas tours in December. Closed January through March. Admission fee includes house tours, haywagon and railway rides, and special programs and demonstrations. (510) 796-0663.

Coyote Hills Regional Park: Patterson Ranch Road, off Paseo Padre Parkway, north of Highway 84. Can be reached by bicycle from Alameda Creek Regional Trail. Park opens 8:00 AM. Visitor center has exhibits of Ohlone history; open daily 9:00 AM to 4:30 PM . Parking fee on weekends during spring and summer. (510) 795-9385.

San Francisco Bay National Wildlife Refuge: South on Thornton Avenue from Highway 84. Visitor center has displays of area wildlife; open daily 10:00 AM to 5:00 PM. Free admission. Grounds open sunrise to sunset. (510) 792-3178.

Bike Rental: Niles Ski and Bike, 37469 Niles Boulevard, Fremont. (510) 793-9141.

See Fremont Ride, page 210, for more resources.

Coyote Hills Park

Another option is to continue from Ardenwood Boulevard west on the Alameda Creek Trail for 2 more miles to Coyote Hills Regional Park, which has a visitor center, picnic facilities, and 3.5 miles of paved trail for cycling. Past Coyote Hills, the trail goes another 2.3 miles along the edge of the San Francisco Bay National Wildlife Refuge before ending at the bay.

26. Woodside – Portola Valley

Distance: 17 miles

Rating: *Moderate*, as most of the terrain is rolling, with only one real climb over Sand Hill. There may be traffic on Woodside Road and Sand Hill Road. Please note: The towns of Woodside and Portola Valley vigorously enforce the vehicle code, and cyclists who do not obey all traffic signs and rules may be cited.

Highlights: One of the most popular routes for area cyclists, this ride takes you through scenic wooded and open countryside. You will trace the history of Woodside, site of

Woodside Store at the intersection of Tripp Road and King's Mountain Road in Woodside. Built around 1854, it became a center of activity for the pioneer lumbering community.

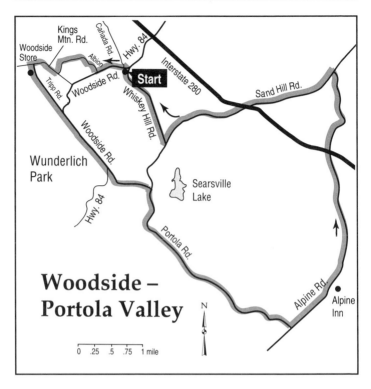

the first English-speaking settlement on the peninsula, from its origins as a lumber town to its more recent emergence as a community of country estates. You will also ride through Portola Valley, home of a historic tavern and old estates of its own.

Location: Woodside is located on Highway 84, less than a mile west of Interstate 280, in San Mateo County.

Ride through Woodside

Begin your ride at the Woodside Town Hall, located behind the Pioneer Hotel, at the intersection of Woodside Road (Highway 84) and Whiskey Hill Road. The hotel was constructed in 1884, although only the façade is from the original building; it still houses a saloon, along with a bank and offices. Independence Hall, dating from the same time, was used for public gatherings. It has been moved from its original location and incorporated into the town hall.

Go left on Woodside Road, heading west toward the mountains. The intersection with Cañada Road, in a block, is the heart of the present town of Woodside and the location of two businesses well known to cyclists: Roberts Market on the left and the Woodside Bakery in the shopping center on the right. Just past the library, you'll see a quaint wooden church built in 1891 that now serves as a chapel for the newer Woodside Village Church next door.

At the next corner, turn right onto Albion Avenue, a quiet country lane that offers a pleasant ride past the impressive entrance gates to several fine estates. When Albion goes to the right in less than half a mile, continue straight ahead on Manuella Avenue to its end. Turn right on narrow King's Mountain Road, a former lumberman's toll road built in 1869. You may encounter some traffic here heading toward Huddart County Park.

Just before crossing Union Creek, notice the Charles Josselyn house on the right, at No. 400. It is situated behind a low stone wall and nearly hidden by trees. This attractive one-story villa, built in 1906, is an example of country estates that were constructed in this area in the early 1900s.

Woodside Store

At the junction with Tripp Road you'll come to the historic Woodside Store, one of the few surviving landmarks from Woodside's pioneer days. Restored and rebuilt by the county of San Mateo, the store now contains a museum operated by the San Mateo County Historical Association.

The present structure was built on land owned by Mathias Parkhurst, who operated a redwood shingle mill with his partner Robert Orville Tripp, a dentist. As more and more mills were established, they decided to give up the lumber business and in 1851 opened a store in a crude lean-to. Three years later they constructed the redwood building you see today.

The store, the only one between San Francisco and Santa Clara, quickly became the center of activity for Woodside. At one time there were 15 sawmills within a five-mile radius of the store, and more than 1,000 lumberjacks bought their food, supplies, and liquor here. The store also served as a post office, bank, library and, of course, dentist's office.

Tripp acquired the property after Parkhurst died in 1863 and continued to operate the store until his death in 1909.

From the Woodside Store, continue riding along quiet, shady Tripp Road. You will again catch glimpses of the estates, mansions, and stables for which Woodside is now known. Its scenic charm and warm climate attracted many wealthy San Franciscans in the late 1800s and have been drawing the rich and famous ever since.

Most of the old estates are hidden from view, but there is a pair of interesting church-like, red brick structures near the road in about half a mile. Built in the 1930s as part of the George and Elia Whittell estate, the larger one was a Moorish style theater where the Whittells held lavish parties. They also had a collection of exotic animals that included lions, zebras, and an African elephant. George was frequently seen driving around Woodside with his pet cheetah in the passenger seat of his automobile. The main house, set well back on the property, was built in 1912 as a summer residence by George's father. The land is still a private estate.

History of Woodside

The early history of Woodside contrasts sharply with the affluent image it presents today. The first settlers, who began arriving in the early 1830s, were deserters who had jumped ship in San Francisco and Monterey. They were a rough but easygoing lot, boisterous, fond of drinking, and not much given to hard work. Some of these fugitives and drifters, however, began lumbering the redwoods using sawpits, a crude forerunner of sawmills.

In 1840 the Mexican governor awarded John Copinger 12,000 acres of prime redwood land, which he called Rancho Cañada de Raymundo. The demand for lumber and shingles was great and provided plenty of work for the local sawyers on the rancho. A number of corn liquor stills also began appearing in the woods and did a lively business— apparently encouraged by Copinger.

Despite occasional attempts by the Mexican and United States governments to evict and deport these "un-desirables," the vagabond community continued to survive until the outbreak of the Mexican War in 1846. At that time U.S. Marines invaded the rancho, conscripting men and seizing horses and cattle. Copinger died shortly after the annexation of California by the United States.

Wunderlich Park

Turn right when Tripp Road rejoins Woodside Road. Traffic may be heavy here, as Highway 84 carries beach goers to the coast, and the shoulder is quite narrow. In just over half a mile, near the end of a gradual downhill, turn right into the entrance of Wunderlich County Park to see the remnants of another fine estate.

This former ranch land was purchased in 1902 by James Folger II, the coffee tycoon, who used it for weekend excursions and campouts. His mansion still stands but is not on park property. You can, however, see the handsome stable he built, which is still in use today. The park is named for Martin Wunderlich, who obtained much of the Folger estate in 1956 and donated the parkland to San Mateo County in 1974.

Leaving the park, continue along Woodside Road for another half mile. Just as Highway 84 begins its climb up the Santa Cruz Mountains, go left onto Portola Road. Use caution as you turn, and watch for traffic coming down the hill.

The land to your left was once part of the 2,000-acre Mountain Home Ranch, which Copinger sold to Charles Brown in 1846. Brown, a deserter from a whaling ship, had built an adobe on the property, possibly as early as 1838. The small square structure, thought to be the oldest building in San

---

History of Woodside (continued)

In 1850 Copinger's widow, Maria Luisa Soto, married a very different sort of man. John Greer was a stern Irish Presbyterian sea captain whose crew had abandoned ship for the gold fields in 1849. To combat the continuing whiskey problem (for which his predecessor no doubt was partly responsible), he helped form a local temperance society and also donated land for a school. Woodside's rough-and-tumble ways were beginning to change.

Lumbering resumed after the gold rush with the aid of the West Coast's first real sawmills. The demand created by the frantic building boom in San Francisco quickly stripped the area of its virgin redwoods and forced cutting to move over the ridge. The little settlement then moved from the base of the Santa Cruz Mountains to its present location. By the 1880s there were several stores, a stage coach stop, and three saloons, giving the area its name of Whiskey Hill.

Mateo County, is still in good condition, and its red tile roof is just barely visible from the road. Brown is best remembered for installing the first sawmill on the peninsula in 1847.

Portola Road is lined with redwood and eucalyptus trees and runs along a creek called Alambique, Spanish for "still," named after one of the illegal distilleries in the mountains. The creek provided water power for Brown's sawmill until a steam boiler was added. Go right at the stop sign, staying on Portola. At the next intersection, across the road and over the embankment, is the site of the former town of Searsville, which is now covered by Searsville Lake.

Searsville

The little town of Searsville grew up around an inn built by John Sears in 1854. The hotel served as a stopover for drivers of mule and ox teams hauling lumber from the mills to the port at Redwood City. It was also the Sunday gathering place for the lumbermen who entertained themselves with such activities as horse racing, cockfighting, drinking, gambling, and brawling.

By the 1870s, the best timber had been cut and Searsville was just a quiet farming village. Its end came in 1892 after the settlers lost a long legal battle with the Spring Valley Water Company, which planned to flood the area by damming San Francisquito Creek. After the work was completed, however, green algae made the water undrinkable. Eventually, the lake was turned over to Stanford University as a source of irrigation water. It was also used for recreational purposes before it became part of Stanford's Jasper Ridge Biological Preserve.

Ride through Portola Valley

Follow Portola Road to the right, and in half a mile, you will pass the turnoff to Old La Honda Road. August Schilling, the spice merchant, once had his estate near this intersection.

You are now riding on what local cyclists call "the Portola Loop," a scenic road with a wide bike lane through the rural area of Portola Valley. You will have 3 miles of gradual incline, but there are several interesting landmarks to see along the way.

After about one mile you will come to the Our Lady of the Wayside Catholic Church, at 930 Portola Road, hidden behind a stand of redwoods on the left. Built in 1912, this charming Mission style edifice was designed by noted architect Timothy Pflueger. Soon the valley widens, and you will have wonderful views of open fields and the Santa Cruz Mountains beyond. Beneath you, however, is the San Andreas Fault, one of the most active earthquake faults in the country. It is the reason much of this land has remained rural and undeveloped.

This area was once remote enough to shelter Indians attempting to avoid mission life. After 1833 it was a cattle ranch called Rancho Corte Madera. Farming and ranching were the predominant activities until the mid-20th century.

Portola Valley's most famous resident of the period was Andrew Hallidie, inventor of San Francisco's cable cars. He used his ranch for further experiments and built an aerial cable tramway from the valley floor into the mountains where his home was located.

In a short distance, you will see the little red Portola schoolhouse, next to the Town Hall and Library. Built in 1909 of redwood in the Mission Revival style popular at the time, it is now an art gallery. (Restrooms can be found behind the school, adjacent to the park.)

Next you'll pass Jelich Ranch, one of the last orchards left in the valley. In operation since the late 1800s, the ranch still produces apples and other fruit for local consumption. The family home dates from 1916.

Willow Brook Gatehouse

Farther along, just after a curve in the road, you'll see an impressive castle-like gatehouse. This was built sometime after 1912 of wood faced with stones from Corte Madera Creek to house the superintendent of the Willow Brook estate, owned by Herbert Law. Law had made his fortune by formulating and selling a patent medicine for "ladies' problems," and bought the land to grow the special plants he needed for the elixir. His Roman style villa was razed in 1945; only the gatehouse remains.

After half a mile, on the left, there is a wooden windmill that formerly housed the pump mechanism for one of the oldest and deepest wells in the area.

When you reach Alpine Road, go left for a long, gradual downhill. Alpine Road was once an Indian trail that linked the south bay clam-digging sites with the coast. During the 1840s, the trail was widened by Antonino Buelna to connect his San Gregorio ranch with his property on the future site of Stanford.

A bike path paralleling Alpine Road may be picked up at the entrance to the tennis club, just past Los Trancos Road. Although the path may take you away from traffic noise, it is narrow, sometimes rough, and must be shared with hikers and equestrians. Many cyclists prefer to ride on the wide, smooth shoulder of Alpine Road.

Alpine Inn

A mile from the turn onto Alpine Road, you'll come to the historic Alpine Inn, California's oldest roadhouse in continuous operation. Go right onto Arastradero Road and immediately right into the driveway.

The history of this establishment dates back to 1852 when it was built by Buelna's son, Felix. The tavern quickly became a hangout for the local inhabitants who enjoyed gambling and bull-and-bear fights here.

In 1868 the building was sold to Irishman William Stanton to settle gambling debts and was renamed Stanton's Saloon. After his death in 1887, Stanton's heirs leased the tavern to a Portuguese immigrant known as Black Chapete. He was a likeable man who enjoyed drinking with his customers, and his hospitality attracted a large clientele, especially after Stanford University opened in 1891. Despite attempts by Stanford officials to have the tavern closed to protect students from its influence, Black Chapete's thrived.

In the early 1900s, the building was leased to a German who changed the name to The Wunder. The tavern survived Prohibition and acquired a new owner in the late 1940s, when it became Rossotti's. It has been the Alpine Inn since 1957, although many still call it "Zotts."

The Alpine Inn, now a State Historical Landmark, remains a popular place, frequented by students, local residents, and cyclists who enjoy sipping beer and eating hamburgers at the picnic tables in back.

Alpine Road is pleasant cycling, with a gentle downhill for 3 more miles. You will pass the unincorporated community of Ladera and go beneath Interstate 280, so watch for traffic at the exit/entrance ramps.

Sand Hill Road

When Alpine merges with Junipera Serra at the traffic light, continue straight ahead and prepare to make a left turn onto Sand Hill Road at the next signal. This is the busiest, most congested part of the ride.

Traffic on Sand Hill may be fast-moving, but there is a wide shoulder. The land to your right was once the site of Sharon Heights, the extensive estate of Fred Sharon, a senator's son. All that remains today is an artificial lake of the Japanese gardens, now a part of Sharon Park.

After a mile of gradual uphill and a brief downhill over the freeway, you will have a moderate half-mile climb. To the left you can see the two-mile-long Stanford Linear Accelerator Center, a subnuclear physics research facility. On your descent, make a right turn at the first intersection onto Whiskey Hill Road, which, after a brief climb, brings you back to your starting location in Woodside.

Alpine Inn on Alpine Road at Arastradero Road in Portola Valley. Built in 1852, it is California's oldest roadhouse in continuous operation.

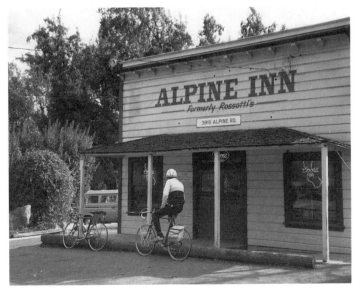

Additional Information

Roberts Market: 3015 Woodside Road. Grocery store with extensive deli. Open daily 8:00 AM to 8:00 PM. (415) 851-1511.

Woodside Bakery and Cafe: 3052 Woodside Road. Bakery opens 7:00 AM. (415) 851-7247. Cafe serves lunch and dinner. Outside tables located behind building. (415) 851-0812.

Huddart County Park: Up King's Mountain Road, 2 miles from Woodside Road (Highway 84). Picnic grounds, miles of hiking trails. Open 8:00 AM to sunset. Free admission for cyclists. (415) 851-0326.

Woodside Store Museum: Intersection of Tripp Road and King's Mountain Road. Open Tuesday and Thursday 10:00 AM to 4:00 PM, Saturday and Sunday noon to 4:00 PM. Free admission. Restrooms open during museum hours. Water available at all times near parking lot. (415) 851-7615.

Wunderlich County Park: 4040 Woodside Road. Open 8:00 AM to sunset. Free admission. (415) 851-7570.

Valley Art Gallery: 775 Portola Road. Open Wednesday through Sunday noon to 5:00 PM. (415) 851-0332.

Jelich Ranch: 683 Portola Road, Portola Valley. Open daily. (415) 851-0482.

The Alpine Inn: Intersection of Arastadero Road and Alpine Road in Portola Valley. Opens daily at 11:30 AM.

Cañada Road: This is a popular cycling route in Woodside, especially on "Bicycle Sunday," held first and third Sunday of each month, April through October, when road is closed to automobile traffic between Edgewood Road and Highway 92.

Filoli: A country estate located off Cañada Road in Woodside; built in 1916 for family of William B. Bourn II. House and gardens open for tours Tuesday through Saturday, February to November. Advance reservations necessary. Admission fee. (415) 364-2880.

Bike Rental: Any Mountain, 2341 El Camino Real, Redwood City. (415) 361-1213. See also Palo Alto Ride, page 238.

27. Palo Alto

Distance: 18 miles

Rating: *Easy*, taking place entirely on flat city streets that frequently have bike lanes. There may be some traffic near downtown and campus.

Highlights: Palo Alto is one of the most bicycle-friendly cities in the nation. On this ride you will explore the spacious campus of Stanford University and see some attractive Palo Alto residential areas dating from the late 19th century, as well as gracious homes from later periods.

Location: Palo Alto is located between Interstate 280 and Highway 101 in northern Santa Clara County, about 30 miles south of San Francisco.

Norris House at 1247 Cowper Street in Palo Alto. It was designed by local architect Birge Clark and still looks much the same as in this photo taken shortly after construction in

courtesy CSS Associates Architects

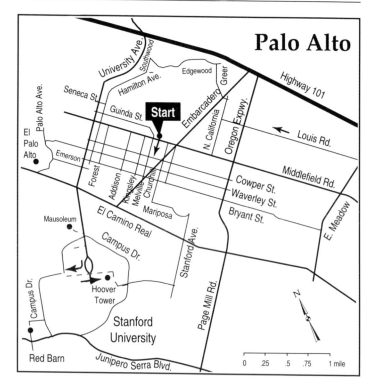

Ride through Palo Alto

Begin your ride at the Lucie Stern Community Center on Middlefield Road at Melville Avenue, one block north of Embarcadero Road. To reach the start from Highway 101, go west on Embarcadero about one mile to Middlefield and turn right. From Interstate 280, exit on Page Mill Road, which becomes Oregon Expressway, and go about 3.5 miles to Middlefield, turning left. (On weekends, when the center is closed, restrooms can be found at Rinconada Park one block east, at Embarcadero and Newell Road.)

The community center, a delightful theater and arts complex built in the 1930s, was a gift to the people of Palo Alto from Mrs. Stern, one of Palo Alto's best-loved philanthropists. It was designed by noted local architect Birge Clark in the Spanish Colonial Revival style for which he is known. Clark lived in Palo Alto all of his life and designed over 400 of its buildings.

From Melville, cross Middlefield Road at the traffic signal. In 3 blocks turn right onto Cowper Street. The remarkable early California style building on the corner, at 1247 Cowper, was designed by Birge Clark in 1927 for authors Kathleen and Charles Norris and has earned a place on the National Register of Historic Places. It is presently the Stanford Newman Center.

Professorville

You are now in the neighborhood known as Professorville. In the late 19th century, this is where the faculty from the newly opened Stanford University built the first homes that made up the original town of Palo Alto. Because of its historic and architectural significance, Professorville has been listed on the National Register as a Historic District.

On the next corner, at 501 Kingsley, you'll see the impressive 1897 home of Professor Fleugel, a Chaucerian scholar who had an 8,000-volume library. It was said that he also had a brick vault in the garden to safeguard his research papers.

Turn left on Kingsley. The Queen Anne house behind the hedge, No. 450, was built in 1894 for physics professor Fernando Sanford, one of the original Stanford professors, who lived here until his death in 1948. The 1893 house on the corner, at 1146 Waverley, belonged to Albert and Mary Smith, both Stanford professors.

Sunbonnet House at 1061 Bryant Avenue, Palo Alto. It was designed by Bernard Maybeck and dates from 1899.

Continuing along Kingsley, turn right on Bryant Street, where you'll find some excellent examples of the Craftsman shingle style of architecture from the early 1900s. At the next intersection, stop at 1061 Bryant to see what has long been called the Sunbonnet House for its gambrel-roofed entry. Designed by distinguished Bay Area architect Bernard Maybeck, it was constructed in 1899 for Emma Kellogg.

Electronics Pioneers

The modest cottage across the street, at 1044 Bryant, was the childhood home of Russell and Sigurd Varian, founders of Varian Associates. In 1937 they invented the klystron tube, the backbone of microwave electronics. The brothers seemed unlikely candidates for such an important invention: one was dyslexic and the other was a college drop-out.

The 1893 home at the far end of Bryant, at No. 1005, belonged to Frank Angell, one of Stanford's original faculty and its first track coach. Turn right here onto Addison Street.

A historic marker at 367 Addison denotes the site where young Stanford graduates Bill Hewlett and Dave Packard founded their electronics company in 1938 in the garage of the house Packard and his wife were renting. Their first big sale was to Walt Disney Studios, who bought nine audio oscillators to improve the sound of its movie *Fantasia*.

Turn left at the corner onto Waverley Street, and in 2 blocks, at the intersection with Homer Avenue, you'll see St. Thomas Aquinas Catholic Church. Built in 1901 in the Gothic Revival style, it is the oldest standing church structure in Palo Alto. This beautiful building was featured in the opening scenes of the 1972 film classic *Harold and Maude*.

Downtown Palo Alto

At the next intersection, go right onto Forest Avenue for one block to 706 Cowper Street, Palo Alto's finest example of Victorian architecture. This splendid house was built in 1894 for T. B. Downing, a member of both the school board and the first city council. After many years of neglect, it has been restored and is now used for offices.

Return to Waverley and continue to the right. One block farther along, to your left and facing Hamilton Avenue, you'll see the Palo Alto Post Office, designed by Birge Clark in 1932.

sharply to the right onto a wide pathway that brings you to the Stanford family mausoleum. Here, guarded by four sphinxes, are the remains of Leland, Jane, and Leland Junior. Beyond the mausoleum, on the roadway to the right, is the grave site of Henry Lathrop, Mrs. Stanford's younger brother, marked by the statue known as Angel of Grief.

Return to Palm Drive and continue across divided Campus Drive. After one block, go right on Museum Way to reach the 1892 Stanford Museum, the oldest museum west of the Mississippi. Under Stanford's direction, it was constructed of concrete reinforced by railroad tracks, which helped it survive the 1906 earthquake, whereas additional sections, built after his death without such reinforcing, collapsed. Today the museum houses mementos of the Stanford family, including the Promontory Point golden spike, as well as an outstanding collection of art. The Rodin Sculpture Garden, to the left of the museum, has a fine collection of the artist's works.

Main Quad

From the museum, go back to Palm Drive, and turn again toward the center of campus. Ahead of you, on the far side of

Memorial Church, Main Quad, Stanford University. Hand-carved stonework and imported mosaics cover the façade of this beautiful 1903 building.

courtesy Stanford University News Service

the grassy Oval, is the Quadrangle, the heart of Stanford University. The sandstone buildings and graceful arches of the Inner Quad date from 1891, while the Outer Quad was completed in 1903. You can walk your bicycle up the ramp to the right of the stairs to explore this part of campus. Visitor information is on the left as you enter the Outer Quad.

Opposite the entrance on the Inner Quad, you'll see Memorial Church, the university's most striking architectural feature. Although the church was part of the original plans, it was not constructed until after Leland Stanford's death in 1893. Mrs. Stanford then decided it should be built as a memorial to her husband and supervised the work herself. The building has hand-carved stonework, stained glass windows, and magnificent mosaics imported from Europe that cover the exterior facade and interior walls. Mrs. Stanford sent back the original mosaics because they depicted only men; because the university was co-educational, she insisted women and children be included. The non-denominational church was dedicated in 1903.

Return to Serra Street in front of the Quad, and ride to the left, away from Hoover Tower, through the barriers.

Red Barn

When Serra ends, turn right onto Via Palou, then left onto Campus Drive West. In about half a mile, go right on Electioneer Road, named for Stanford's most famous horse. (Restrooms are located next to the tennis courts.) You will soon see the magnificent Victorian Red Barn, one of the few remaining buildings of the Stock Farm. Dating from the late 1870s and restored in 1984, it is still used for boarding horses. A white brick "fireproof" stable, located farther down the road, was built in 1892 after a wooden stable burned and several horses were killed.

The Stock Farm began to decline after Stanford's death, and its horses were sold off to help the financially troubled university. The ranch officially closed in 1903.

The only other building left from the farm is an old winery that has been converted to shops, now called the Stanford Barn. It is located on Quarry Road near the Stanford Shopping Center.

Retrace your route back to campus, continuing on Serra Street past the Quad and the Art Gallery, built in 1917 with funds donated by Leland Stanford's brother Thomas.

Hoover Tower

Ride through the barriers to Hoover Tower, which stands 285 feet tall. An impressive landmark since 1941, it houses the Hoover Institution on War, Revolution and Peace. Its rare collections were begun by Herbert Hoover, president of the United States from 1929 to 1933 and Stanford University's most famous alumnus. Hoover memorabilia are exhibited in two rooms on the ground floor, and an observation platform is located at the top.

Continue along Serra and, at the next stop sign, turn right onto the walkway that cuts through campus. To the left is Encina Hall, built as the men's dormitory in 1891 and now used for offices. (Roble Hall, the original women's dormitory, was located on the other side of campus, far from where the men lived.) Ride 2 blocks straight ahead, staying to the left, and then turn left onto the wide pathway that exits onto Escondido Road. Watch out for cyclists if school is in session, as there are thousands of bicycles on campus.

Continue on Escondido across Campus Drive East. This area was formerly the center of Ayrshire Farm, the dairy operation of Matadero Ranch, owned by a mysterious Frenchman who used the assumed name Peter Coutts. Once a wealthy banker and publisher of a French newspaper, his liberal political views forced him to leave his country in 1874. His true identity was not revealed until after he returned to his homeland six years later. The estate was acquired by the Stanfords in 1882 and became part of the Palo Alto Farm and, later, the university. Only a few buildings remain of Coutts' extensive ranch. Immediately after the barriers, on the left, you can see the cottage Coutts built in 1875, which became the home of David Starr Jordan, the university's first president. Today, with numerous additions, it serves as the administrative building of Escondido Village, a complex of student apartments. A short distance farther, at No. 860, is a two-story painted brick structure that housed Coutts' fine library and farm office.

College Terrace

Continue to the end of Escondido and make a left turn onto Stanford Avenue. You have now left the grounds of the university and are riding along the edge of College Terrace, a late 19th century housing development.

In 1887 Alexander Gordon bought 120 acres of farmland near the construction site of the new university and divided it into lots, hoping to attract faculty and fraternities. It became known as College Terrace because all of its streets had been named after colleges and universities. In 1891 it was annexed by the neighboring town of Mayfield.

The Stanfords had originally thought Mayfield would be the resident village for the university, but they insisted it be dry. The local inhabitants, however, refused to give up their 13 saloons. Stanford then established a separate, and dry, town called University Park, which was incorporated as Palo Alto in 1894. Mayfield gradually faded in importance and was annexed by Palo Alto in 1925. The prohibition on alcohol was finally lifted after World War II.

Stay on Stanford Avenue, across congested El Camino Real, until it ends at Park Boulevard. Turn left and, just past the Peers Park restrooms, go to the right, through the barriers onto Mariposa Avenue. When this street ends, make a right turn onto Churchill, crossing the railroad tracks and Alma Street.

In 3 blocks, at the intersection with Waverley, you can see the stately Gamble House to the left. It was built in 1902 for Edwin Percy Gamble, son of the co-founder of Proctor-Gamble Company, and was given to the city of Palo Alto by Gamble's daughter, who lived here until her death in 1981. The house and grounds are operated by the Elizabeth Gamble Garden Foundation. The gardens are open to the public.

Bryant Bike Boulevard

Go right onto Waverley, right again at Coleridge, then left in one block onto Bryant Avenue. This is part of Palo Alto's "bike boulevard," a direct route through the city for bicycles.

Ride along Bryant for about 2 miles, past interesting homes, through barriers, across Oregon Expressway, and over a little bridge. When you reach East Meadow Drive, turn left. This will take you by the grounds of Mitchell Park (restrooms are located here) and across Middlefield.

Soon you'll go by another, smaller park, named for Don Jesus Ramos, a Mayfield pioneer from the 1850s. Make the first left past the park onto Louis Road, as you head back toward the center of town. Most of south Palo Alto was developed in the 1950s, but you can still spot an occasional older structure amid the tract housing. In 1.6 miles, after crossing Oregon Expressway, turn right at North California Avenue. Go left onto Greer Road at the stop sign, cross Embarcadero, and when Greer ends at Edgewood Drive, turn left. The 1937 house that architect Birge Clark designed for himself and his family is at No. 1490.

When Edgewood ends, turn left onto Southwood Drive, and at the second stop sign, ride ahead and to the right onto Hamilton Avenue. You'll see many lovely homes as you ride through this part of town.

Squire House

In less than a mile, go right onto Seneca Street. At the far end of the block, at 900 University, you'll come to the striking Squire House, a perfect example of Classical Revival architecture. It was built in 1904 for John Adams Squire, a classics buff, amateur weatherman, and heir to a Massachusetts meat-packing fortune. The towering palm trees along the driveway were only four feet tall when they were first planted. This beautiful house was scheduled for demolition in the 1960s, but it was saved by a citizen fund-raising drive and is now a State Historic Landmark.

From the Squire House, return to Hamilton and continue to the right. After one block, turn left onto Guinda Street and, when you reach its end, go right at Melville. This brings you

Squire House at 900 University Ave., Palo Alto. The palm trees were only four feet tall when initially planted in 1904.

back to the Lucie Stern Center, where you began your tour of
Palo Alto.

Additional Information

Prolific Oven Bakery and Coffeehouse: 550 Waverley
Street. Opens daily 7:30 AM, except Sunday opens 9:00 AM.
(415) 326-8485.

Stanford University Visitor Information Center: On the
Outer Quad. Open daily 10:00 AM to 4:00 PM. Campus
tours start here. (415) 723-2560.

Memorial Church: Stanford University Inner Quad. Open
weekdays 8:00 AM to 5:00 PM. Sunday service at 10:00 AM.
(415) 723-1762.

Leland Stanford Junior Museum: Museum Way, off Palm
Drive, Stanford University. Due to damage suffered in the 1989
earthquake, it is closed until further notice. (415) 723-4177.

Stanford Art Gallery: Serra Street. Open Tuesday through
Friday, 10:00 AM to 5:00 PM, weekends 1:00 to 5:00 PM. Free
admission. (415) 723-2842.

Hoover Tower: Serra Street, Stanford University. Open
daily 10:00 AM to 4:30 PM. Closed during finals week and
Christmas and spring breaks. Fee to go up in the observation tower, ground floor exhibits free. (415) 723-2053.

Museum of American Heritage: 275 Alma Street. Displays of early electrical and mechanical devices. Open
Friday through Sunday 11:00 AM to 4:00 PM. Free admission. (415) 321-1004.

Palo Alto Junior Museum: 1451 Middlefield, next to the
Lucie Stern Community Center. Natural history museum for
children. Open Tuesday through Saturday 10:00 AM to 5:00
PM, Sunday 1:00 to 4:00 PM. Free admission. (415) 329-2111.

Palo Alto Chamber of Commerce: 325 Forest Avenue, Palo
Alto, CA 94301. Open weekdays 9:00 AM to 5:00 PM. (415) 324-
3121.

Bike Rental: Action Sports, 401 High Street, Palo Alto.
(415) 328-3180. Bike Connection, 2086 El Camino Real,
Palo Alto. (415) 424-8034.

28. Santa Clara

Distance: 6 miles

Rating: *Easy*, short, and flat. This ride follows quiet city streets, many with bike lanes. Traffic may be heavy midweek on main roads but is generally light on weekends. It is a pleasant ride for the whole family at any time of year.

Highlights: Santa Clara, incorporated in 1852, is one of the Bay Area's earliest cities and the home of California's first college, now the University of Santa Clara. This ride offers a sampling of Santa Clara's rich heritage, including the Santa Clara Mission, a Carmelite monastery, adobes, Victorians, and a pioneer cemetery.

Location: The city of Santa Clara is located midway between Interstate 280 and Highway 101 in Santa Clara County.

Morse Mansion at 981 Fremont, Santa Clara. It was built in 1892 for the owner of a seed company.

Ride through Santa Clara

Begin your ride of "the Mission City" at Henry Schmidt Park, located at the intersection of Saratoga Avenue and Los Padres Boulevard. Facilities here include restrooms (closed winter weekends), picnic tables, a playground, and tennis courts. To reach the park from Interstate 280, take the Saratoga Avenue exit and go about 1.5 miles toward Santa Clara.

From the park, ride left onto divided Saratoga Avenue. After less than half a mile go straight ahead onto one-way Bellomy Street (Saratoga angles left). As you cross Winchester Boulevard, you will see the Santa Clara Mission Cemetery ahead and to the right. At the next corner, Lincoln Street, make a sharp right turn into the entrance of the cemetery, where many early Santa Clara Valley pioneers are buried.

This cemetery was established in 1851 when the one near the mission became overcrowded. The chapel with its copper roof was completed in 1906. Nearby is the burial place of Judge Myles P. O'Connor, who donated money for O'Connor Sanitarium, now O'Connor Hospital, in San Jose. He died in

1909. Other famous names you may recognize as you wander among the tombstones are Pedro de Saisset, the French vice consul in San Jose in whose name the de Saisset Art Museum was established at the Santa Clara University; Hiram Morgan Hill, founder of the town of Morgan Hill; Martin Murphy, Sr., a major landholder in Santa Clara Valley and father of the founder of Sunnyvale; Maria Soledad Arguello, wife of California's first governor under Mexican rule; and Antonio Suñol, *alcalde*, or mayor, of San Jose in 1841.

When you're done studying tombstones and reading inscriptions, leave the cemetery and continue on Bellomy. In one block go right onto Jefferson Street to No. 373, the Berryessa Adobe. Built in the 1840s on former mission land, this modest dwelling is one of the few early adobes remaining in the valley. Its name derives from the family that purchased it in 1861.

Return to Bellomy, go right, and then make a left turn onto Monroe Street at the traffic light. After 2 blocks, go right at Santa Clara Street. At the end of the block, at No. 1217, is a charming Victorian Gothic cottage built in 1848 by Andrew Landrum, a local carpenter. It is one of the oldest and best-preserved houses in Santa Clara.

In another block, at the intersection with Main Street, there are two more historic residences. The large 1886 house at 714-716 Main once belonged to Dr. H. H. Warburton, who settled in Santa Clara in 1848 and was the town's first physician. His original medical office is now part of the San Jose Historical Museum in Kelley Park, but during his later years he maintained his office here at his Main Street home.

Across the street, at 1085 Santa Clara, is the stately Arguello house, built about 1860 for the widow and family of Luis Antonio Arguello, the first governor of California under Mexico. Although it has been converted into apartments, the exterior remains nearly unchanged.

Santa Clara Mission

Continuing along Santa Clara, turn left in one block at Washington Street. When it ends at Homestead Road, go right, and cross Lafayette Street at the traffic light. This will take you into the rear of the University of Santa Clara, where Mission Santa Clara de Asis is located. To reach the front of the mission church, ride straight ahead and around the walled rose garden, formerly the mission cemetery.

The Santa Clara Mission was established in 1777 near the Guadalupe River, the first of several different locations. After earthquakes damaged the previous church and buildings, the fourth and last mission compound was built between 1822 and 1825, but it fell into decay following secularization of the mission system in 1836. In 1851, at the request of the bishop of California, the Jesuits founded Santa Clara College in the old mission buildings and thus established California's first institution of higher education. The college was granted a university charter in 1855 and has maintained a long history as one of the top-ranked Catholic institutions in the country.

The arbor path on the other side of the church leads to more gardens and the remains of the 1822 mission compound. The Old Adobe Wall was probably part of a kitchen, and the Adobe Lodge, now the remodeled Faculty Club, was once the granary. A fire in 1926 destroyed the old mission church; the present replica was constructed in 1929.

To leave the campus, ride on the road directly opposite the front of the church. On the left is the de Saisset Art Gallery and Museum, which houses a collection of early California and mission artifacts. Make the next possible left turn after the museum. Continue through the barricade at the end of the street onto The Alameda, being careful to avoid the spikes in the roadway.

Stop in half a block to see the Woman's Club Adobe, on the right at No. 3260, built about 1790. The sole surviving building of the third mission compound, it was probably living quarters for Indian families. Don José Peña received this building in 1840, along with several others, as part of his land grants. It remained in his family until it was acquired by the Santa Clara Woman's Club and dedicated as their headquarters in 1914. It is a State Registered Landmark.

At the next corner, make a right turn onto Benton Street. A block after crossing El Camino Real, you will come to the Santa Clara Railroad Depot, the oldest operating passenger station in California. It dates from 1863 and has been restored by the South Bay Historical Railroad Society. Inside there is a small museum of railroad artifacts and photographs.

Historic Homes

Return on Benton and cross The Alameda. In 3 blocks, go right at Washington Street to explore another neighborhood of historic homes. The 1897 structure on the corner, No. 1116, belonged to Dr. Judson Paul, who saw patients in his office at the back of the property. Carpenter Calvin Russell built his house at No. 1184 in 1861. Across the street, at No. 1179, is a lovely Colonial Revival style house, constructed in 1905 for the son of Senator Frederick Franck, whose family originally owned this entire block.

At the corner of Washington and Fremont, at 981 Fremont, you'll find the magnificent Morse Mansion, an elaborate Queen Anne style house dating from 1892. Charles Copeland Morse was the founder of the seed business that eventually became the Ferry-Morse Seed Company, so this wonderful building is known as "the house that seeds built." There is an old carriage house in back.

Ride on Washington to the next corner and turn left onto Harrison Street, a block of well-maintained houses typical of the late 19th century. The red house at No. 1051 was built in 1891 by a carpenter from Maine and is a fine example of "wedding cake" Victorian architecture.

Main Street, to your left, is also part of Santa Clara's historic district and has a number of early homes, the oldest being the Johnson house at No. 1159. It was constructed in 1851 of precut lumber shipped from Maine around Cape Horn.

Continue on Harrison for 2 more blocks, then turn right onto Monroe Street, which will soon take you across El Camino Real. In another 3 blocks, go left at Warburton Avenue, toward the Civic Center.

To see more of Santa Clara's history, turn right into the large public parking lot before the Triton Museum and ride to the back, where you will find the Jamison-Brown house with its wide verandah. The house was built in 1866 and remodeled extensively in the 1930s. The porch, which was added at that time, came from a ranch house where Jack London was a frequent visitor. (You will visit the site of the ranch later in your ride.)

Across the lawn is the Headen-Inman house, constructed in 1913 and moved here in 1984 when its original site, two blocks away, was sold for development. It is now the Santa Clara Historical Museum. Don't miss the lovely sculpture garden behind the Triton, the city's art museum.

Continue riding past the Jamison-Brown house and through the parking lot. Turn left at Don Avenue, left again at Warburton, and then right onto Lincoln Street. The stainless steel and mosaic sculpture in front of the Santa Clara City Hall is by the famous San Francisco artist Benjamin Bufano.

Lincoln will take you past Civic Center Park on the left with its pools, fountains, and bronze statue of Saint Clare, the city's patron saint.

A couple of blocks after crossing El Camino, on the corner of Catherine, at 1380 Lincoln, is a charming home built in 1897 by real estate magnate John Center for his niece. It was originally three stories high but was lowered in the 1920s.

Carmelite Monastery

As you cross Benton Street, you can't miss the pink plaster walls of the Carmelite Monastery. Turn right into the entrance, and ride down the tree-lined driveway.

In 1895 Judge Hiram Bond, a self-made millionaire from New York, purchased part of New Park Ranch from lumber and mining tycoon James Pierce. Here he established an estate and built a large home where Jack London, who knew the Bond sons from his days in the Klondike, was a frequent visitor. The ranch was supposedly used as one of the settings in London's *Call of the Wild*, and the Bonds' dog is reputed to be the model for Buck.

In 1905 Judge Bond suffered financial reverses, and New Park was put up for sale. The property was purchased in 1913 by Senator James Phelan, owner of Villa Montalvo in Saratoga, for the Carmelite nuns in memory of his sister, Alice Phelan Sullivan, who founded the monastery and is buried in a room off the ornate chapel. This beautiful structure, erected in 1917, is considered to be the most perfect example of Spanish Renaissance ecclesiastical architecture in the New World.

Carmelite nuns are a cloistered order, living in silence and solitude and devoting their lives to prayer. So, although there are nuns in residence here, you are unlikely to encounter any on the grounds, as only a few are allowed to be seen in public or to leave the monastery.

You can still see evidence of the old Bond ranch in the gardens, barn, water tower, and carriage house (where the nuns now live). The main house, however, was razed to make room for the chapel. Its verandah eventually became part of the Jamison-Brown house you saw earlier.

As you leave the shady monastery grounds, continue to the right on Lincoln, which becomes Winchester Boulevard as it curves right.

Harris-Lass Museum

At Market, a right turn will bring you to one last stop, the Harris-Lass Historic Museum, at No. 1889. This Italianate style home was built in 1865 for Henry Harris and his family. Additions were made in the 1890s, and later the entrance was moved from the front to the side. In 1906 the home was purchased by Captain Christian Lass, a retired sea captain, and members of his family continued to live here until 1985. Now owned by the city, the house and grounds have been beautifully restored by the Santa Clara Historic Preservation Society as a living history museum dedicated to the area's agricultural past.

To return to your starting point, continue along Market, which immediately becomes Saratoga Avenue. Follow it back to the park to complete your tour of historic Santa Clara.

Harris-Lass Historic Museum at 1889 Market Street in Santa Clara. The 1865 house and surrounding property represent the city's last remaining farm site.

Additional Information

Santa Clara Mission Church: On the campus of the University of Santa Clara. Open daily. The de Saisset Art Gallery and Museum, located nearby; open Tuesday through Sunday 11:00 AM to 4:00 PM. Free admission. (408) 554-4528.

Railroad Depot: 1005 Railroad Avenue. Museum operated by South Bay Historical Railroad Society. Open Tuesday 7:00 to 9:30 PM, Saturday 9:30 AM to 4:00 PM. (408) 243-3969.

Triton Museum of Art: 1505 Warburton Avenue. Open weekdays 10:00 AM to 5:00 PM (Tuesday open until 9:00 PM), Saturday and Sunday, noon to 5:00 PM. Free admission. (408) 247-3754.

Santa Clara Historical Museum: 1509 Warburton Avenue, off Don Street, behind the Triton Museum. Open Sunday 1:00 to 4:00 PM. Free admission.

Carmelite Monastery: At the corner of Lincoln and Benton. Grounds open daily 6:30 AM to 4:30 PM, Sunday 8:00 AM to 5:00 PM. Chapel usually closed except for services (Sunday Mass 10:30 AM), but you may ask to have it opened.

Harris-Lass Historic Museum: 1889 Market Street. Open for tours on weekends 1:00 to 4:00 PM. Admission fee. (408) 249-7905.

Santa Clara Chamber of Commerce and Visitor Information Center: 1515 El Camino Real, Santa Clara, CA 95050. Open weekdays 8:00 AM to 5:00 PM. (408) 286-7111.

San Jose Historical Museum: Kelley Park, 1600 Senter Road, San Jose. Open weekdays 10:00 AM to 4:30 PM, weekends noon to 4:30 PM. Numerous restored and reconstructed historic buildings, including hotel, stable, firehouse, trolley barn. Admission fee. (408) 287-2290.

Bike Rental: Any Mountain, 10495 N. DeAnza Boulevard, Cupertino. (408) 255-6162. Stan's Bicycle Store, 19685 Stevens Creek Boulevard, Cupertino. (408) 996-1234. Calabazas Cyclery, 6156 Bollinger Road, San Jose. (408) 366-2453.

29. Los Gatos

Distance: 23 miles

Rating: *Strenuous*, with several gradual to demanding climbs. Traffic is often heavy and fast-moving on Highway 9, but the road has a good shoulder. Downtown Los Gatos may also be congested, especially on summer weekends.

Highlights: Nestled near the base of the Santa Cruz Mountains, Los Gatos provides a beautiful setting for its numerous late-19th century homes and commercial buildings. You can also visit two museums and Villa Montalvo in Saratoga and ride into the wooded hills on the outskirts of town.

Location: Los Gatos is located at the intersection of Highways 9 and 17 in Santa Clara County near the Santa Cruz Mountains.

Begin your ride at West Valley Community College at the intersection of Fruitvale and Allendale avenues in Saratoga. To reach the college from Highway 17, exit onto Saratoga–Los Gatos Road (Highway 9), go about 2.5 miles to Fruitvale and turn right. From Interstate 280, take Saratoga Avenue about 4 miles, then turn left at Fruitvale Avenue. Parking is available at the college for a fee (Lots 3 and 6), but it's free on Saturday afternoon and all day Sunday. Restrooms can be found to the left of the tennis courts behind Lot 6 on Fruitvale.

Villa Montalvo

From the college, ride south on Fruitvale Avenue. After the road narrows, take the first right turn onto Farwell Avenue and, when you get to Saratoga–Los Gatos Road (Highway 9), turn right again, heading toward Villa Montalvo. After less than half a mile, go left at Montalvo Road.

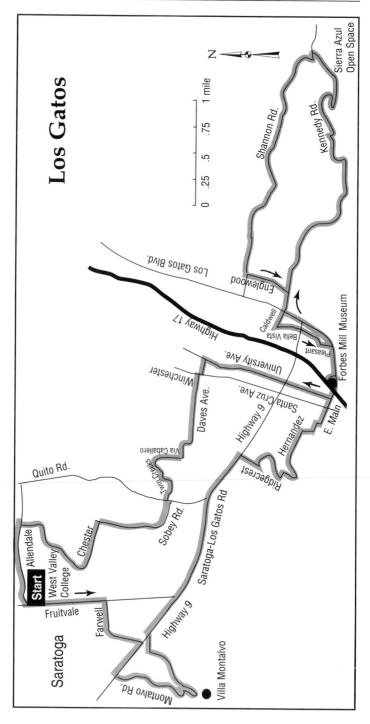

This was once the long driveway to the Villa Montalvo mansion, and you can still see the pillars that marked the entrance to the estate of James D. Phelan, three-time mayor of San Francisco and a U.S. senator. Ride one mile up the hill, passing some beautiful Saratoga residences. The last block past the Arboretum Center is quite steep.

Phelan spared no expense in building this 19-room Mediterranean style villa. The main doors came from a Spanish palace, the rooms were filled with priceless works of art, and the gardens were laid out by John McLaren, the landscape architect of Golden Gate Park. It was completed in 1912, shortly before Phelan began his term as senator. Once the scene of many a lavish party, Villa Montalvo is now an art gallery and cultural center, as specified in Phelan's will. The carriage house has been turned into a theater, and outdoor concerts are held in the garden.

After exploring the buildings and grounds, ride past the house and down the steep, narrow one-way exit road (restrooms are located at Parking Lot 4), which merges with Piedmont Road at the bottom of the hill. When Piedmont ends, turn right at Mendelsohn Lane. Go right again at Saratoga-Los Gatos Road, where you may encounter a lot of traffic but will have a wide shoulder, downhill riding, and wonderful views of the nearby Santa Cruz Mountains.

After less than a mile you'll pass La Hacienda, a large inn and restaurant. In 1902 the Nippon Mura Inn was developed here as a Japanese-style resort for San Franciscans. The inn was part of the once-bustling settlement of Austin Corners, but little remains of the community today.

Soon you will enter the town of Monte Sereno. Just as the road begins to narrow, turn right onto Ridgecrest Avenue. After a rather strenuous climb of several blocks, the street ends

History of Los Gatos

In the 1850s, James Alexander Forbes built a flour mill along Los Gatos Creek on land that was once part of Rancho Rinconada de los Gatos (named for the wildcats in the mountains). The mill was the focal point of a tiny community that became known as Forbestown. The coming of the railroad in 1878 established Forbestown as a lumber center, and, during the building boom that followed, it was renamed Los Gatos.

at Beck Avenue where you'll go left, following the road as it curves to the right for a downhill along the wooded canyon on Hernandez Avenue.

Ride through Los Gatos

Continue on Hernandez through a neighborhood of interesting, large old homes. On the corner of Palm, at 55 Hernandez, you'll pass the 1887 residence of Alfred Malpas, manager of the Los Gatos Fruit and Wine Company. Quite innovative for its time, the house featured two bathrooms, gas heating, and piped-in hot and cold water.

At the end of the street, turn right onto Glen Ridge Avenue. Here again you'll see many fine period homes. At the corner go left on Pennsylvania, right on Bayview, and left onto West Main Street. The shingled house on the corner, 312 Main, dates from the early 1880s but has undergone substantial renovation over the years.

At the next intersection, on Tait Avenue, is the Los Gatos Museum, located in the town's first firehouse, built in 1927. The museum has an art gallery and local history exhibits.

Continuing along West Main for 2 more blocks, you will reach Santa Cruz Avenue, the heart of downtown Los Gatos. Traffic is likely to be heavy here, especially on weekends. Cross Santa Cruz, using the right lane, and pause at the Town Plaza, where the stagecoach used to stop.

The Plaza is a pleasant place to relax or have a picnic under the trees. Here you can also view the 200-pound fire bell used to summon volunteer firemen and to toll curfew back at the turn of the century.

At one time, when Santa Cruz Avenue was the only way to transport redwoods from the mountains to the mills and markets in the valley, it was a toll road with a gate and toll house located a few blocks up the street toward the hills. Between 1857 and 1877, lumber haulers were charged from 50¢ for a two-horse team to $1 for a six-horse team. The road was made public after the haulers rebelled over the high tolls.

Los Gatos suffered extensive damage during the 1989 Loma Prieta earthquake, but the downtown area has been beautifully restored. Diagonal from the Plaza, facing Santa Cruz, is La Cañada Building, constructed in 1894 as a corner drugstore. Its most notable feature is the candle-snuffer turret.

Across Main Street from the Plaza are two former bank buildings and the 1904 opera house.

When you are ready to leave, continue along Main Street. You may see cyclists taking a break outside the popular Los Gatos Coffee Roasting Company or buying goodies at the bakery on the corner. A comfortable bike lane begins after a block.

Just on the other side of the bridge over Highway 17, you will pass the entrance to the Los Gatos Creek Trail, a 1.8-mile dirt and gravel road that leads to the dam at Lexington Reservoir.

Notice the decorative facade of the 1883 Beckwith Building located on the left. Recently restored, it now looks much as it did when it was a hotel at the turn of the century. A short distance farther on, East Main begins a gentle uphill and becomes Los Gatos Boulevard.

An important early residence can be found on the left at the top of the rise, at 49 Los Gatos Boulevard. This home was built around 1875 by Peter Johnson, a teamster and early mayor, and has undergone little structural change in over 100 years.

On the next corner, at No. 22, there is a lovely Victorian cottage that was once the summer home of Alma Spreckels of San Francisco. Across the street, at No. 207, is an impressive Italianate style house from about 1890.

Kennedy-Shannon Loop

When you reach Kennedy Road, a short distance past the point where Saratoga Avenue (Highway 9) intersects from the left, make a right turn at the traffic signal. This is the beginning of the Kennedy-Shannon loop, a challenging 6.5-mile route with two significant hills that is well known to local cyclists. The 2.25-mile ascent to the top of Kennedy starts gently, but soon you'll begin a steady, mile-long climb. The road is quite narrow in places and has little shoulder, but the route is very scenic as it winds along a canyon, through the trees, and up the hill. You'll see many fine homes spread out along the way.

At the summit, on the right, is the entrance to Sierra Azul Open Space Preserve where bicycles are permitted, although the dirt trails are very steep.

The one-mile descent on Kennedy is fast, but watch out for switchbacks near the top. You'll enjoy impressive views over the hills before dropping back down into a wooded canyon and a more rural area. At the bottom of the hill, be prepared to stop at the sign, gear down, and make a left turn onto Shannon Road, where you must immediately begin climbing again.

The steep ascent on Shannon is just over half a mile, and there may be some fast-moving traffic on the narrow road. Amid the newer homes scattered on the hillsides, you can still see an occasional old ranch and horse pasture.

From the top of Shannon, you'll have an easy 1.5-mile downhill that takes you back through residential neighborhoods. At the stop sign near the bottom, angle left to stay on Shannon. You'll pass Blossom Hill Park on the right, which has restrooms on the far side. After a few blocks, turn left at Englewood Avenue, following the Bike Route sign. This brings you back to Kennedy Road where you'll go right.

Cross Los Gatos Boulevard, riding straight ahead onto Caldwell Avenue, and turn left on Bella Vista Avenue. This keeps you away from traffic for a bit, as you make your way back to the main part of town. Bella Vista crosses over Highway 9 and becomes New York Avenue on the downhill. A left on Pleasant Street (following the Bike Route signs) and a right on East Main will take you back into downtown Los Gatos.

Forbes Mill Museum

You will again ride past the 1924 Neoclassical style high school, whose alumni include actresses Olivia de Havilland and her sister Joan Fontaine. A block past the school, turn right onto Church Street, and when Church curves to the right, go left down the hill to reach the Forbes Mill Museum.

The museum is housed in an 1880 annex, the only building that remains of the Forbes flour mill where the town of Los Gatos originated. After serving a variety of uses over the years, the annex was renovated and turned into a regional museum dedicated to preserving the heritage of the Santa Clara Valley. (Another entrance to the Los Gatos Creek Trail is located behind the museum.)

From the museum, return to Main Street, go right and recross the Highway 17 bridge. At the traffic signal, turn right onto University Avenue. Note the decorative arches on the 1906 stone Fretwell Building on the corner.

You'll ride by Old Town, an interesting complex of shops and restaurants that were built around a 1925 stucco schoolhouse. (Public restrooms can be found near the bell tower of the Old Town Theater.) University Avenue has many pretty 19th century Victorian cottages, but the most interesting structure is the red brick Honeymoon House at No. 315. It was built by Harry Perrin in 1896 for his bride and is a rare example of the Romanesque style of architecture used for a private residence rather than a public building.

Ride along University through the congested junction with Saratoga Avenue (Highway 9), and after half a mile you will come to the intersection with Blossom Hill Road. (The entrance to Lake Vasona County Park is down the hill to your right. A paved bike path extends from the park, along Los Gatos Creek, 6.5 miles to Leigh Avenue in San Jose.)

Daves Avenue

Continue straight ahead on University, taking the second left turn onto Farley Road (at the Bike Route sign). After one block, when you come to Winchester Boulevard (the continuation of Santa Cruz Avenue), turn right, and then immediately go left uphill onto Daves Avenue. The second house on the left, No. 17560, was built in 1873 by John Daves, who traveled across the plains to the Santa Clara Valley with his parents in 1852.

Another dwelling with a more unusual history is located at the end of an unmarked narrow road just opposite Kirkorian Way, less than half a mile farther along. The house was built in 1890 by a retired seaman and later owned by the Hitts, who installed a pipe organ in the water tower and held church services in the barn. Hitt ordained himself a minister and called his church group the "Hittites." The Hitts also manufactured fireworks here until World War II, when they switched to rodent bombs.

Continue riding on Daves and, just before the road curves left, turn right at the stop sign onto Via Caballero (at the Bike Route sign), which becomes Twin Creeks Road. This part of Los Gatos has many lovely newer homes. When the road ends, turn left at Quito Road, named for the rancho located here in the 1840s, and immediately go right onto Sobey Road for more up and down.

After less than a mile, turn left onto Chester Avenue, which takes you up another hill and through another affluent neighborhood. As you ride along, you can see the Mission Revival style buildings of the Odd Fellows Home for the Aged. The oldest was constructed in 1912. John McLaren, landscape architect of Golden Gate Park and Villa Montalvo, was a member of the I.O.O.F. and designed these gardens as well.

Continue on Chester, which now is mostly downhill, and turn left when the road ends at Allendale. West Valley College will soon appear on your left, and Fruitvale Avenue is just ahead.

Additional Information

Villa Montalvo: End of Montalvo Road, off Saratoga-Los Gatos Road (Highway 9) in Saratoga. Art gallery open Thursday and Friday 1:00 to 4:00 PM, Saturday and Sunday 11:00 AM to 4:00 PM. Free admission. House tours given Thursday and Saturday, April through September. Admission fee. (408) 741-3421. Grounds maintained by county as an arboretum, open daily 9:00 AM to 5:00 PM. Free admission. There are walking paths, but picnicking prohibited. Public restrooms next to Parking Lot 4 on exit road. (408) 867-0190.

Los Gatos Museum: 4 Tait Avenue. Open Wednesday through Sunday noon to 4:00 PM. Free admission. (408) 354-2646.

Los Gatos Coffee Roasting Company: 101 West Main Street. Open daily 6:00 AM to 7:00 PM. (408) 354-3263.

Forbes Mill Museum: 75 Church Street, Los Gatos. Open Tuesday through Sunday 10:00 AM to 4:00 PM. Free admission. (408) 395-7375.

Los Gatos Chamber of Commerce: 50 University Avenue, Los Gatos, CA 95030. Open weekdays 9:00 AM to 5:00 PM, Saturday 10:00 AM to 4:00 PM. (408) 354-9300.

Bike Rental: See Santa Clara Ride, page 246, or San Jose–New Almaden Ride, page 261.

30. San Jose – New Almaden

Distance: 14 miles plus 3-mile bike path

Rating: *Moderate*, due to some traffic and narrow roads. The route is mostly flat or gently rolling and portions along bike paths are easy. Only part of the route is shaded, and this section of Santa Clara Valley can be hot on a summer day.

Highlights: This ride follows pleasant bike paths and country roads into scenic Alamitos Valley to the little town of New Almaden, which once supported the largest quicksilver (mercury) mining operation in North America more than a century ago.

Casa Grande, 21350 Almaden Road, New Almaden. Built in 1854 as the home of the quicksilver mine superintendent, it still looks much the same as this 1890s photograph.

courtesy New Almaden Quicksilver County Park Association.

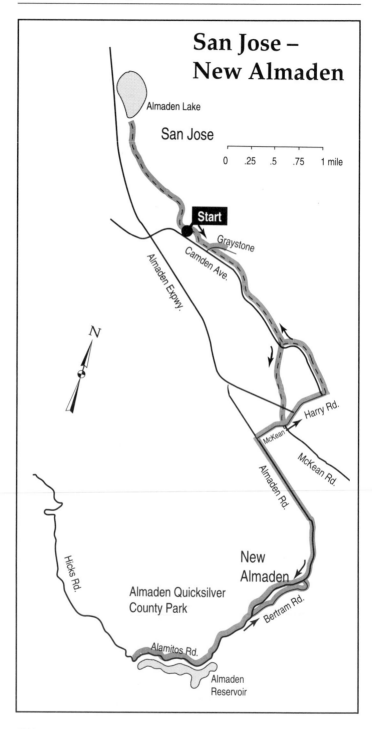

Location: New Almaden is located south of Interstate 280 and west of Highway 101 in southern Santa Clara County.

Pfeiffer Park

Begin your ride at Pfeiffer Park on Camden Avenue in south San Jose. From Interstate 280, go south on Highway 87 to Almaden Expressway, continuing south. At Camden Avenue (about 8 miles from I-280), turn left, and in half a mile you'll come to a small parking lot on the left. Water and picnic tables can be found about a quarter mile along the paved trail that goes to Pfeiffer Park and Almaden Lake on the other side of the tree-lined creek, but there are no restrooms.

The route to New Almaden does not go over the bridge, but heads southeast on Los Alamitos Creek Trail. The first block is paved, but after Graystone Lane the path turns to dirt and gravel for half a mile. You may either continue on the unpaved trail or ride along Camden, which has some traffic but enough room for bicycles. Return to the path when the pavement resumes.

About 1.5 miles from the start, the trail exits onto Camden. Go left, crossing over the bridge. Just on the other side, make a right turn onto the bike path that follows the east side of Alamitos Creek. When the trail ends in less than a mile, go right onto McKean Road. (McKean, at this intersection, also goes straight ahead.)

After the road narrows, turn left at the stop sign onto Almaden Road where you'll have gently rolling terrain, some rough shoulder, and light but fast-moving traffic. Although suburban development is spreading south, much of this area is still rural, and you will see a number of old farms and ranches interspersed with newer homes.

The Country Store, the only place on your route to buy food or drink, is a mile down the road.

Ride through New Almaden

You'll soon come to the quiet little town of New Almaden, nestled in the narrow canyon along Alamitos Creek. The most impressive building in New Almaden is Casa Grande, the home of the mine supervisor, at 21350 Almaden Road. This imposing brick structure was built in 1854 with walls two feet thick and magnificent hand-carved fireplaces. James Randol, who was manager of the mine for over 20 years and was responsible for the mine's peak production, lived here with his wife and five children until his retirement in 1892. After the mine went bankrupt in 1912, the house was abandoned until the 1920s, when it became a roadhouse where bootleg whiskey was sold. A dance hall was added later. Today Casa Grande is Club Almaden and has an "opry" house theater.

New Almaden, under the strict control of Randol, was a mining town unlike any other. Company-sponsored organizations took care of the residents' health, wealth, and cultural and social life. There were 25 company-owned cottages built along the main street that were rented at a nominal fee to management-level employees. The thousands of miners lived in Englishtown (for Cornish workers) or Spanishtown (for Mexicans) high on the hill near the mines.

Just beyond Casa Grande is Cottage 1 (No. 21472), where the head mining engineer lived. Cottage 2 (No. 21474) was first occupied in 1847 by John Young, superintendent of the initial

History of New Almaden

The history of this area goes back to ancient times when the Indians of the Bay Area came to the hills above the poplar-lined creek for the red cinnabar earth they used to paint their bodies. In 1824, when Antonio Suñol of San Jose made the first attempt at mining in California in his search for silver and gold, he found the same red ore used by the Indians.

It wasn't until 1845 that Andres Castillero, a Mexican cavalry officer, filed a mining claim to this deposit of cinnabar, the ore that produces mercury, or quicksilver.

The following year, he and his partners sold controlling interest in the mine to the Barron-Forbes Company of Mexico, who named it the New Almaden Mine after the great quicksilver mine in Almaden, Spain. After years of litigation over its ownership, the mine was taken over by the Quicksilver Mining Company of New York.

The discovery of gold in 1848 created a tremendous demand for mercury, an essential ingredient in the reduction of gold ore. New Almaden, the largest source of mercury in North America, eventually became the most famous and one of the most productive mercury mines in the world. The town that developed around the mine is now a National Historic Landmark District.

mining operations, and has undergone substantial remodeling over the years. The best-known resident of Cottage 3 was H. J. Huttner, a mechanical engineer who in 1874, along with Robert Scott, designed and built an ore-extracting furnace that revolutionized the reduction of quicksilver. Scott lived next door in Cottage 4.

Farther down the block is the Bulmore House, Cottage 12 (No. 21560), which dates from 1854. Bulmore moved here in 1878 when he was cashier and foreman at the mine. Later he became general manager and was the last mining official to reside at Casa Grande. The adobe next door is named for George Carson, who arrived in 1883 and served as company telegrapher, bookkeeper, and postmaster. The New Almaden Quicksilver Mine Museum, which has an interesting collection of mining artifacts and photos, is located behind the Carson House.

At the far end of town on the left, at No. 21744, is the tollgate house where the gate-keeper lived and collected tolls from travelers wanting to use Almaden Road. It is now apartments.

Quicksilver County Park

Across the road you'll see the entrance to the 3,600-acre Almaden Quicksilver County Park, the site of the actual mining operations. The massive ore-reduction works was originally located nearby but has been dismantled and removed. Only a few mining structures of any sort remain in the park, and all the shafts have been sealed for safety.

During the summer months, the oak-studded hillsides of the park may be hot and dry, but in the spring they are covered with native wildflowers and exotic blossoms planted long ago by miners. The old mining roads are now trails for hikers and equestrians. (A portable toilet is located next to the parking lot.)

For a scenic ride to the Almaden Reservoir, continue past the park on Almaden/Alamitos Road. There is a moderate incline to the dam. You'll have views of the park on the right, then the reservoir to the left, and the beautiful wooded Santa Cruz Mountains ahead in the distance. It is hard to believe that Silicon Valley is just a short distance away.

When you reach Hicks Road after about 1.5 miles, turn around and retrace your route back to town. As the road starts to curve left, just before the entrance to the county park, go straight onto Bertram Road, a very narrow residential street that parallels Almaden Road. On the right is St. Anthony Church, a quaint brown shingle building dating from 1900.

Past the church, you'll see a restaurant located on the site of the old Hacienda Hotel, which housed unmarried mine employees. The original structure was destroyed by fire in 1878. It was later rebuilt and then remodeled into a restaurant in the 1930s.

Hacienda Cemetery

After a short distance, you'll come to the Hacienda Cemetery, overgrown and nearly hidden behind white picket fences. The cemetery was used from the 1850s until the 1920s when some of the mine company's land was sold and subdivided. The developer put Bertram Road right through the middle of the cemetery and over an unknown number of graves. The cemetery is now maintained by the California Pioneers of Santa Clara County.

To complete your tour of New Almaden, ride along Bertram until it brings you back to Almaden Road. Go to the right to leave town, and retrace your route for 1.7 miles, turning right at McKean. When McKean goes to the right after a short distance, continue straight ahead on Harry Road, where there is still some open countryside.

After about half a mile, turn left onto Camden and pick up the paved bike path at the corner. From here it's just over 2 miles back to Pfeiffer Park. Along the way, when the trail exits onto Camden, go to the right across the bridge, where the path continues.

At Graystone Lane, just before the park, turn right over the creek. There you will find a small structure called the Pfeiffer Stonehouse, built in 1875 of rock quarried from the hillsides. Food and tools were stored here during the days when Pfeiffer's quarry was in operation. Sandstone from this location was used to build the San Jose Hall of Justice, Old Post Office (now the San Jose Museum of Art), St. Mark's Church, and the original buildings of Stanford University.

Bike Path to Almaden Lake

Return to Pfeiffer Park. From here you can ride along the flat, paved path that continues northwest along Alamitos Creek to Almaden Lake Park, a pleasant 3-mile round-trip.

Additional Information

The Country Store: 20421 Almaden Road. Open daily 6:30 AM to 7:00 PM.

Club Almaden: 21350 Almaden Road. Available for special events. (408) 268-7036. The Opry House has vaudeville shows and melodramas. (408) 268-2492.

New Almaden Historical Museum: 21570 Almaden Road. Open Saturday noon to 4:00 PM. Small admission fee. (408) 268-1729.

Almaden Quicksilver County Park: Open 8:00 AM to dusk. Bicycles not allowed on trails. Pit toilet located near visitor center. (408) 268-8220 or 268-3883.

La Forêt Restaurant: 21747 Bertram Road, New Almaden. Opens for dinner at 5:30 PM. Sunday brunch at 10:30 AM. (408) 997-3458.

Almaden Lake Park: Almaden Expressway at intersection of Coleman Avenue. Swimming, restrooms, and a snack bar. Fee parking. Park closed during winter season. (408) 277-5130.

Bike Rental: Action Sports, 1777 Hillsdale Avenue, San Jose. (408) 978-8383.

Rides by Rating

Easy:

Alameda, 10 miles, p. 173

Alameda – Bay Farm Island, 6 miles, p. 181

Fremont – Alameda Creek, 19 miles (or less), p. 211

Half Moon Bay, 7 + 6 miles, p. 125

Napa, 8 miles, p. 33

Palo Alto, 18 miles, p. 227

Pleasanton, 6 miles, p. 187

San Francisco – Golden Gate Park, 7.5 + 4 miles, p. 117

Santa Clara, 6 miles, p. 239

Sausalito, 10 miles, p. 91

Sonoma, 10 + 3.5 miles, p. 13

Moderate:

Angel Island, 7 miles, p. 99

Benicia, 12 + 4 miles, p. 145

Fremont, 18 miles, p. 203

Livermore, 26 miles, p. 195

Napa Countryside, 31 miles, p. 41

Petaluma, 21 miles, p. 51

San Jose – New Almaden, 14 + 3 miles, p. 255

Sonoma Valley, 25 + 3 miles, p. 25

West Marin, 30 miles, p. 75

Woodside – Portola Valley, 17 miles, p. 217

Moderately Strenuous:

Petaluma Countryside, 40 miles, p. 61

San Francisco, 21 miles, p. 107

Strenuous:

Berkeley, 40 + 8 miles, p. 165

Half Moon Bay Countryside, 14 miles, p. 133

Los Gatos, 23 miles, p. 247

Marin Headlands, 14 miles, p. 83

Martinez, 22 miles, p. 155

Pescadero – San Gregorio, 28 miles, p. 137

Point Reyes, 34 or 42 miles, p. 69

Bike Paths
(paved paths, separated from traffic)

North Bay and Marin

Sonoma: East Fourth Street to Sonoma Highway, pp. 20–22
West Marin: Samuel P. Taylor – Cross Marin Trail, p. 78
Sausalito: Sausalito, p. 94;
Mill Valley, pp. 97–98)
Angel Island: Angel Island, pp. 99–106

San Francisco and the Coast

San Francisco: Golden Gate Bridge, pp. 113–114;
Great Highway, p. 123
Half Moon Bay: Francis Beach, p. 129

East Bay

Alameda: Robert Crown Beach to Fernside Boulevard, p. 176;
Bay Farm Island, Shoreline Park, pp. 182–185
Berkeley: Nimitz Way, p. 171
Benicia: Benicia State Recreation Area, p. 153
Livermore: Sycamore Grove Park, p. 200;
Stanley Boulevard to Almond Avenue, p. 201
Fremont: Alameda Creek, p. 211–215;
Central Park, p. 205

South Bay and Peninsula

Woodside – Portola Valley: Alpine Road, p. 224;
Cañada Road, p. 226
Palo Alto: Stanford University, pp. 231–234
Los Gatos: Los Gatos Creek Trail to San Jose, p. 253
San Jose – New Almaden: Los Alamitos Creek, pp. 257,
260, 261

Bike Rental Addresses

1. Sonoma,
2. Sonoma Valley

Goodtime Bicycle Company,
18503 Sonoma Highway,
Boyes Hot Springs. (707)
938-0453.

3. Napa,
4. Napa Countryside

Bryan's Napa Valley Cyclery,
4080 Byway, East Napa.
(707) 255-3377.

5. Petaluma,
6. Petaluma Countryside

Bicycle Factory,
110 Kentucky Street,
Petaluma. (707) 763-7515.

7. Point Reyes

Trailhead Rentals,
88 Bear Valley Road, Olema.
(415) 663-1958.

8. West Marin

Caesar's Cyclery,
29 San Anselmo Avenue,
San Anselmo. (415) 258-9920.

9. Marin Headlands

See San Francisco or
Sausalito.

10. Sausalito

Bicycle Odyssey,
1417 Bridgeway, Sausalito.
(415) 332-3050.

Any Mountain,
71 Tamal Vista Boulevard,
Corte Madera. (415)
927-0170.

11. Angel Island

Ken's Bike and Sport,
94 Main Street, Tiburon.
(415) 435-1683.

Planeaway, Cove Shopping
Center, 1 Blackfield Drive,
Tiburon. (415) 383-2123.

See also San Francisco.

12. San Francisco,
13. San Francisco – Golden
Gate Park

Golden Bike,
407 O'Farrell Street,
San Francisco. (415) 771-8009.

Lincoln Cyclery, 772 Stanyan
Street, San Francisco. (415)
221-2415.

Marina Cyclery,
3330 Steiner Street, San
Francisco. (415) 929-7135.

Park Cyclery,
1865 Haight Street, San
Francisco. (415) 221-3777.

Velo City,
638 Stanyan Street,
San Francisco. (415) 221-2453.

14. Half Moon Bay,
15. Half Moon Bay
Countryside

The Bicyclery,
432 Main Street, Half Moon
Bay. (415) 726-6000.

16. Pescadero

See Half Moon Bay or
Woodside – Portola Valley.

17. Benicia

See Martinez.

18. Martinez

Martinez Cyclery,
4990 Pacheco Boulevard,
Martinez. (510) 228-9050.

Any Mountain,
1975 Diamond Boulevard,
Concord. (510) 674-0174.

19. Berkeley

Backroads Bike Shop,
801 Cedar St., Berkeley.
(510) 527-1888.

Berkeley Cycle,
2020 Center Street, Berkeley.
(510) 845-7560.

Karim Cyclery,
2801 Telegraph Avenue,
Berkeley. (510) 841-2181.

Encina Bicycle Center,
2891 Ygnacio Valley Road,
Walnut Creek. (510) 944-9200.

20. Alameda,
21. Alameda – Bay Farm Island

Cycle Sports,
2238A South Shore Center,
Alameda. (510) 521-2872.

22. Pleasanton

Paquette's Cycle,
1991 L Santa Rita Road,
Pleasanton. (510) 846-4788.

Dublin Cyclery,
7001 Dublin Boulevard,
Dublin. (510) 828-8676.

23. Livermore

Livermore Cyclery,
2288 First Street, Livermore.
(510) 455-8090.

See also Pleasanton.

24. Fremont,
25. Fremont – Alameda Creek Trail

Niles Ski and Bike,
37469 Niles Boulevard,
Fremont. (510) 793-9141.

26. Woodside – Portola Valley

Any Mountain,
2341 El Camino Real,
Redwood City.
(415) 361-1213.

See also Palo Alto.

27. Palo Alto

Action Sports,
401 High Street, Palo Alto.
(415) 328-3180.

Bike Connection,
2086 El Camino Real, Palo
Alto. (415) 424-8034.

28. Santa Clara

Any Mountain,
10495 N. DeAnza Boulevard,
Cupertino. (408) 255-6162.

Stan's Bicycle Store,
19685 Stevens Creek
Boulevard, Cupertino.
(408) 996-1234.

Calabazas Cyclery,
6156 Bollinger Road, San
Jose. (408) 366-2453.

29. Los Gatos

See Santa Clara or San
Jose–New Almaden.

30. San Jose – New Almaden

Action Sports,
1777 Hillsdale Avenue, San
Jose. (408) 978-8383.

Bibliography

Arrigoni, Patricia. *Making the Most of Marin*. Fairfax, CA: Travel Publishers International, 1990.

Boisvert, Conrad J. *East Bay Bike Trails*. Penngrove, CA: Penngrove Publications, 1992.

——. *San Francisco Peninsula Bike Trails*. Penngrove, CA: Penngrove Publications, 1991.

——. *South Bay Bike Trails*. Penngrove, CA: Penngrove Publications, 1990.

Bloom, Naomi. *Favorite Pedal Tours of Northern California*. Bishop, CA: Fine Edge Productions, 1992.

Butler, Phyllis F. *Old Santa Clara Valley*. San Carlos, CA: World Wide Publishing/Tetra, 1991.

Dunham, Tacy. *Marin Bike Paths*. Marin County, CA, 1988.

Edwards, Don. *Making the Most of Sonoma*. Novato, CA: Presidio Press, 1982.

Evans, Nancy M., and Neil A. Evans. *Exploring Half Moon Bay and the San Mateo County Coast*. El Granada, CA: Worldview Associates, 1992.

Golden Gate National Park Association. *Park Guide*. San Francisco, 1990.

Gullard, Pamela, and Nancy Lund. *History of Palo Alto: The Early Years*. San Francisco: Scottwall Associates, 1989.

Heig, Adair. *History of Petaluma: A California River Town*. Petaluma, CA: Scottwall Associates, 1982.

Hoover, Mildred Brooke, Hero Eugene Rensch, Ethel Grace Rensch, and William N. Abeloe. *Historic Spots in California*. Revised by Douglas E. Kyle. Stanford, CA: Stanford University Press, 1990.

Hosler, Ray. *Bay Area Bike Rides*. San Francisco: Chronicle Books, 1990.

Lane, Bob and Pat. *The Amador-Livermore Valley*. Norfolk, VA: The Donning Company, 1988.

Martinez Historical Society. *Martinez: A California Town*. Martinez: RSI Publications, 1986.

Minor, Woody. "A History of Bay Farm Island." Alameda, CA: *The Alameda Journal*, July 15-September 2, 1988.

Miller, Austin. *Bicycle Rides in and around Napa*. Napa, CA: Napa Bicycling Club.

Neumann, Phyllis. *Marin County Bike Trails*. Penngrove, CA: Penngrove Publications, 1989.

———. *Sonoma County Bike Trails*. Penngrove, CA: Penngrove Publications, 1990.

Paul, Ken, and Alexandra Gautraud. *San Mateo!* Palo Alto, CA: CastleRock Press, 1989.

Peterson, Dan. *Petaluma's Architectural Heritage*. Santa Rosa, CA: Architectural Preservation Associates, 1978.

Petersen, Grant, and Mary Anderson. *Roads to Ride*. Berkeley: Heyday Books, 1984.

Petersen, Grant, and John Kluge. *Roads to Ride South*. Berkeley: Heyday Books, 1985.

Pitcher, Don. *Berkeley Inside/Out*. Berkeley: Heyday Books, 1989.

Powers, Peter. *Touring California's Wine Country by Bicycle*. Eugene, OR: Terragraphics, 1990.

———. *Touring the San Francisco Bay Area by Bicycle*. Eugene, OR: Terragraphics, 1990.

Regnery, Dorothy F. *An Enduring Heritage: Historic Buildings of the San Francisco Peninsula*. Stanford, CA: Stanford University Press, 1976.

Richards, Rand. *Historic San Francisco: A Concise History and Guide*. San Francisco: Heritage House Publishers, 1991.

Rusmore, Jean, and Frances Spangle. *Peninsula Trails*. Berkeley: Wilderness Press, 1989.

Spangle, Frances, and Jean Rusmore. *South Bay Trails*. Berkeley: Wilderness Press, 1991.

Wayburn, Peggy. *Adventuring in the San Francisco Bay Area*. San Francisco: Sierra Club Books, 1987.

Whitnah, Dorothy L. *An Outdoor Guide to the San Francisco Bay Area*. Berkeley: Wilderness Press, 1989.

Wilson, Mark A. *A Living Legacy: Historic Architecture of the East Bay*. San Francisco: Lexikos, 1987.

Woodbridge, Sally B., and John M. Woodbridge. *San Francisco Architecture*. San Francisco: Chronicle Books, 1992.

Index

Title	Author	US Price
All Terrain Biking	Jim Zarka	$7.95
The Backroads of Holland	Helen Colijn	$12.95
The Bicycle Commuting Book	Rob van der Plas	$7.95
The Bicycle Fitness Book	Rob van der Plas	$7.95
The Bicycle Repair Book	Rob van der Plas	$9.95
Bicycle Technology	Rob van der Plas	$16.95
Bicycle Touring International	Kameel Nasr	$18.95
The Bicycle Touring Manual	Rob van der Plas	$16.95
Bicycling Fuel	Richard Rafoth	$9.95
Champion	Samuel Abt	$12.95
Cycling Europe	Nadine Slavinski	$12.95
Cycling France	Jerry. H. Simpson, Jr.	$12.95
Cycling Kenya	Kathleen Bennett	$12.95
Cycling the San Francisco Bay Area	Carol O'Hare	$12.95
Cycling the U.S. Parks	Jim Clark	$12.95
The High Performance Heart	Maffetone & Mantell	$9.95
In High Gear (hardcover)	Samuel Abt	$21.95
In High Gear (paperback)	Samuel Abt	$10.95
Major Taylor (hardcover)	Andrew Ritchie	$19.95
The Mountain Bike Book	Rob van der Plas	$10.95
Mountain Bike Magic	Rob van der Plas	$14.95
Mountain Bike Maintenance	Rob van der Plas	$9.95
Mountain Bike Maint. and Rep.	Stevenson & Richards	$22.50
Mountain Bike Racing	Gould & Burney	$22.50
The New Bike Book	Jim Langley	$4.95
Roadside Bicycle Repairs	Rob van der Plas	$4.95
Tour de France (hardcover)	Samuel Abt	$22.95
Tour de France (paperback)	Samuel Abt	$12.95
Tour of the Forest Bike Race	H. E. Thomson	$9.95

Buy Our Books at Your Local Book Shop or Bike Shop
Book shops can obtain these titles for you from our book trade distributor (National Book Network for the USA) and from Ingram or Baker & Taylor, bike shops directly from us.

If you have difficulty obtaining our books elsewhere, we will be pleased to supply them by mail, but we must add $2.50 postage and handling (as well as California Sales Tax if mailed to a California address). Prepayment by check (or credit card information) must be included with your order.

Bicycle Books, Inc.
PO Box 2038
Mill Valley, CA 94942
Tel: 1-800-468-8233 (toll free)

In Britain: Bicycle Books
463 Ashley Road
Poole, Dorset BH14 0AX
Tel: (0202) 71 53 49